FROM CHURCHILL'S
WAR ROOMS
Letters of a Secretary 1943–45

It did not occur to us that we were being brave, we just felt lucky that we had this marvellous, exciting job which took us all over the world.

Olive [Christopher] Margerison, 2005.

FROM CHURCHILL'S WAR ROOMS
Letters of a Secretary 1943-45

JOANNA MOODY

FOREWORD BY PHIL REED

DIRECTOR OF THE CHURCHILL MUSEUM AND CABINET WAR ROOMS

TEMPUS

For Olive's friends and colleagues in the Cabinet War Rooms: Joan, Elizabeth, Jacquey, Wendy, Sylvia, Betty, Jo and Ruth

Cover illustrations: Female typist, image courtesy Imperial War Museum; Franklin D. Roosevelt, Stalin, and Churchill in Teheran, Iran, image courtesy Franklin D. Roosevelt Presidential Library and Museum. Other images, Author's Collection.

First published 2007
This edition first published 2008

Tempus Publishing
Cirencester Road, Chalford
Stroud, Gloucestershire, GL6 8PE
www.tempus-publishing.com

Tempus Publishing is an imprint of NPI Media Group

© Joanna Moody, 2007, 2008

The right of Joanna Moody to be identified as the Author
of this work has been asserted in accordance with the
Copyrights, Designs and Patents Act 1988.

British Library Cataloguing in Publication Data.
A catalogue record for this book is available from the British Library.

ISBN 978 07524 4608 0

Typesetting and origination by NPI Media Group
Printed and bound in Great Britain

Contents

Foreword

In the study of history we rely on historians for our understanding of past times and events. They, with their vast compass of wide reading and sage interpretation, facilitate for us insights into bygone eras that we lack the resources to explore in detail. In the case of ancient history they locate, translate and extrapolate scarce sources; in more modern times they distil the super-abundance of data available in the form of official and personal reports. But what, in every case, the historian relies on, particularly in this age of experiential demands, is the first-hand account of the intelligent and reliable witness who was there and whose testimony speaks to us from those times with an actuality and a humanity that no amount of studied analysis can equal.

Olive Margerison was there. She was at the epicentre of affairs of state at a juncture in history, which, uniquely, shaped the lives of living and future generations across the planet. She was not a decision maker, not a leading player, nor even an influence on the outcome of any events (though, with her tales of crucial secret folders mislaid by others, she might have risked being!) She was a close bystander, privy not merely to secrets, but to the personalities and foibles of the individuals who managed the course of events, as far as it was within their power. She is a living witness to the main players and the thoughts, emotions and actions, which drove them.

But Olive is no nameless scribe with no record beyond her witness statement. She was a woman with a life before, during and after the whirlwind events that she describes. And if we are to give credence to such witness, we feel a human need to know something of the lives of such close observers. Olive's life extends well beyond that short, but seismic period of history and, happily, encompasses the microcosmic ordinariness and the personal highs and lows of an individual and of a real life, led in a period long since passed, but, for all the distance of time, relevant to any age and any human life.

If I learned one thing from my friendship with Olive – and there is much that will stay with me long after she has become a delightful

reminiscence in my own life – it is her recounting how she and her husband, in the early days of their marriage, keenly agreed to employ their
scarce resources to 'go and buy a memory' and do something which,
regardless of their lack of money, they could one day reflect upon, retell
and cherish. We are privileged, not only to look back on, and to relive,
the memories and experiences of one who was at the hub of historical
events, but to see those events in the context of a life full of memories
even more valuable than just the mere movements of history.

Phil Reed
Director, Churchill Museum and Cabinet War Rooms
Imperial War Museum
London, June 2006

Preface

In the summer of 1982, following the government of the day's decision to open the Cabinet War Rooms to the general public, I was retained as a researcher working on contract in the Research and Information Office of the Imperial War Museum. My task was a fascinating one: to find out as much as possible about the exact wartime appearance of the individual rooms, and just as importantly, to discover how, when and by whom they had been used at different times during the conflict.

For those who have either forgotten or are too young to have had first-hand experience of the period, Britain in the early 1980s was only just emerging from a prolonged economic recession and the first shock of what has come to be known as 'The Thatcher Revolution'. Not only museums but government departments in general had been on short commons for some time and it was only due to Mrs Thatcher's personal interest in the project (the Falklands War was still fresh in the public mind) that the restoration of the Cabinet War Rooms had been given a fair wind by the spending watchdogs in the Treasury.

At the time, what remained of the underground, wartime complex, located beneath a massive, turn-of-the-century, neo-classical structure, with the unlovely soubriquet GOGGS (Government Offices Great George Street), was in the care of the Property Services Agency of the Department of the Environment. Privatised a few years later and now long-forgotten, the PSA was the direct successor to the pre-war Ministry of Works that had originally put the War Rooms together on instructions from the Assistant Secretary (Military) of the Cabinet, General Ismay, and his deputy, 'Jo' Hollis (Olive's future wartime boss). While a majority of rooms in the complex had been returned to normal civilian usage (I recall that one of the bedrooms set aside for Mr Churchill's colleagues in the War Cabinet had become the HQ of the Ministry of Defence Amateur Dramatic Society!) or been left empty and abandoned, a handful of key rooms, the Central Map Room, the Prime Minister's bedroom and the Cabinet Meeting Room itself, had been preserved almost untouched since the end of the war in August 1945. In addition, the PSA had managed to hold onto a complete set of photographs taken in the principle rooms of the complex at the time of their evacuation and the Imperial War Museum, brought in to advise on the historical aspects of the restoration, had commissioned Dr Nigel de Lee of the War Studies Department at RMC Sandhurst, to trawl through the official files held in the Public Record Office.

So there was already a considerable body of evidence for me to build on when I commenced work at the beginning of July 1982. It soon became apparent, however, that the kind of detailed information required to restore the CWR to its former glory was only likely to be obtained from individual members of the War Cabinet Secretariat and related bodies such as the staff of No. 10 Downing Street, who had actually lived and worked in the underground complex during the course of the war. With a few notable exceptions, such as Wing Commander Gwylim Lewis, a First World War fighter 'ace', who in his own words had been 'dug out of retirement' to serve as a Map Keeper in the Central Map Room, all of my informants had been young and relatively junior at the time. Nevertheless, there were still a good number of retired civil service mandarins of vast seniority and pillars of the British political establishment, such as the former Establishment Officer of the War Cabinet Office, Sir John Winnifrith, and Churchill's favourite wartime Private Secretary, Sir John Colville, who contributed to my research. But by far the most useful and detailed information came, as it was likely to, from the ranks of the Secretariat proper, the often very young women who had worked as personal assistants or members of the central typing pool.

One of these, the formidable Joan Astley, who as Miss Bright had presided over the Central Information Centre on the second floor of GOGGS, was already known to me as a result of her book *The Inner Circle*, and it was not long before I learned that Lord Ismay's former PA, Miss Elizabeth (Betty) Green was still working part-time on the vetting of Cabinet Office papers for public disclosure. Through them I soon got to meet the rest of 'the girls', including Olive, and to put faces to the names that I had seen on the accommodation plans for the CWR and for the Dock, the horribly cramped sleeping quarters located beneath the main complex of underground rooms: Miss Christopher, Miss Hartley, Miss D'Orville, Miss Wallace, Miss Meade, and many others. And with the faces came memories, sometimes rather hazy but mostly incredibly vivid, of people and places, times and events when they were all young, full of hope and found themselves at the very centre of the nation's war effort.

Armed with these recollections, the restoration proceeded at pace and by early 1984, the Museum, which had been invited to manage the War Rooms on behalf of the Secretary of State for the Environment, was well in the throes of final preparation for the grand opening by Mrs Thatcher herself. By this time, I had been appointed first Curator of the Cabinet War Rooms, but if the thought of having to deal with a visit from the Prime Minister was somewhat daunting, it was nothing compared to my nervous anticipation when just before the opening we invited a choice selection of our informants, amongst them Olive and 'the girls', to view the site and to comment upon the accuracy of our restoration efforts. Fortunately we passed muster, but even more heartening was the knowledge that the Museum had won for itself and the CWR a body of staunch and true supporters, while in turn providing a focal point for the renewal of old and valued friendships forged in unique and unrepeatable circumstances.

My own time as Curator CWR came to an end in 1993, when I handed over to my erstwhile colleague Phil Reed. But I was delighted to learn that Olive and some of her old friends had been able to attend the opening of the Churchill Museum in 2005 and it was with immense pleasure that I accepted Joanna Moody's invitation to write this brief preface to her book highlighting the wartime correspondence of Olive and her equally charming and sadly missed husband Neil.

Jon Wenzel
Tonbridge, June 2006

Acknowledgements

I owe an initial debt to Mona Killpack who first suggested this project and put me in touch with her distant cousin, Olive Margerison. I am deeply grateful to Olive for sharing such a valuable collection of letters and wartime memorabilia, and for her informative interviews and extensive telephone conversations. Her sister Enid Wilson, her nephews and their wives, Neil and Sue Margerison, Andrew and Elizabeth Wilson, showed me old family documents and files. Derek Attridge, of the Department of English and Related Literature, University of York, was generous with his time when needed, and Gordon Smith gave assistance with photographic prints. The British Academy provided me with a small research grant, which enabled me to spend time with Olive in her own home and thus complete the book. At the Imperial War Museum, London, Phil Reed, Director of the Churchill Museum and Cabinet War Rooms, agreed at a very busy, award-winning, time to write the foreword, and I appreciate the interest of Elizabeth Bowers and the cooperation of Yvonne Oliver and Chris Plant. I am also grateful to Jon Wenzel, formerly of the IWM, for his interest and prefatory comments, and to Olive's good friend, Rosalyn Swindells, who helped her with typing extra information. Sophie Bradshaw of Tempus Publishing efficiently and enthusiastically took the book through to its final stages. David Moody, as always, has given expert and helpful criticism of style and presentation, and special thanks are due to the following for their discussion and warm hospitality: Ingrid and Edward Popkin, Belinda Coppock, and Richard Fulford.

Chronology

		to the Inter Services Security Board (MI5)
		Planning of 'Operation Torch' (invasion of Africa, 1942)
		Planning of 'Operation Overlord' begins (invasion of Europe, 1944)
	April	Germany invades Yugoslavia and Greece
	May	Neil becomes a major
	June	Germany invades Russia
	7 Dec.	Pearl Harbour
	8 Dec.	Britain and USA declare war on Japan
	Dec.	Olive transferred to the offices of the War Cabinet, Great George Street, as shorthand-typist attached to the Joint Planning Staff in the Cabinet War Rooms (CWR), remaining there as one of only 8 civilian girls
1942	*2 Oct.*	Battle of El Alamein begins defeat of Axis forces in North Africa
	31 Oct.	Olive meets Neil
1943	*Jan.*	Olive interviewed for a job at the Special Operations Executive (SOE) as secretary on the staff of Captain Buckmaster, in their offices in Baker Street. Application successful, but she is told they are unable to release her, and she will be promoted to the offices of the Chiefs of Staff Committee to work as secretary, later personal assistant, to Brigadier, later General, Hollis
	Jan–Feb.	Battle of Stalingrad, defeat of German army there; retreat of German forces from Russia
	May	Washington Conference (2 weeks)
	10 July	Allied invasion of Sicily
	1 Aug.	1st Quebec Conference
		Plans for Moscow Conference changed due to Churchill's illness
	3 Sept.	Allied landings in Italy; followed by surrender of Italy
	9–20 Oct.	Moscow Conference

12 Nov.	Olive embarks in *HMS Renown* for Cairo & Teheran
17–19 Nov.	Delay at Malta
21–26 Nov.	Cairo Conference
27–30 Nov.	Teheran 'Three Power' Conference
30 Nov.	Olive attends Churchill's 69th birthday in Teheran
1–8 Dec.	Back working in Cairo
9 Dec.	Olive embarks in *HMS Penelope*, sails for Malta and home
11 Dec.	Arrives Malta (Churchill ill in Tunis), 3 days there; *HMS Penelope* goes on to Bizerta to await instructions; invitation to dine on *HMS Jervis*
17 Dec.	Hollis goes on to Tunis; Olive returns by air to UK via Gibraltar
26 Dec.	Olive summoned to Marrakech to rejoin Hollis team; secret trip to Lyneham airfield to meet Lord Beaverbrook's plane going to join Churchill; Olive misses plane and is put on another, then joins Hollis at Hotel Mamounia; works there and at Villa Taylor
	Brigadier Hollis promoted to Major General
Dec.	Marrakech Conference; Olive attends Churchill's New Year's Eve party at the Villa Taylor, meets Gen. Eisenhower
1944 *Jan.*	Flight home, touches down in Gibraltar where Olive meets up with Neil; Olive sails back in *HMS King George V*, in which Churchill is travelling
6 June	D-Day: 'Operation Overlord' Allied landings in Normandy, invasion of North-West Europe
late June	Neil injured when jeep blown up in Italy; hospitalised for 3 weeks
Aug.	Liberation of Paris
Sept.	Olive embarks in *Queen Mary* for 2nd Quebec Conference

	11–16 Sept.	2nd Quebec Conference at Chateau Frontenac Hotel; Olive meets Mrs Roosevelt; return to UK in *Queen Mary*
1945	*Feb.*	Yalta Conference
	12 April	Truman becomes US President on death of Roosevelt
	4 May	Germany surrenders
	8 May	VE Day: end of Second World War in Europe
	June	Neil promoted to lieutenant colonel; moves to work in Austria
	5 July	British General Election
		Olive flies to Germany for Potsdam Conference
	15 July	Potsdam Conference (3 weeks)
	26 July	Election Results. Churchill voted out; Hollis summons Olive back to London
	27 July	Clement Attlee becomes PM, and completes matters at Potsdam
	6 Aug.	Atomic bomb dropped on Hiroshima,
	9 Aug.	Atomic bomb dropped on Nagasaki; followed by surrender of Japan
	15 Aug.	VJ Day marks end of war with Japan
	16 Aug.	Cabinet War Rooms closed
	Nov.	Neil sends Olive notice of forthcoming leave
	1 Dec.	Neil arrives home, after two years absence
	15 Dec.	Olive and Neil marry; confirmation of her MBE
1946	*Mar.*	Neil demobbed; Olive gives up work to become a full-time housewife
1984		Opening of the Cabinet War Rooms to the general public
1988		Neil dies from a heart attack
2005	*10 Feb.*	Opening of the Churchill Museum; Olive presented to Her Majesty Queen Elizabeth II

Introduction

The letters and wartime memorabilia included here are to be found in the personal possession of Mrs Olive Margerison MBE. The correspondence charts a romantic story of sixty years ago, when, as young Olive Christopher, she and her fiancé Neil Margerison wrote to each other for two years whilst separated during the Second World War. Olive worked as a secretary in the Cabinet War Rooms, in London. He was an officer in the Army Ordnance Corps, in Gibraltar, North Africa, Italy and Austria. Their story of separation may not be uncommon, but their situation was undoubtedly special.

Olive was not an ordinary secretary. She was a member of Winston Churchill's team in the crucial period 1943–45 when momentous decisions were being made for Allied victory in Europe. Having begun as a stenographer in the War Office she was soon promoted, first to the office of the Joint Planning Staff in the War Rooms, and then to become personal assistant to General Sir Leslie (Jo) Hollis, RM, Secretary to the Chiefs of Staff, later to become post-war Commandant General of the Royal Marines. Working long hours, writing and typing confidential papers and memos, spending much of her time in the underground bunker opposite St James's Park, Olive was party to secrets known only to a few important people. She was one of a limited number of civilians employed alongside men and women from the three armed forces, together efficiently undertaking the work of recording, filing, and generally supporting the War Cabinet's operational planning. Churchill particularly favoured the civilian workers, believing they brought a different kind of order and well-being to the formality of the office. He maintained that the civilian secretaries in the War Rooms were every bit as good and as necessary as the uniformed staff, and he insisted, against much opposition, that they travel to conferences because they were familiar with the modes of working of the Chiefs of Staff. They were trusted, got on well with their seniors who regarded them highly, and there were never any security leaks from their offices during the whole course of the war. We can now find out more about their busy and eventful lives by visiting the Churchill Museum and Cabinet War Rooms, at the Imperial War Museum, London, where we can see for ourselves the conditions in which they lived and worked throughout the Second World War.

It meant that, during the period when Britain was at war, Olive led two lives. She was a competent, high-flying secretary, with the astonishing benefits that came with the job, including certain luxuries and a substantial dress allowance with coupons that defied wartime austerity. At the same time she was an ordinary and rather impoverished young woman, in love with someone far away, longing for his return and trying to raise his spirits by sending news from home. A warm, generous young woman sat before the typewriter creating these missives, which are valuable not only for what they reveal on the page but also for what has had to be kept hidden. Readers must fill in the gaps. Alongside the expressions of desire and talk of friends and family, we must bear in mind the progress of the war, how much is not being said, and what may happen to these young people when it is all over. We read between the lines, inserting our own knowledge of the wider picture as their relationship blossoms. In the period in which this correspondence was written Churchill was working long hours in the War Rooms and travelling hundreds of miles to see the British troops and, amongst others, US President Roosevelt and Soviet Premier Stalin. Germany and Russia fought at Stalingrad; the Allies invaded Italy and then North-West Europe; flying bombs fell on London, and the atomic bomb was dropped on Hiroshima. Yet these events are not to the foreground; instead, they form the backdrop to the letters at the heart of the book, which, apart from being a personal history of the time, offer a key cultural site for the construction of the self in wartime Britain.

Olive first met Major Neil Margerison in late October 1942, when he was working at the War Office. They became engaged in December 1943, hoping to marry a few weeks after her return from a trip she had to make for her work. Neil could not know that Olive was leaving London for Cairo and then going on to the important 'Three Power' Conference in Teheran; but she was due back some time in January 1944. However, before they could meet again, he was posted abroad with no date set for his return, and, apart from one brief unexpected encounter, they would not see each other for two long years. Their correspondence, therefore, became the only way they might grow to know and understand each other more intimately, and it is here that the particular interest lies. The letters show how both Olive and Neil developed, emotionally, socially, and personally, throughout this troubled period. The mode of writing is concerned, chatty, sometimes intimate, guarded about work and politics, but, above all, the language and phrasing are friendly, loving and longing, and distinctively of that time. Their individuality and sense of self are strongly asserted through an epistolary mode which is their sole means of expression and communication.

Part One in this volume tells first of Olive's early years when her grandfather did all he could to form her into a young 'lady' with the necessary social grace and competence to get on in the world. Having made it himself into the milieu of the rich and famous, with their luxurious lifestyle, he wanted the best for his granddaughters and thus involved himself in their upbringing and training. Extracts from his letters indicate how important his role was to be in preparing Olive for society, and they show how generously he took on what he must have considered the greater responsibilities of a grandparent. For example, he paid for schooling and clothes, told her to practise her handwriting (29 March 1934), to offer proper apology if she refused an invitation (29 April 1936) and he encouraged her to buy a book on etiquette (7 March 1936), and work on her deportment. His influence was extensive, so much so that Olive, benefiting life-long from this early training, never forgot how much she owed to him. Part One also relates her search for employment, the start of the war and her subsequent arrival in the Cabinet War Rooms, from where she eventually moved upstairs to become personal assistant to General Hollis. Life in the underground bunker is related in some detail, and Olive's recollections of being a young woman living in London during this time are fully described, based on later recollections. We also hear of her meeting with Neil, their decision to become engaged, the parting when she left London, and his posting abroad, ending with his sad letter of farewell (3 December 1943).

Part Two focuses on Olive's social life and wartime experience working for General Hollis, seen not only through letters exchanged with Neil but also through a complementary narrative which gives details of the main stages of the war, including the Allied conferences where she was a delegate. Olive accompanied Hollis, who was travelling with Winston Churchill, to Cairo, Teheran and Marrakech (December/January 1943–1944), Quebec (September 1944), and Berlin/Potsdam (July 1945), and there are letters charting her progress and travels, including a long one following the second Quebec Conference sent to Neil's mother (24 October 1944). The correspondence then focuses mainly on her social world in London, and on her developing relations with his family, and we hear something of Neil's life in Italy, where he met Pope Pius XII (6 July 1944) after Rome was liberated. The emotional upheavals of waiting and unfulfilled desire become increasingly evident, especially after his posting to Austria in 1945, and Part Two closes with lengthy letters about his search for employment and their future together. She was hoping to find him a job through her contact with General Hollis (27 August and 2 September 1945), whilst he worried that she might not settle down (26 September 1944), and he was anxious about earning enough to live on (3 May 1945). A Postscript tells of his return and their marriage in December 1945, and then briefly relates what happened to Olive and Neil from 1946 onwards.

Because of her exceptional status Olive could not fully share things with her new fiancé. Little could be said about work, nothing about the political world, and no mention made of where she was or might be going, but she did write to keep her love alive. An avid correspondent, she was constantly aware of the Official Secrets Act, signed by her when she entered the War Rooms. Everyone had to be alert to careless talk, and she particularly had to be wary. Writing often to keep in touch with Neil she was always trying to find ways of letting him know how she was, and how much she loved and missed him, but without giving too much away. Her letters are, therefore, full of personal and family detail, and they delight in the affectionate concern of a lively individual. We read of her engagement with those around her, of her mother and sister, and of her social life in London and beyond, as well as of her thoughtful interests and her responses to places visited, and – above all – her desire to share these with Neil in a life together. In contrast to a diary, letters establish a dialogue as a means of communication, and, here, that dialogue is kept alive and strengthened even where distance and censorship might well have discouraged other writers.

All forms of writing were security bound, either by the Act, by official or self-censorship, or by common understanding. No one in Olive's office was allowed to write a diary, nor make notes, nor write a book; and when she was first appointed she was told never even to read a newspaper, nor to think about what she might hear or be told. Her world was simply different and she must not think about it but just get on with whatever she was given to do. Anyone who contravened this risked being moved on or perhaps imprisoned. Her training was such that she did not gossip, so even when writing during quieter moments in the office she said nothing about what was happening at work, although she could happily refer to her colleagues and the fun they had together (from the 'Workhouse', 9 February 1945). Neil used to complain later that she was too quiet in a social situation, but she put it down to that early formation, and was, in fact, a good conversationalist and known for her sense of humour. Her liveliness comes across in the correspondence, and is complimented by Neil who appreciated what he termed her 'bubbling effusion of high spirits' (14 June 1944).

Other people's letters inevitably make engaging reading, for no other literary product can project us so intimately into the personal lives of their writers, nor provide us with such an immediate sense of the past. It is in the human detail we begin to touch the real texture of the times. Olive's letters are significant for the re-evaluation of women's experiences in wartime Britain, and they shed some light on relations at a senior level in the Cabinet War Rooms. She did in many ways have a 'good war', and there is a sense of regret as life quietened down once the nerve centre of operational planning was no longer in use (31 August 1945). Privately, she took an intellectually engaged interest in Neil's inner life, commenting on his reading and poetry, and responding to his artistic sensibility. She is revealed as a self-conscious writer, able to pluck a story from the minutiae of life and tell it with wit. Publicly, she was an extremely efficient and successful clerical officer, who carried considerable responsibility in confidential government affairs, while, at the same time, she remained a lively girlish typist, with lots of friends and simply thrilled with all that happened to her. As if balancing between her formal secretarial activity and her wholehearted enthusiasm for a good time, she wrote about the diverse nature of life, and, amongst the joyful, excited celebrations of her private and social world there are, nevertheless, strong hints of the stresses and strains of absence and sadness. There is here both fantasy and clear-sighted realism. The Olive Christopher revealed in the letters is a complex woman, with a strong sense of her own identity which she was unwilling to lose in that of her fiancé, although she was ready to make a full commitment to him. A 'true' voice emerges as we read her letters in response to his, thus increasing our understanding of her efforts to fulfil and to empower herself as a thinking subject in her different roles. Clearly she revelled in the fact of Neil's talent and the potential it offered for their future prospects, but it is evident that the construction of her self was paramount. What emerges, therefore, as most distinct in Olive's letters as opposed to Neil's is the presence of gentle assumptions about a passive way of life. She could write, for example, about objects in her bedroom (3 October 1944) and the tranquillity of her grandfather's house (11 November 1944), or visiting friends with children (27 August 1945), and thus anticipate her future as Neil's wife; even though, at the same time, she was in fact quietly getting on with her considerably active engagement in the War Rooms, silently observing the action coming to a close under Churchill's skilful government. General Hollis relied on her and she stayed working with him until Neil's demobilisation in March 1946, when she finally became the full-time housewife she had long anticipated.

Olive and Neil were fortunate in being able to exchange many of their letters through the useful facility of the diplomatic bag, though some were sent by normal air and sea mail. Neil occasionally spoke of hold-ups, and groups of letters arriving at once. There were inevitable delays, and mention is made of not having heard from each other for some time. The letters are placed here in the chronological order in which they were written, but, because of delays, they do not necessarily follow on from each other in terms of content; it is not hard, though, to make the necessary connections. Olive generally wrote from work, or from her grandfather's house 'The Brackens' at Dormans Park in Sussex. She seldom addressed the letters from her mother's home in Croydon where she lived when not sleeping in the War Rooms dormitory. She usually wrote at length, and one letter (29 September 1944) continued through three airmail covers. There are only twenty-five of her letters extant, dating from 12 February 1944 to 18 September 1945, many being lost in transit. Fifteen of these are airmail, and mainly typed. They are all to Neil, except two to his mother (12 February 1944; 24 October 1944) and one from Potsdam to her colleague, Jacquey (23 July 1945). There is some repetition between this and another sent not long after to Neil, but I have left in both as the tone and content differ interestingly between writing to a friend and to her fiancé.

Neil also was a good correspondent, although for a time in Italy he had the use of only one air lettercard a week. As he wrote to his parents as well as Olive she heard from him just fortnightly for a while. In the period immediately after being wounded in Italy (Summer, 1944) he wrote almost daily, though without telling her what had really happened. He sometimes drew small, usually humorous illustrations (4 October 1944), and occasionally enclosed his own poems and songs. He also wrote at length about the mundane life of the mess, though he rarely touched on what he was doing, but his emotional response to the bombardment of Monte Cassino is evident (6 July 1944; 13 October 1944), and there is one exception where he could tell of an ammunitions crisis which was already in the public domain (18 April 1945). The earlier letters are handwritten, both sea and airmail. Those from Austria are typed. Olive kept ninety-nine of his letters, dated from 14 May 1943 through to 23 February 1946, of which I have included thirty-two. They are particularly selected to balance Olive's, and to offer the developing dialogue and shared concern for a future together, which never seemed in doubt despite the long separation. I have omitted sections that are not directly relevant to Olive's own story, and, to avoid interrupting the narrative flow, annotation is brief.

Many times over the years Olive began to record her story and wrote down ideas, memos, lists, or typed brief passages that now show several false starts. Extracts from some of these are included, such as a record of the events immediately preceding and following the Marrakech episode with Winston Churchill (January 1944), and transcripts from an interview given in 2001. She carefully stored papers, pictures, and other ephemera of the period, including the grim souvenir of a piece of Hitler's red marble desk, picked up from the floor of the ruined Berlin Chancellery. Her prize possession is a signed photograph of Churchill himself. Neil had told her many times that she should write her memoir, and even early on, in his letter of 4th October 1944, he recognised how exceptional her experience had been:

> I read your news with the same attitude that one adopts when reading "Alice in Wonderland" – it all sounded so utterly fantastic …When I came across a casual reference to 'walking down Broadway' I damn nearly subsided with a contented gurgle beneath the desk. You are a lucky blighter, cherub, & to say that I am <u>green</u> with envy inadequately describes my reactions. One thing you simply <u>must</u> realise is, that you will NOW WRITE A BOOK; perhaps some fine day I may be allowed to illustrate it. Your experiences are outstanding whether you accept them simply as a travel record, or whether you can go much higher and relate them historically to the progress of the war and as evidence of a group of nations establishing what we all hope to be the basis of a new and better order. Yours is the rare opportunity of meeting these peoples, seeing their cities, watching their enthusiasms, noting the conduct and attitude of our own representatives, being able to describe it all in terms of intimate example & detail which in time implies history. Hell! I wish I could see you & help. There's nothing I would like more than to settle down in a deep chair by the fireside, and listen to your story.

It is indeed intriguing to come across such a record, and Olive's letters and memorabilia place her story apart from those of her close friends and colleagues Joan Bright Astley and Elizabeth (Layton) Nel, whose own earlier accounts are here drawn on, as are some of the better known diaries and letter collections of the more famous players of the time. The story is also supported by recollections garnered through more recent discussions with the author. The reader is able to recall the significant events of the period whilst sharing in the friendly intimacy of this couple, and it is here in the small gestures of an ordinary romance that we begin to get close to what it must have been like during those momentous years.

The illustrations include letter facsimiles, photographs, passes, and a lavish dinner menu from Chateau Frontenac, Quebec. They are deliberately mixed, being chosen to highlight certain extraordinary features of Olive's own varied experience during the war. All, except three, are still treasured in her home, but she always felt they should go into the public record and the material will go into the archives of the Imperial War Museum. The Second World War is of course well documented, and the select bibliography offers simply the texts consulted for this book. It is, however, through a visit to the Churchill Museum and Cabinet War Rooms themselves that one can learn most about the life led by Olive and her colleagues in that now famous underground bunker in central London.

Olive's and Neil's letters offer perpetual life to their authors, for correspondence, with its diverse worlds recorded and refashioned for the recipient, gives open expression to the conscious efforts of those who seek to inform others of their own thoughts, feelings and actions. Although Olive has given short interviews to her local media, was presented to Her Majesty Queen Elizabeth II at the opening of the Churchill Museum in February 2005, and is one of the few remaining veterans of the War Rooms who knew and worked for Churchill, this is the first time her correspondence and memorabilia have fully come to light, brought together to illustrate a rich wartime narrative.

Part One: 1915-43
Early Years

'Nothing seems to have changed. It's very like it was then'.

It was February 2005 and Mrs Olive Margerison MBE once again made her way through the underground corridors of the Cabinet War Rooms, near Clive Steps, King Charles Street, London.[1] Although she had not used the old entrance from Great George Street she sensed that nothing had changed in sixty years; it seemed as if the renovations for the CWR museum had hardly altered things at all. The restoration was meticulous and it simply looked and sounded the same. She remembered how she had felt then and heard the echoes of distant voices, the tap of machines and the ringing of telephones. It all came back: the exhaustion of work, but the fun and the camaraderie, the fug of smoke, the bright lights and varnished walls, the sound of typewriters and the voices of young marines. There was the fear of air raids, anxiety about forces overseas, and always the sense that everyone was struggling together to save the country. Winston Churchill[2] had led his team down here to a great victory, and she, Miss Olive Christopher,[3] had played her own small part. She felt very proud, and yet humbled by the surroundings and all they had meant to her and the others who had been there during the Second World War.

How was it that a young secretary such as herself had come to work in this famous underground bunker? What had enabled her to take up this special career all those years ago?

1915-30

Olive Christopher was born in Bromley, Kent, on 12 February 1915. Her father, Herbert, was a 'will o' the wisp' figure and a bit of a rebel. His older brother Charles died when Olive was three, leaving Herbert as the only heir to Grandfather William's business in hotel and catering. But he never wanted to join him, and was told he must therefore have a trade. His choice was interior decorating and he became apprenticed to a high-class firm. Herbert talked about it often to his daughter when she was young. He loved the work, and enjoyed being part of a team. For example, they had redecorated the ballroom at Osterley House, where he worked on the ceiling having been taught to gold leaf.[4] He was undoubtedly skilled, but unfortunately careless with money, and never did what his parents wanted. According to Olive later, it made his father exasperated and consequently hard on him.

Whilst still quite young Herbert married Margaret Brightwell, a talented singer and pianist, whose mentor was Frank Bridge.[5] She would one day play at the Dome in Brighton although she never made a career in music. They opened an antique shop in Bromley High Street, advising on interiors and selling furniture, some of which went into Chartwell, Winston Churchill's country home. Much later Herbert told his daughter: 'I had to show father what I could do for myself'. Although father and son were never amicable, Grandfather William liked his daughter-in-law and loved the children who brought him great joy. He became very involved with them – as much as he could around his work commitments – and he devoted himself to their secure upbringing in the light of their father's mercurial nature. His considerable influence on Olive, as she grew up under his protective guidance, was instrumental in preparing her for the life she would eventually lead. In fact, he was to have a profound effect upon her development and formation, and her ability to fit in with the world of the War Office and Cabinet War Rooms was largely as a result of the social training she had received under his benevolent direction.

When Olive was five years old the family moved to Paris.[6] Her father was a good cook and he decided to acquire a business there. Grandfather William said he should have his wife and daughter with him so they all went, and Herbert opened a restaurant in the Place de l'Odéon. Margaret liked Paris, and it was a happy childhood there for little Olive; but at the end of 1922 they came back to England and her sister Enid was born in January 1923. Herbert returned alone to Paris, having taken on a new partner, but this unfortunately proved to be a disastrous move. The business floundered, and when the restaurant was sold the partner disappeared with the proceeds forcing Herbert into bankruptcy. His pride was such that he would not turn to his father for help, and from that time on never had any contact with him, although Grandfather William maintained a regular link with his daughter-in-law. Olive forever felt sad that they never got on.

Herbert's return to England to join his family was not a success. Having declared that he was really in love with a French girl, his wife – a rather withdrawn, austere woman – was, perhaps not unnaturally, cold and unwelcoming, and life became very unsettled. The family moved to Broadstairs where Margaret opened a guesthouse, and Olive went by tram to school in Cliftonville. Herbert, however, did not like the town, so they moved again to Poole in Dorset, where Olive won a scholarship to the grammar school. She was not there long for in 1928 the family moved again, to Bournemouth. Here Olive, aged thirteen, successfully passed an entrance examination to Bournemouth School for Girls, where her fees were paid by her grandfather.

Olive was always on excellent terms with Grandfather William whom she frequently visited as she grew older, later accompanied by her sister. Separated from his wife, William lived alone at 'The Brackens', a small-ish house with beautiful garden and woods in extensive grounds, close to his business in Dormans Park, near East Grinstead, Sussex. He was a self-made man who had worked extremely hard all his life to build an immensely successful business from quite simple beginnings, when he had pushed a cart around with cooked food to sell at race meetings. Not only was he owner of the Dormans Park Hotel, but, more importantly, he was the founding director of Letheby and Christopher Ltd., High Class Caterers and Confectioners (with the Royal Warrant), caterers to Royal Ascot and the Royal Agricultural Society of England, as well as to many other functions.[7] Its offices were based in the centre of East Grinstead, over the Whitehall restaurant and ballroom and Radio City cinema (a magnificent copy of the one in New York), which he also owned.[8] William Christopher was a man of great warmth, considerable force and tremendous energy, but also with a strong sense of duty and a work ethic second to none. He had a huge range of contacts and was a member of the Founders' Company in the City of London. The Cheltenham Christopher Cup, named after him, gives due recognition to his importance in one of the main events of the social calendar. It is, therefore, perhaps unsurprising that he was disappointed in his remaining son's lack of ambition and apparent fecklessness, and it may go some way to explain his exceptionally close interest in the upbringing and formation of his two bright granddaughters. He wished to see them develop into young ladies like those he saw at Ascot, and he aimed to set them up well in good marriages. He kept an eye on their schooling, he paid attention to their dress, he ensured they had good manners and that their deportment was correct, he helped them financially, and kept in contact via correspondence. Because he travelled often to different events around Britain he was always a fund of stories about the rich and famous, and the girls enjoyed visiting him at 'Brackens'.

Olive's grandmother, in contrast, was a bit of a martinet. She lived with their only daughter Daisy, first in Sidcup, Kent, then in a large house at Elphinstone Road, Hastings, Sussex. She died there in 1930, and Daisy eventually had to leave when war was declared, moving to 'Brackens' where she would feel safer if and when the Germans invaded. Olive was a little scared of her grandmother but adored Aunt Daisy, and loved seeing her when she visited 'Brackens' for its house parties, especially the large ones during 'the season'. Her grandfather grew all the strawberries for Ascot in his own gardens, and Olive once went with him into the Royal Enclosure where the fruit was much admired. The famous Mrs Topham, owner of Aintree Racecourse, was a regular houseguest at the weekend party before Ascot.

When Olive was fifteen she left school and the family moved to London. Her mother ran a small hotel in Anerley, East Croydon, and Olive attended South London Secretarial College for a year. Herbert and his father were still not on good terms, but her grandfather was kind to his granddaughters, though sometimes, it was felt, perhaps not always as generous as he might have been! On one occasion he said to Olive: 'I want you to buy yourself a nice frock – your Aunt Daisy recently bought a very pretty frock at Marshall and Snelgrove'. He gave her a cheque for three pounds, nineteen shillings and elevenpence, which, to Olive, seemed a huge sum; but her mother was cross, as there was actually not enough for the shoes, stockings, and handbag needed to complete the outfit.

Grandfather William, concerning himself particularly with his grand-daughters' personal conduct, used to send instructions in letters, always signing 'Yours affectionately, W. Christopher'. For example, on 29 March 1934, when Olive was already nineteen so out of school and into employment, he nevertheless wrote:

> With regard to your handwriting, it is very poor indeed – I can see that with a little practice you could easily write quite nicely, which is very important from a social point of view. No matter how polished you may be so far as education is concerned, bad handwriting gives the impression of being illiterate. Take my advice and attend an Evening School to learn writing & away from business, write as much as you can. You can buy a Copy Book & try to imitate the writing, this causes you to form your letters properly, & you soon get to write properly, & you will be pleased with yourself.[9]

With her secretarial training Olive was of course an efficient typist and clearly found typing quicker, so a couple of months later he wrote:

> Darling Olive, when you communicate with me again, please write the letter, as I shall like to see how you have got on with your handwriting. I am pleased to hear from you & it will give me great joy to have you with me for an hour or two.

He could sometimes be cross with her, though, for not thinking of others. For example, on 29 April 1936 he wrote:

> Darling Olive,
>
> When you find you are unable to keep a suggested appointment, always state the reason, no matter to whom it may be, do not just baldly write that you "cannot keep the appointment", but write "I am sorry I cannot be with you for lunch as I am still in my engagement, & do not leave until next Saturday, but I can meet you etc". Had you explained how you were situated I should have understood, moreover you have delayed replying to my letter until this morning.... You young people are too casual, but I am too busy a man for that sort of thing, & if you want consideration, you must be considerate yourself, by giving decisive, prompt replies, & the reasons for not being able to do certain things.

I will let you know when you can bring your young friend to see me.[10]

Yours affectionately,
W. Christopher

He followed this in May expressing further displeasure:

I quite understand that it was impossible for you to meet me on the Friday as I suggested, & having regard to your explanation I should not expect it, but I was under the impression that you were doing nothing, & thinking that I put the day aside for you, & thought you ought to have made an effort to come & that is why I wrote that you ought always to give a reason why you cannot keep an appointment, whether with me or anyone else. Never write that you cannot keep an appointment without first kindly stating the reason why you cannot do so.

As Olive grew older he began to invite her to accompany him, in place of his absent wife and daughter Daisy who was too delicate, to formal luncheons at Dormans Hotel and later to City banquets of some distinction. In May 1936 Olive received the following:

I understand you have been able to get a nice little dress for next Monday, and I am looking forward to having you with me at the banquet. I gave you, in a former letter, the particulars as to the train you are to catch at London Bridge, due at Dormans Station 1.11 & I will send a car to meet you & bring you to the Brackens. After dinner we shall return to the Brackens & you will leave Tuesday morning. I think you had better let me know what time you have to be at business Tuesday, so that I can arrange accordingly. I enclose the receipt for Enid's schooling which please give to your mother ....You must let me know of any expenses you may have in connection with this matter.

Accompanying her grandfather to banquets became more frequent; Olive was well known by the society attending them and her role increased in importance. A letter from him in January 1936 states:

I may want you to act as hostess at the LADIES banquet next year (not this). What you want to do is to get a little training in speaking, deportment etc, & not to be 'shy', but to be able to converse easily with the gentlemen who may be on the right & left of you, who will be the company's most important guests. One will be the Lord Mayor of London and the other probably the Lord Chief Justice … you will see the importance of trying to get a good training from someone who is a Lady and knows what she is about.

He followed this up on 7 March with:

I will try & find out if I can find a suitable Lady to give you a few lessons. I will let you know. Meanwhile you can buy a book on <u>Etiquette</u>, which may be all that is necessary, & just a lesson or two on deportment may be all that is required. I will pay for the book, but you had better get a good one.

And when it finally came round to September, nearing the date of the banquet, he prepared her with the following:

Darling Olive,

Referring to you coming to the dinner next Saturday, I want you, if you will, to respond to the Toast of the Ladies. It is not a very difficult matter & I enclose you a suggested little speech which you can add to or alter as you like — it is only a suggestion, perhaps you can get an added inspiration from some of your girl friends, or you can <u>learn</u> this off if you like & just give it. In any event it must not be long.

With love & looking forward to seeing you,

Yours affectionately,

W. Christopher

You will be Hostess of one of the tables.

The speech he sent read as follows:

Master Wardens, Members of the court of Assistants, Ladies & Gentlemen:

We cannot be other than grateful for the kind way Mr Hatswell has proposed the Toast of the Ladies, and while I am unused to after dinner speaking & feel that this Toast deserves a better response than I am able to give it, I gladly do so, and thank you all, the Ladies in particular, for kindly coming here this evening, and I hope you will not be long before you come again, as then, perhaps, I shall get another invitation.

In the end Olive wrote her own short speech, for which she received many compliments.

By this time, of course, she was a fully-fledged secretary, independent, living in a flat of her own, and with all the accoutrements needed by a young 'lady' destined for the world of society. Her father had effectively moved out of his wife's hotel in Croydon, and was buying property, such as rows of houses, to sell after renovation. They finally agreed to divorce, and by the time war began he was remarried and had moved to East Grinstead. It was a traumatic time for all the family, but, though Enid kept her distance, Olive did manage to keep in touch with her father and see him occasionally.

1931-39

Olive's first secretarial employment was with George Court and Sons Ltd., a New Zealand company of merchants and importers, in Chiswell Street, EC1. She was not there for long but enjoyed herself and when she left their testimonial read:

> To WHOM IT MAY CONCERN. This is to record that Miss Olive Christopher of 154, Lower Addiscombe Road, East Croydon, was in our employ as Shorthand Typist and filing Clerk from 30 June 1930, to September 18 1931, on which latter date she left of her own accord. During this period we found her extremely willing and courteous, thoroughly trustworthy and competent. We are sorry to lose her and extend our best wishes for her future.

This trustworthiness and competence were to stand her in good stead later on, especially after the onset of war.

She then took a job with Lloyds Underwriters, firstly Robert Bradford and then C.E. Heath and Co. By the age of eighteen she felt completely independent and had become a chorus member of the Lloyds Operatic and Dramatic Society, taking part in productions such as *Bittersweet*, *White Horse Inn*, and *Music in the Air*. She loved being on her own, and she really felt she was 'going somewhere'. Life in London at this time was sociable and fun for a young secretary such as herself, and there was so much to do; but she kept in touch with family, visiting her mother and sister in Croydon, and, when she craved country air, heading off on the train to see her grandfather at Dormans Park, or joining him for lunch when he came up to town.

In 1935 she moved again, being appointed secretary to Henry Pollock, a bright young sales director with Remington Dry Shavers, in Leadenhall Street. She developed a close friendship with his wife and family, and stayed with them sometimes at their home in Brighton. When, in 1937, he was offered a better job, she went with him to an American firm,

ShaveMaster Electric Dry Shavers in Oxford Street, finding herself in nicer offices, bigger premises, and settled happily for the next year and a half. She particularly remembers lunchtimes spent in the 'sensational' Marks and Spencer in Oxford Street. Her grandfather, though, was concerned about all these changes, and particular about whom she went out with. Seeking his approval proved a complex business, and in May 1936 he had written:

> With regard to the young man about whom you write, you must let me know who & what he is. If he is the right sort I shall be delighted for you to bring him to me, but I must know who I am going to receive before I can consent. I do not like you leaving your jobs so frequently, it does not help you in getting another one. For important reasons I want you to be particular about your employment & with whom you associate, & under no circumstances make yourself cheap with a young man. I do not, dear one, mean to suggest that you do, but I can tell you that a man, no matter how fond of a woman he may be, always despises her if she allows him to be too free with her, hence you see so many sad cases in the newspapers.

In fact, Olive had one steady boyfriend, Denis Ford, whom she had known for many years, since they had met on family holidays at Bracklesham Bay and East Wittering. She and her sister used to lark about with him and his brother Brian, joking, swimming and playing tennis, and she would become engaged to Denis in 1940.

This gentle sociable world was, however, about to change beyond all recognition. The weeks and months of 1938-39 passed by and, with increasing anxiety, Olive and her office colleagues followed events as they rapidly developed in Europe. In March 1938 Germany occupied Austria. On the 29 September agreement was reached in Munich, where Britain and France ceded the Czechoslovakian Sudetenland to Germany, thus securing Chamberlain's 'peace for our time';[11] by March the following year Germany had annexed the Czech provinces of Bohemia and Moravia and invaded Poland on 1 September. On 4 September 1939, the day after Britain and France declared war on Germany, the foreman in Olive's office, a cockney called George, arrived with a huge wooden placard hanging around his neck reading: 'ARISE YOUR COUNTRY NEEDS YOU'.

Instead of meeting for their regular lunch date in London at Frascati's Restaurant, Grandfather William wrote to Olive asking her to join him at the Dormans Park Hotel. He needed her help, for he was losing the Italian staff who were being taken for internment on the Isle of Man. Rather reluctantly she left town, having agreed to do the hotel's books and generally help for a couple of weeks, and she did this so successfully that he invited her into the business. She declined, however, and returned to her job with ShaveMaster, knowing that sort of life was not for her. She left behind her mother and sister Enid, who had decided to evacuate from Croydon to 'Brackens' for a while, remaining there until the hotel was taken over by the Americans.[12] Olive would visit regularly for weekends throughout the war, walking through woods to the railway station at Dormans Park, but 'Brackens' being a smallish house, with only two bedrooms upstairs, it was a bit of a squeeze with six occupants. Nellie, the old nanny, and housekeeper Nora had been there for as long as Olive could remember. Grandfather William arranged for the drawing room to be rearranged for her mother and Enid to have as a bedroom, and he slept downstairs, but he now often used to go to the flat over the Whitehall cinema and restaurant complex in East Grinstead. This remained open throughout the war, and the cinema was immensely popular with the local community who came to see films and newsreels. It was, however, bombed during the air raid of 9 July 1943 when over a hundred people were killed.[13] Grandfather William was there at the time, though not injured, and he never recovered from the trauma of the occasion. To Olive's dismay he died the following April. She had seen him only a day earlier but never had the chance to say a proper goodbye to the one person who had such an effect on her life.[14]

1940-43

In these early war years Olive continued working in London for Henry Pollock, and became engaged to Denis Ford who had joined the Royal Air Force and was posted overseas. She had given up her flat and was living at her mother's house in East Croydon, eventually joined again by Enid, who came back to London to look for a job. Many of their friends had signed up and were now in Europe with the British Expeditionary Forces. Like others they followed the news on the radio: April 1940 saw Germany invade Denmark and Norway, and in May it began the surge into Belgium, Holland, and France. On 10 May Churchill became Prime Minister, to the relief of many, taking over at last from Chamberlain; but little did Olive realise then that one day she would find herself working for the great man, taking minutes, typing, and filing secret memos related to the operational planning that would follow the evacuation from Dunkirk and the fall of France.

Olive and Enid were at home in Croydon throughout July when the Battle of Britain, with its large-scale daylight air attacks launched by the Germans, filled the skies. They decided to stay put even when the concentrated direct Blitz on London began in early September. This tempest of heavy raids went on throughout the winter with varying intensity until May 1941, and at the end of 1940 Olive faced a change of employment when, as a result of the bombardment, her American employers decided to wind up their London office. Pollock told Olive it was time to move on. He encouraged her to look for something to do with the war effort, otherwise, as he said: 'You may be posted somewhere you may not like'. He generously gave her days off to job-hunt, and she visited the Mayfair Secretarial Bureau in Sackville Street, which sent her for interview at the War Office, Whitehall. Her excellent clerical skills and good references now came to the fore, and she was there informed: 'Well Miss Christopher, we may have just the job for you. Ask for Miss Bright'.

Joan Bright was a very special executive assistant.[15] She held a unique position in the British Intelligence community, organising the clerical staff and maintaining a highly confidential service of information to the Commanders in the field; this enabled them to keep themselves briefed on the secrets of what was happening or about to happen. She was on terms of mutual confidence with many in the War Cabinet, and it became her function to organise any special arrangements for senior officers in Whitehall and on conferences. She liked Olive, was impressed by her record, and so, in December 1940, she offered her work in the War Office. Particularly noticing her trustworthiness, she then moved her into the Department of MO9[16] as typist and stenographer, attached to the Inter-Services Security Board (MI5). In an interview Olive described it thus:

> I was just a secretary in the beginning in the War Office. Then I moved to work in the Inter-Services Security Bureau, part of MO9 – all very secret. We used to recruit agents, notably for Dunkirk, to pick up the stragglers and bring them back. David Niven,[17] the famous actor and film star was one of these. I was often rather bored: one of my jobs was to sort out code names in alphabetical order in groups of ten.[18]

Like Joan Bright, whom she got to know well, Olive appreciated the rarefied atmosphere in which she found herself. Joan later observed that, initially, it had been unusual for civilian women to hold any sort of personal assistant or private-secretary type of job in a military stronghold like the War Office. She, however, cherished her position and what she revealingly termed 'its ancient ways, its unwashed walls, the uneven water-marks length of the office-cleaner's arm, the ceilings thick with dust and the dim evenings in blacked-out rooms which held the stale smell of scores of smokes and dozens of thick-cupped, thick-made teas'.[19] She found the officers polite to women, and when air raids came the girls were sometimes allowed to hide behind doors rather than descend immediately to the shelters in the basement. She observed how young women in the War Office in those early days sat merely at their typing-tables, guarded by older women supervisors, with eagle eye and scratchy pen, noting their movements and relationships. But by the time of the Blitz there was scarcely a senior officer without his female personal assistant – a temporary civil servant for the duration of the war. It was to this exceptional band that Olive found herself attached, and they became known as 'the girls'.

Not long after her appointment Joan Bright suggested Olive apply to be transferred from MO9 to the offices of the War Cabinet, as shorthand typist attached to the Joint Planning Staff. She had signed the Official Secrets Act by this point and now became one of only a few civilian women working there alongside the uniformed men and women from the armed forces. Their offices were underground in a relatively secure 'central War Room' which had been created in the basement of the Offices of Public Works building, facing St James's Park and Horseguards Road on one side and Great George Street on the other.[20] Known properly as the 'New Public Offices' – so called when it was constructed at the turn of the century – this building offered the strongest structure of any in Whitehall and was conveniently situated between Parliament and the Prime Minister's office-residence at No. 10 Downing Street. Work had begun in June 1938; a vast concrete block was later set in at ground level and eventually, ten feet below, humble storage areas were adapted to house the central core of government and a unique military information centre to serve the Prime Minister and the Chiefs of Staff of the air, naval and land forces. It was the general headquarters, officially called the Cabinet War Rooms or CWR, and affectionately known as 'the bunker' or 'the hole'. This was to become almost a second home to Olive for the next few years, and the friendships she made there were to last a lifetime.

General Sir Leslie Hollis,[21] to whom Olive would later become personal assistant, had been largely responsible for situating and planning this underground centre. When work began in June 1938 he was at the rank of Major and he subsequently wrote of how he had been given the complex task of designing an underground headquarters containing meeting rooms for the War Cabinet, the Chiefs of Staff, and the minimum essential junior staffs and sub-committees concerned with the direction of the war.[22] The accommodation provided was to include air conditioning, secure communications, an independent water and lighting supply, hospital arrangements, and sleeping quarters. They also had to supply a map room which could be manned day and night by an inter-service staff. Top secret and below ground, it would be reached by guarded stairs from the government building above, and offer its important occupants shelter from the bombing.

What emerged was a labyrinth of brightly lit rooms, with cream painted walls and passages. Air supply ducts were painted yellow and stretched the length of the passageways, and, apart from the offices, there were conference rooms, a canteen in the sub-basement and bedrooms. The events of the Munich crisis had speeded up the process and the rooms, constructed under the watchful eyes of both Hollis and Major-General Sir Hastings Ismay,[23] became fully operational on 27 August 1939, exactly a week before the German invasion of Poland and Britain's declaration of war. By 1941 they had been extended to three times the original size, including the Courtyard Rooms, comprising the Churchills' dining room and kitchen, Mrs Churchill's bedroom, and office/bedrooms for Churchill's closest staff. There was also a large complex of rooms used by the Joint Intelligence Staff as well as the Joint Planning Staff.[24] Churchill, however, was mainly housed in the so-called Annexe, which had been established on the relatively solid ground floor of the block of Government offices in Storey's Gate, directly above the War Rooms and facing St James's Park, as an extension to No. 10 Downing Street. He and his family moved in there during the Blitz because No. 10, just five minutes walk away, was such a fragile building and a well-known location.

Planners at first visualised it all as a temporary refuge, but it was used throughout the war. Shortly after assuming the office of Prime Minister in May 1940 Churchill had visited this secret installation to see for himself what preparations had been made to allow him and his War Cabinet to continue working, if, as was widely expected, heavy enemy air raids on London were to make life above ground intolerable. He stood in the Cabinet Room and declared, 'This is the room from which I will direct the war', and some one hundred and fifteen War Cabinet meetings were indeed held there, and four of his speeches were broadcast from within. Churchill, who daily took an afternoon nap and then stayed up till late, often called evening meetings as well. Few outsiders were allowed to pass the armed guards who kept constant watch on its entrances, buried deep in Whitehall cellars, but any one who did might have found the most remarkable concentration of Great Britain's senior political and military figures ever imaginable in one place at one time. It was here, therefore, that Winston Churchill, his War Cabinet, the heads of the three branches of the Armed Services and the top echelons of military intelligence and planning found shelter to work undisturbed by the heavy bombing raids which made daily life so difficult above ground. As war went on the site had additional reinforcements. The underground rooms survived every raid that the Luftwaffe mounted on London, and only one bomb fell close enough to cause any concern. By 1943 it was a hive of activity by day and night, and everyone concerned with the operational planning would come and go. What had been intended as a temporary expedient was to serve as the central shelter for government and the military strategists for the next six years. Joan Bright later observed: 'This [was] where the country's leading figures ate, slept, sought refuge from the bombs and made momentous decisions about the course of the war'.[25]

The premises were never luxurious. There was no gas cooker and not even running water nor a flush lavatory. In fact, probably the worst aspect of life was this complete lack of proper facilities. Chemical toilets, known as Elsans, had to be used, and washing was done in bowls and buckets. Many essential workers like Olive slept in a sub-basement dormitory, an even less comfortable area known as the 'Dock'. Reached by a slatted staircase, it was bare with brick walls, and the typists, clerks and others tried to sleep in bunks covered with army blankets. These crowded dormitories were barely four feet high and cramped, with insects, rats and a noisy ventilation system. The women had bunks allocated to them, where they could keep just a few things, especially decent housecoats, and Olive later observed that it was a source of great innovation to retain modesty and decorum when they had to pass the Royal Marine guards, from whom they had to seek permission to visit the bathrooms on the first floor. She particularly remembers a Sergeant Rummery who would tease the girls as they scurried by. Staff needed torches in order to see, and for those working long hours without ever seeing daylight, ultra-violet lamp treatments were given as vitamin D boosters to keep them healthy. Some, like Olive, occasionally braved the air raids to journey home rather than endure such conditions.

The Cabinet Secretariat was headed by Sir Edward Bridges,[26] Secretary to the Cabinet and Head of the Civil Service, and Major-General Ismay, at this time Deputy Secretary (Military) to the War Cabinet and Chief Officer to Churchill in his capacity as Minister of Defence. Joan Bright notes that together they 'kept the War Cabinet Offices compact and flexible, as expeditious as a well-oiled machine'.[27] Bridges, particularly, ensured that the machinery of government was well prepared and that the reports and memos typed and filed by Olive and her colleagues were succinct and proper records of the decisions made by the Prime Minister and his Chiefs of Staff. There was a harmony that pervaded every corner of the War Rooms, and Hollis later commented to Olive that under less experienced leadership, or with men less selfless or less devoted to their work and cause, this might not have been so, for during the war military problems tended to override many civilian issues, even though the two were interdependent in a good number of cases. On the military side at the centre sat the Chiefs of Staff Committee, responsible for joint military opinion and the day-to-day direction of the military effort, subject only to the overriding authority of the Prime Minister and War Cabinet.

Apart from Ismay, this committee included, at various times, General Sir Alan Brooke, Chief of the Imperial General Staff, Admiral Andrew Cunningham, the First Sea Lord, General Sir Robert Laycock, Admiral Louis Mountbatten, Sir Charles Portal, Chief of the Air Staff, and Admiral Sir Dudley Pound.[28] Ismay was once heard to say about Olive's colleague, Jacquey d'Orville,[29] 'There goes a very fine filly', but there were never any forms of indiscretion, and the girls always felt the happy collaborative atmosphere more than compensated for the long hours of hard work.

Olive found working in this underground warren of offices and corridors, and with such eminent officers, very strange at first. She was in a room[30] with a few others typing up minutes for rapid distribution, particularly following the important late night meetings of the Cabinet and the Chiefs of Staff. The typists had also to meet the heavy demands of the ever-increasing numbers of Joint Planning Staff who occupied more and more rooms in the basement. The minutes and reports had to be accurate, with two carbon copies, and made available for circulation within a matter of hours, regardless of the time of day or night. They worked hard, sometimes on duty for twenty-four hours, without ever seeing daylight, and the only mechanical sound was the patter of heavy, but noiseless, typewriters[31] and the hum of the ventilation fans. They often had to type a document several times, and the technology was cumbersome by modern standards, but they churned out reports around the clock and ran off duplicates on Gestetner stencil copiers. Messages were sent between buildings along vacuum pressure tubes.

During the period 1941–42 they were working consistently on the planning of 'Operation Torch', the simultaneous landing of British and American forces on the north-west coast of Africa under the supreme command of General Eisenhower.[32] The detailed plans for this first joint operation were of such secrecy that only the three Chiefs of Staff had full copies. Olive and the other stenographers saw them only in parts, and they would type them with someone more senior standing over or behind them. There were also the very early plans for 'Operation Overlord', the invasion of Europe. The girls had a sense of what was being planned, but paid no close attention beyond what was needed for their own clerical work, and they never talked about it with each other. If anyone asked too many questions they were likely to be moved elsewhere, and Olive remembers being told: 'Refrain from reading the press because it would be easy to confuse what you do in your work with what you read in the daily newspapers'. They all saw this as a wise precaution, and it never occurred to them anyway to discuss their work outside the office.

The girls were under the beady eye of Mr George Rance, the civilian representative of the Office of Works and the provider of the complex; he kept them informed about anything going on outside and sustained a convivial and happy atmosphere. In particular, in the Cabinet Room, he had a notice board which showed them if it was 'fine', 'wet', or 'windy' outside, with red or green lights if an air raid was 'on' or 'off'. Elsewhere an electric bell was used. If the red light was 'on' they heard nothing of the air raid till they finished work and went outside the heavy doors that led to the street world above. Joan Bright comments on their additional work in 1942 as air raid wardens and fire watchers, when, aside from their clerical duties, they 'patrolled the building, checked that the black-out was complete and in incendiary raids carried bucket and spade ready to scoop up each small fire bomb and shove it into the sand-filled buckets.'[33] Elizabeth (Layton) Nel[34] later observed that it seemed as if every night raiders arrived, even when the worst was over. Air raids for her were not as alarming as her imagination had pictured them, but she was never involved in a hit like Olive, who one night received a telephone call that her home had been firebombed. She was allowed off her evening shift at 10p.m. and walked all the way back through the raids to Croydon as there was no transport still running. The firebomb had come through the roof and landed in the airing cupboard, with much damage all round. The family had to relocate to 'Brackens' until it was removed and repairs completed, so for a while, when not sleeping in the dormitory, she travelled up to town by train from Dormans Park. She had an even luckier escape in March 1941, when she had a date with an old friend, Bill Sutherland. There was to be a gathering of Canadians at the Café de Paris after drinks in their mess, but Bill could not go as he was in charge of the mess. Olive said she would stay with him, rather than join the rest as expected, so they were both fortunate – it was the night a bomb fell on the building, killing eighty people including the performers on stage.

Everyone was told not to keep diaries and all letters were censored, so this became a closed and secure world where regulations were enforced and the strictest secrecy prevailed. Olive was writing occasionally to her fiancé Denis, in North Africa with the RAF, but she never told him exactly what she was doing nor where she worked. Their Generals used to say to them that the lower ranks were always better at keeping secrets, whereas the senior ranks would go off to their clubs and 'spill the beans' playing bridge! But venturing out, to get your hair done for example, was also, as Joan Bright observed, like a 'punctuation mark of reality' after long periods of confinement during the bombing.[35] Olive discovered they might be on duty for so long that they could lose sense of night and day. Almost everyone smoked, and there was a dense haze. For occasional diversion, a favourite game was to race toilet rolls along the floor down the corridor, and when, very occasionally, there was no work to do she wrote letters or made clothes for the others out of silk remnants which could be purchased without coupons.

Olive later described a 'typical day' in the Cabinet War Rooms as follows:

> Official time of arrival – 9 a.m. The hours of work were dictated, of course, by the demands of the wartime regime. Any personnel on night duty, such as the Map Room officers, for instance, would have to respond to urgent signals and emergencies of any kind which would have repercussions occurring through 24 hours, or even longer. So, one might arrive on duty at 9 a.m. only to find that "all hell was breaking loose"! The Committee Rooms would be occupied by the Joint Planning Staff and the Joint Intelligence Committee, the Cabinet Room by the Chiefs of Staff and, also, sometimes the Prime Minister. Officers would be rushing up and down corridors and in and out of the typing pool with urgent draft papers for copying, etc. Operation TORCH (invasion of North Africa) comes to mind! Interspersed with all this activity were breaks for tea, lunch, dinner, etc., in the Staff Canteen. If we were very busy, the Royal Marine Guards would take pity on us and bring us the odd "cuppa" from their kitchen. If all was peaceful we were sometimes allowed out for fresh air or dinner, which was usually taken at Lyons Corner House at Charing Cross in their Salad Bowl Restaurant – cost 5/-! One has to remember that our working hours were officially three days on duty (sleeping in the C.W.R. dormitory) and two days off.

As the girls were civilian they were not in uniform but in ordinary day-to-day wear. Looking smart and glamorous was important, but a challenge for them in these times of rationing. For several there was real hardship, so making their own clothes helped to save coupons. Tweed, wool cloth, silk and velvet were all expensive, and Courtaulds rayon was not in abundance after 1939; Stevenson's moygashel fabrics were popular, but they usually required two coupons a yard. Happily, though, the girls discovered that there were certain curtain fabrics that did not need coupons so they bought them for clothes, and this sort of fabric was good for housecoats. Sleeping in the 'Dock' dormitory was an excuse to have a decent housecoat, and necessary with the guards there for going to the bathrooms. John Lewis had a famous materials department and would have the remnants they were after – without coupons. Everyone was on the lookout for fabrics, and one girl even had a fine winter coat made out of an army blanket. Olive used to get pure silk remnant pieces and make them up into underwear, for others as well as herself, which was a real saving. To buy new she might have to pay as much as four guineas for cami-knickers and six guineas for a nightgown. There was a culture of 'make do and mend', so that clothes near their end could take on a new lease of life – for example, a hand-knitted sweater was altered into a 'weskit' with a front of washable chamois, by ripping it down and re-knitting the sleeves with a short back, then joining up with the hand-cut front. Turning and remodelling their clothes was not unusual for the girls, and Olive's mother had an old fashioned Singer Sewing Machine which 'worked wonders'. It was even possible to get hold of couturier patterns, priced around seven shillings, so that special designs could be made up. Eventually, though, when some of the girls began to go on conferences as part of the administrative team, they were given a generous dress allowance and were advised by Joan Bright always to have at least one exceptionally smart outfit for receptions, and to purchase decent trousers for wearing on the battleships that would carry them overseas. The extra funding, with its valuable coupons, was unquestionably one of the best 'perks' of the job, and they all loved being able to shop for ready-made clothes in the city's big stores.

Hats were often worn in London during the war, and the girls loved the faultless workmanship of Scotts, Reslaw Hats, and Aage Thaarup, which were thought the most fashionable. Shoe mending was difficult, because of the shortage of leather, so they appreciated the luxury of new shoes, especially Brevitt 'loafers' which they looked for in Lilley and Skinner in Oxford Street. Olive relied on her loafers for the long walks to work through rubble-strewn streets. The girls regularly kept an eye out for new hats and shoes coming in to Dickens and Jones in Regent Street, and those who went home, out of London, used to look into the Marshall and Snelgrove country shops. Slimma skirts and slacks were widely worn, and Selita models were popular; there was a particular outfit in silver grey flannel with bands of scarlet and navy known as 'Veronica' which they all wanted. Olive loved the elegant simplicity of Dereta and Berketex models, and the coat department at Harvey Nichols in Knightsbridge was a particular haunt. It was not rare to struggle saving coupons for something ordinary like a Utility model jacket for around sixty-seven shillings and twelve coupons, though everyone longed for one of the more exquisitely tailored Dorville dresses in shantung or a smart Brenner Sports suit. There was one, Olive remembers, priced at twenty-six pounds nine shillings, which needed eighteen precious coupons; but an ordinary dress in wool corduroy from Lillywhites, Piccadilly, could be picked up for five pounds one shilling and ninepence, and took up only eleven coupons. Those who had previously shopped at couturiers such as Digby Morton would be contacted when a sale was on, so they might spend their long-saved coupons in one go. The message would go out that new styles were in, and someone would sneak out to shop. They had a wonderful network keeping each other informed, and they covered for each other if someone rushed out to get something just in.

Make-up was not on coupons, but was rationed, and they were usually on the look out for Yardley and Elizabeth Arden beauty products in pretty pots for the dressing table, so often bought for that reason. Ardena face powder was used by many of the girls, and Arden's 'Blue Grass' perfume was popular; but Olive loved the ever famous Chanel 'No. 5' when she could get hold of it, such as when she went to the conference in Cairo. The most difficult and craved item was the silk stocking, rationed in Selfridges huge store, and costing as much as two pounds a pair. Aristoc Utility and Kayser-Bondor stockings could be bought at Russell and Bromley, but these were limited and shared fairly around the different dealers, so the girls were on the look out for new stock coming in. They mended and mended their own with a hook as soon as a ladder appeared, crocheting up in any free moment, and some girls went bare-legged, even in winter. Silk was better than nylon, and had better colours; but nylons were tougher, and a treat. When the girls went to Quebec they bought dozens of pairs to carry home – Olive had twenty pairs alone for herself, family and friends.[36]

With the austerity of rationing, meals in the CWR canteen were most likely of the soup, sausage and mash variety, so to eat out was always a welcome alternative. Sometimes they went to the breakfast bar just around the corner from Clive Steps, where they could get fresh scrambled eggs. The two girls that ran it were from the country and would bring back food from the farm after the weekend, so there would be fresh rather than powdered eggs for breakfast on Mondays. Sometimes the girls went out to find a rich wartime steak and kidney pie at the Antelope, in Eaton Terrace Mews, near Sloane Square;[37] but Lyons Corner House by the Strand was the most frequented. On one occasion it was decided to allow Olive and her colleague Sylvia Arnold off for the afternoon and evening – to come back on duty later that night. They went to the cinema in Piccadilly, but as it was winter and dark early they lost each other in the blackout coming out. Neither of them had turned on their torches because they were so security minded, and both jumped when they heard a strange voice behind them in the dark say: 'Have you got your torch, dear?' The word 'torch' had a special resonance for them, as they were working on 'Operation Torch' at the time. They giggled and went on, arm-in-arm, to Lyons.

Friendship, fun and keeping up the camaraderie were important to all of them, and the fact they did all manage to get on so well is evident in a light-hearted memorandum which was compiled by the female staff for senior officers in the Joint Planning Staff who were going to the USA with Churchill.[38] As a parody of greater things it was known as 'Operation Desperate' and in it the girls listed their particular requirements as to 'war supplies' and what should be brought back. Happily all requests were met. A note clipped above the document read:

May 1942 MOST SECRET Ref: J. P. (T) (42) 1
10ᵗʰ May, 1942
OPERATION "DESPERATE"
The attached Report and Draft
Directive to Force Commander,
Together with his Memorandum in
Reply, is circulated for record
purposes and for future guidance.
<u>Cabinet War Room</u>

The document itself was in three pages as follows:

[page 1]
MOST SECRET – TO BE BURNT BEFORE READING
<u>J. P. (To (42) 1 (FINAL)</u>
9ᵗʰ May 1942
WAR CABINET
JOINT PLANNING TYPISTS
OPERATION DESPERATE
Report by the J. P. Typing Pool

In view of the recent changes in the Government policy of distribution of coupons *, we have examined the situation, and the following conclusions have been reached:–

a) The limitation of supplies in the U.K. has resulted in the following acute shortages –

    (i)   silk stockings;
    (ii)   chocolates;
    (iii) cosmetics.

b) The lack of these vital commodities is regarded as extremely serious and may, in consequence, become a source of extreme embarrassment. This must be avoided at all costs.

c) It is felt that immediate steps should be taken to explore the possibilities of U.S. resources.

2. In the light of the above, it is considered that the most expedient method of implementing the proposal in (c) would be the early despatch of a mission to the U.S.A.; a Force Commander has already been appointed, in anticipation of instructions.

Accordingly, we attach a draft directive+ to the officer concerned.

(Signed)   NAUSEA D. BAGWASH
                         LIZZI LIGHT-FOOT
                         MAGGIE DEUCE
                         DEADLY NIGHTSHADE
                         JUNE WINTERBOTTOM (Mrs)

★ As from May 31st – <u>only 60</u> in 14 months!
+ Annex

<u>Cabinet War Room</u>

[page 2]
ANNEX
<u>DRAFT DIRECTIVE TO FORCE COMMANDER</u>
OPERATION "DESPERATE"

YOU have been selected to command Special Mission to U.S.A. for the purpose of exploring the rich resources, believed to exist in the West, of certain vital commodities. These are:-

    (i)   Silk Stockings

    (ii)   Chocolates

    (iii)   Cosmetics.

You are to assume command as soon as possible, and in the implementation of this Operation the co-operation of the acolytes of the Joint Staff Mission will no doubt prove of great value.

For your guidance we append a Table giving detailed information of commodities required.

Commodity	Size	Colour
Silk Stockings	10 ½	Mist Beige
Chocolates	Large	Usual
Cosmetics:-		
Powder	"	Ochre Rose
Lipstick	"	Garnet
Creams	"	Natural

[page 3]

OPERATION "DESPERATE"

Memorandum by the Force Commander.

I have examined the directions issued to me with my usual unremitting attention and wish to bring to the Chiefs' of Staff attention the following important points:-

    (a) I have so far been allotted only one aeroplane. In order to carry out my task to the satisfaction of all concerned, I shall require a special fleet of transport aircraft, suitably modified to carry

    (i)   Silk stockings (10 ½).

    (ii)   Chocolates (large).

    (iii)   Cosmetics (Usual).

    (b) if the Chiefs of Staff cannot see their way to providing me with this essential prerequisite, there will be no alternative but to carry out the following modified plan.

2. Before leaving the United States, it is my intention secretly to remove all my normal clothing and substitute for it a complete covering of silk stockings. By this simple ruse de guerre I confidently expect to hoodwink the immigration authorities, the pilot of the aeroplane, and the Customs officials. My disguise will be rendered even more effective by a liberal application of cosmetics.

3. This will not altogether obviate the difficulty of providing transport for the chocolates. I anticipate, however, that I shall be expected to bring back some unimportant documents, and it should be an easy matter to substitute chocolates while no one is looking. A detailed plan will be submitted in due course.

10th May, 1942

Life in the War Rooms continued as usual throughout the summer of 1942, with the secretaries filing reports and typing memos for 'Operation Torch' in North Africa. Olive was following events closely because of her fiancé Denis being in the desert. In the autumn, she found herself spending much of her precious off-duty time with her close friend Evelyn Low.[39] Not only were they involved with voluntary activity at the central London church of St Martin-in-the-Fields but they also maintained a lively social life. They often went for drinks in the evenings when they were free, and would drink whatever they could get hold of, but had to be careful in those clubs where 'moonshine'[40] might be sold. It was a period when there were lots of evenings out to balance all those nights spent on duty. Olive, with Denis in mind, was usually on her own in the crowd, but Evelyn was going out with Bruce Hutchinson, a Canadian officer. They were all original members of Merries at Number 1 Baker Street, a club started up by a jolly naval officer and named after himself. It was a Friday evening, at the end of October, and they were going to the upstairs bar – downstairs was the restaurant and piano. The club was practically empty, but there was an army officer playing the piano and they took their drinks down to listen to him. He stopped playing and came over, with his eye on Evelyn. His name was Major Neil Margerison[41] and could he join them? For Olive it was love at first sight.

On the following Saturday Neil called her: 'This is a terrible thing, but see if you can help me. I'm trying to get in touch with Evelyn. Do you have her number?' 'Yes', said Olive, and was able to ring off having given Neil the means to contact her friend. Shortly afterwards he rang back to say there was no response to his call so would she be free on the weekend to go out. He was from the North. He was mad about film, and was working in films. Olive said she loved walking and suggested Box Hill in Surrey; so on Sunday they met at Victoria Station and caught the train for Dorking. It began to pour with rain, and they were so drenched they had to take shelter at the Westcot Hotel, just outside the town. They were there all day – sitting chatting in borrowed garments whilst their own clothes dried beside a huge log fire. Although the hotel was not doing lunches that day they did get something to eat – Neil could speak Italian to the waiter, who gave his name as Alphonse Maligambar. Time passed quickly and after tea they took the train home. A few days later Neil invited Olive to dinner at the Royal Empire Society where he was living, and from then on they began to see each other regularly.

Neil Diarmid Margerison was the second of three sons to the Chief Valuation Assistant of Blackburn Corporation. His father played the organ in Blackburn Cathedral and his mother was involved with education. Their family home was at 'The Swallows', Adelaide Terrace, Blackburn. Neil had been in the cathedral choir and attended the Grammar School where, following in his father's footsteps, he had shown not only artistic and musical talent, but also a flair for composing poetry, which his parents appreciated and encouraged. He had gone to Blackburn Technical College and the Manchester School of Art, hoping to take up art as a career, but he joined the army the day after war was declared, to serve as a private with the Royal Army Ordnance Corps in France. There he had risen to the rank of sergeant, and just before the Dunkirk evacuation was recalled to take a commission – a rapid rise in so short a time. He came home to become a staff captain, and since then he had been on an assignment at the War Office making films about ammunition and designing munitions factories.[42] He would later become a senior technical expert on ammunition, and, before demobilisation, advised on the development of mines in Austria. He was a lively and popular member of his unit, which he regularly entertained with his music and by writing short plays and constructing programmes for their amusement. He was terrific company and Olive loved being with him, and with his brothers Alan and Jimmie. His wide artistic talents complemented her own sensibility, and they found themselves very much in sympathy with each another, despite her engagement to someone else.

For the next three months she was in an indecisive state. She attended the New Year's Eve 'Watch Night' service at St-Martin-in-the-Fields with Neil and his younger brother Jimmie, and as the year tipped into 1943 she agonised about what to do. Denis was still in Africa, and she decided she must do something to end the engagement. She felt guilty as she finally wrote to him, much to his, their families', and to her own distress. Her future she knew must be with Neil, although their relationship did come under pressure when he began to resent the commitment she had to make to her confidential work. Life for Olive in the War Rooms grew more and more demanding as the year drew on, and distance began to develop between them.

Early in January 1943 Olive had dinner with Joan Bright to whom she confessed that, much as she liked the work, she was a little bored and wasn't there more she could do? Joan was close to MI5 and on her recommendation Captain Buckmaster[43] interviewed Olive for a secretarial post in his office at the Special Operations Executive in Baker Street. Although she was told her application was successful, the personnel officer in the Cabinet War Rooms, Mr Winnifrith, said they could not release her. His response to Olive was to suggest that she went on leave for a week, and there would be something else for her on her return. When she got back in early February Mr Winnifrith called her back into his office and told her to go upstairs to see Brigadier Hollis, who was in need of another secretary to join Jacquey d'Orville.

Olive was overwhelmed. Brigadier Hollis was a major figure in the Cabinet Offices. Everyone knew him, and to work for him would be not only a great pleasure but also a significant promotion. Although she was sorry to leave the underground bunker with all its camaraderie, it would give her a new challenge and bring her even closer to the excitement (for the secretaries) of secret wartime planning. She took the lift from the ground to the second floor where Hollis was to be found in the Chiefs of Staff secretariat in the offices of the War Cabinet. She knocked and entered, to find him standing by his huge desk, going through some papers. As soon as he saw her he rather gruffly asked: 'Can you shorthand and type?' To which she responded: 'Well yes – I'm assuming that's why I am here!' He then looked at her rather boldly, and suddenly said: 'May I say what very fine legs you have'. A cleaner was outside working on the open window, and there was laughter, from him, from Olive, and from Hollis himself. She got the job, and thus Olive found herself working in the special office of the Chiefs of Staff, joining a small select group which was responsible for the preparation of papers for War Cabinet meetings, the production of minutes from these, and general communications by memo, letter and telephone with other departments. Joan Bright later wrote in detail about how she set up an appropriate system of secret filing for the Chiefs of Staff Committee, and how her girls maintained order and discretion there throughout the war years.[44] There were six girls on and six off – twelve civilian secretaries – and this generally meant two days on duty and two days off. Neil would subsequently address his letters to Miss Olive Christopher, c/o Room 52A, Offices of the War Cabinet, Great George Street, London, SW1, but all the girls called it simply Storey's Gate.[45]

January 1943 witnessed the Battle of Stalingrad, the defeat there of the German army, and the retreat of its forces from Russia. The Allies' position was strengthening and, with Churchill's programme of frenetic travelling, the offices were kept exceptionally busy not only with British War Cabinet matters but also reports arising from his meetings overseas. Another move came for Olive when she was again promoted, this time to become personal assistant to Brigadier Hollis on the retirement of Mr Jones, his ADC, whilst also being co-secretary with Jacquey d'Orville. She moved into the large central office, with Hollis's room on one side, and Ismay's on the other. At this time there were several girls on at a time in this inner sanctum: Olive and Jacquey, now working more closely together, with Maggie Sutherland for Hollis; others included Sylvia Arnold, Mollie Brown, Betty Green and Margaret Fairlie; Wendy Wallace worked for General Sir Ian Jacob. The hours were long; Hollis notes that it was the usual routine for those working close to Churchill to be on duty to receive his instructions up to three o'clock in the morning and sometimes even later.[46] Olive and the others were there too, typing up reports or memos. The officers of the defence staff, senior and subordinate, thought nothing of working fourteen or fifteen hours a day over long periods without a day off, let alone a weekend or a spell of longer leave. The normal pattern here was three days on, sleeping in shifts, and two days off, so, as Olive was still living in Croydon, more time was taken up with travelling. She reckoned this had many repercussions in her relationship with Neil, and was the reason why, in spite of everything, they tended to drift apart as the spring turned into summer.

Brigadier 'Jo' Hollis was very informal – attractive, and great fun. Olive called him 'Jo' in private, but always referred to him in public or in letters as 'my Brigadier' – and eventually 'my General' – whenever she wrote to Neil, her family and friends. She later called his wife 'Lady Jo' after he was knighted. Joan Bright noted that both Hollis and Ismay possessed a 'rich sense of the ridiculous' and an 'ability to descend to the level of their juniors without losing their respect', which was not necessarily true of other senior staff in the War Cabinet Offices.[47] They liked to flirt with the civilian girls but, as Olive said later, in the nicest possible way. They would ruffle their hair or give them a kiss, but the girls understood how they felt and never took advantage. It never really meant anything and anyway they were a bit flattered. When Olive was alone with Hollis he was always utterly charming. During one air raid she remembers walking down the corridor past his open door and seeing all three Chiefs of Staff on the floor flat on their faces, with Brigadier Hollis under a desk. She was astounded when she heard him say, looking up at her: 'Why aren't you afraid? You're the bravest person I've met!' Olive's reply was: 'I'm not frightened, just foolhardy!' and Hollis and the Chiefs of Staff crept out from their shelter. He laughed and said: 'Let's have a drink', and opened up the bottle of gin he kept tucked away in the cabinet for emergencies.

The summer of 1943 raced by for the War Cabinet secretaries, as they typed up memos and reports concerning both the Allied invasion of Sicily, which began in July, and the continuing preparations for the following year's invasion of France. The situation became more pressured still with the surrender of Italy in September, and Olive could see little of Neil – there simply was not enough time to socialise. Excitement grew in the office whenever the possibility of a conference was raised, and a few colleagues disappeared to Canada in August to attend what became the First Quebec Conference at the Chateau Frontenac.[48] The rumour existed that life at conferences offered luxurious contrast to the austerity of daily life in Britain, and Olive and Jacquey hoped that one or more of them might one day accompany Hollis if he were ever to travel abroad with the Prime Minister.

The first opportunity for Olive came when she heard she would go with him in October to a conference in Moscow, and she had to apply for a passport.[49] She was also given a generous dress allowance to buy suitable outfits and warm clothes, for it was expected that it would be cold and they must dress well. The plans, however, altered because Churchill was ill and Hollis stayed back to be with him; Ismay departed with Anthony Eden,[50] his own secretaries, Betty Green and Mollie Brown, and Jacquey D'Orville. Olive could not have been more envious, but there was to be an enjoyable consolation. Feeling very put out, Hollis compensated with a dinner at the Connaught Hotel the next day. 'Oh, we must do something', he had said, and asked Olive to join him and his wife for a party. Lady Ismay was invited, as were Averell Harriman[51] and his daughter Kathy, and the evening began with cocktails at Lady Ismay's house in Lowndes Square. Neil was amused to hear the story from Olive of what happened.

When they arrived Lady Ismay commented on how glum Hollis looked, and asked if it was because he was not going to Moscow. He replied that he was not bothered by that, but rather by an interview he had just had with Churchill: 'I was summoned to the PM's suite. He was in his bath and there was steam everywhere'. Hollis had been ruffled by this as he was all dressed up to go out, and not only got steamed up by the heat but received what he termed: 'the biggest dressing down I've ever had in my life'. 'Well, my darling Jo,' said Mrs Hollis, 'Surely you're the only man who has been given a dressing down by the PM in the nude!' Then they all went on to dinner at the Connaught Hotel and enjoyed a delightful evening.

In November, however, Olive did at last get the opportunity she dreamed of, for she heard that she would be going to Cairo as part of Hollis's team, even travelling on *HMS Renown* with the Prime Minister. She heard from Hollis that Stalin[52] refused to go anywhere that involved more than one day's flying from Moscow, and Roosevelt[53] was not anxious at this time to come to England. Since Churchill had already been to America on several occasions, it was decided that he and the President would meet first in Cairo, at the Mena House Hotel, eight miles outside the city and near the Pyramids. There would be a full-scale Anglo-American Conference, and then they would go on to meet Stalin at a 'Three Power' Conference in Teheran.

Olive was so excited. The few days in the office before departure were a hectic race to sort out the filing and shop for clothes. She had already spent her Moscow allowance and had, of course, purchased warm clothes which would not be suitable for Cairo, so she had to start again. Extra coupons were provided, and the girls were advised to buy trousers to wear on the battleship, and get new 'loafer' shoes to look smart. Joan Bright commented with some delight on the presence of civilian women on battleships, for she had had the experience earlier in the year on the way to Casablanca:

'Civilian women must not go in battleships', sang the Board of Admiralty. Behind them swelled in harmony a chorus of generations of men of the British Navy who had guarded their ships as jealously as they had guarded our shores. ... Aboard, to do the work, would be girls in the uniform of the Women's Royal Naval Service (Wrens), Auxiliary Territorial Service (ATS) and Auxiliary Air Force (WAAFS). In our civilian clothes we typed, flagged, tagged, filed, slapping the papers into folders, and feeling nasty about the girls in khaki and blue who would do the same at the other end. [54]

By the time of the Cairo Conference, however, the tensions between forces and civilian secretariat had eased and the right mixture of efficiency and discipline had become well established. The Chiefs of Staff found it was not necessary to have only uniformed staff, as the Americans did, and General Eisenhower was once overheard remarking to Hollis: 'You don't put your girls in uniform then?' Hollis replied: 'It wouldn't make them any more reliable if we did.'[55] What to wear therefore became an endless topic for speculation for the girls, and Olive particularly remembers buying a pair of elegant and very expensive maroon trousers,[56] and then making a blue linen blouse to wear with them. The joy of all this preparation, however, was held in check by the fact that she would be leaving Neil, and simply could not let him know anything about where or why she was going.

Olive and Neil had been deliberating for a while about their future, Neil especially, and there was a time in the summer of 1943 when, much to Olive's regret, the relationship had seemed to be over. Her job seemed to intimidate him, and he felt that Olive was too committed. Their meetings were few and far between, for although he was still at the War Office he was working with the Director of Army Cinematography as technical adviser on the handling of ammunition, and would often be away on location. This was the case when he called Olive in late October – almost a year after they first met – and she told him, discreetly, that she would not be around for a while. It seemed to induce panic in Neil. He had to see her and, under pressure, Olive travelled down to where he was filming near Hook in Hampshire. She stayed at the Wellington Arms at Stratfield Sturgis, and they met to say farewell. The outcome of this visit was that the relationship revived and Neil came up to London to see her again the night before her departure. They said goodbye at Kensington High Street tube station, where he suddenly said: 'I think this is it, don't you? We'll get married when you come back'. As they finally parted company they spoke of telling their families and inviting everyone to a wedding in the New Year.

There was an unwelcome shock though yet to come. When she was overseas Olive received a cable informing her that Neil had been posted abroad, and the following letter arrived for her, in Cairo, via the diplomatic bag:

Blackburn
3rd December 1943

Dear Olive,

By the time you return home, I shall have left England. A simple sentence, if one reads it out of context. Simple also when one does not appreciate its implications. I have delayed a long time before writing to you. Because we shall not meet, & no amount of letter-writing can alter this fact, the urgency of this message no longer applies, & I feel rather that I should like to nurse the thought of writing until the last possible moment. How strange to remember the presentiment of our last evening together, and to sit somewhat helplessly, and watch events taking shape. Despite myself, I cannot help commenting on a feeling of finality; as if yet another chapter, in the book of our joint experience had been completed. Like a small boy who has watched the Lord Mayor's Show go by, and finds himself gathered up in a great crowd of people intent on dispersal. A somewhat bewildered & frightened child who has to be content with the thought of "next time". I feel that "something has happened to you" whilst you have been away. Something rather strange, & something which has altered your life?

For myself, I sit amongst a muddle of loose ends, most if which will never be tied. ....

I leave Blackburn on the 8th Dec., for mobilisation centre. After that – silence, until I arrive at my destination. I think I shall be out of the country before Christmas....

I do not propose to embark on a discussion of yourself & myself. Experience in the past has taught me the value of allowing events to shape their own course. If the war lasts two years I shall be away from England & yourself for that period. Two years is a very long time, Olive. Much will happen during that period, to both of us. I must leave you with your views, & I with mine. That I think is the most sensible plan. Your own views will no doubt follow in your next letter to me.

How I hate the "finality feeling" of this letter – rather like writing a will. It is impossible to depart Overseas without some slight comment on a change of air, experience and environment. It is logical to blot one page of life before starting on a new one, but within me is the wish that things should flow on, as peacefully & sensibly as possible.

How well I know you, and how dismally inadequate is the medium of letter-writing to express one's sensations. Because I cannot try to tell you all the things you mean & have meant during the past year, I will say little else, than goodbye.

So many things left unsaid, so many ambitions to discuss, so many miles to walk, so many times when I must close my eyes & try in some dim & clumsy way to sense the intimacy & ecstasy of holding you.

My best wishes to Enid & mother – to all our mutual friends, the very best of luck & good fortune.

Goodbye, & God Bless you.
Neil

Apart from a brief and unexpectedly lucky encounter in Gibraltar in January 1944, they were not to see each other again for two long and eventful years.

Part Two:
Letters

(I) 1943-44 Cairo, Teheran, Marrakech

Early in the morning of 12 November 1943 a fleet of cars departed from Storey's Gate, carrying the delegation for the Middle East to attend both the Cairo and Teheran Conferences. The occupants were dropped at Addison Road Station to catch the train for Plymouth, where they would await the arrival of the Prime Minister. Olive, who was travelling with Brigadier Hollis, was to join Winston Churchill's party on *HMS Renown*. She was therefore given a yellow label for her luggage, and there were different colours for the other battleships. No passenger's name was written on the labels, only a code number.

Three civilian girls, Olive, Elizabeth Layton and Margaret Fairlie, lined up to greet Churchill as he came aboard, and his eyes twinkled when he spotted them, surrounded by uniformed naval officers.

Olive later wrote this memo:

> The drabness of Addison Road Station could not entirely conceal the air of suppressed excitement of the passengers who boarded the special train on the 12th November, 1943.
>
> For the most part they had had little, if any, sleep on the previous night, being engaged in a last minute rush to collect papers, boxes, typewriters, reports, files, pack bags and make last minute telephone calls. The excitement was in no way abated when morning came and the party assembled at a secret rendezvous, thence to drive through the dark and deserted streets of London.
>
> There was indeed some reason for excitement. Once again it had been decided that the heads of the two great English-speaking nations should meet together with their Staffs in Conference. It was almost exactly three months since they had met at the Chateau Frontenac, Quebec, but much had happened in the meanwhile, and the need for further collaboration to plan what was hoped would be the closing stages of the struggle in Europe was urgent. But this time it was not to be merely a Conference between the President of the United States and the Prime Minister of

Great Britain. Marshal Stalin had signified his willingness to meet the other two, and this was not all. General Chiang Kai-Shek[1] and his Madame had been invited to attend the Conference and were to travel from China. Thus we were setting forth on a unique venture, where the heads of the four most powerful of the United Nations were to meet in Conference, not all at the same time, but nevertheless, at some time.

Perhaps the full import of their journey was not known to all those boarding that special train. Be that as it may, all knew that great events in which they were to take part were impending.

The train left punctually at 9 a.m. and one felt that much curiosity was aroused at the sight of what was obviously a special train sliding through the outskirts of London and the towns and villages. We arrived at Plymouth soon after 2.30. Poor bombed Plymouth. How derelict parts of it looked as the train creaked over the many points which separate North Road from Millbay.

Out in the Sound lay RENOWN and LONDON. The former is one of the most beautiful ships in the Royal Navy. Although she was built in 1915 and has since been modernised, she still retains lines possessed by no other ship of her Class in the Fleet. She is also the last of the battlecruisers, her sister REPULSE having been lost in the South China Sea in December 1941 and her big brother HOOD sunk in action with the BISMARCK.

How many famous people had this ship carried in her time. Kings, princes and heads of State.

LONDON, although less attractive in line, is a sturdy 10,000 ton cruiser recently modernised.

Our party was split into two, some going to RENOWN and some to LONDON. We were to go to RENOWN and after a short passage in the sound, passing Drake's Island on the starboard beam, we were soon aboard, to be made wonderfully welcome by the officers and ship's company.

Everything had been thought out for our comfort, cabins relinquished and a notice for all with information on all kinds of details – some of quite intimate character.

At 4.30p.m. the principal figure and his party had still not arrived, and a message was received saying that the train had been stopped at Taunton for a Conference. This sounded ominous, especially as the Prime Minister was known to be suffering from a temperature due to an inoculation for typhoid. At 6 o'clock, however, our fears were dispelled and a boat could be seen approaching the ship with, it was alleged, the great man on board. Soon the well-remembered figure came over the side and was received by the Captain, the Commander and other officers. It was not long before anchor was weighed and RENOWN, with LONDON in company and a destroyer escort, put to sea in the gathering darkness.

The passengers might roughly be divided into the following categories. Mr. Churchill and Party in the cuddy. Officers attending the Conference, who had decided to make the passage by sea, a Cypher Staff of W.R.N.S. Officers and last but not least, the staffs of the No.10 Downing Street Office and of the Minister of Defence's Office.

The passage south through the Bay to the straights of Gibraltar was relatively uneventful, if life in a battlecruiser in wartime could ever be regarded as such. Nevertheless, with the great events to come and in the absence of any scares from above or below, life on board RENOWN was a pleasant round of not too hard work, good comradeship, unstinted kindness and hospitality, mixed with large volumes of extremely hard work.

The crossing of the Bay of Biscay was in fact very rough and everyone felt rather seasick, so not much work was done and there was little typing and filing for the secretaries. Their office was in a specially converted washroom, and Olive remembers the typewriter carriages rolling with the ship. The crew were wonderful, and helpful as anything. It was exciting travelling on a battlecruiser and being spoiled by the officers. Olive remembers the 'Saturday-night-at-sea', when there was a dinner followed by toasts; they drank lots of pink gin cocktails, and there was the debagging of a naval officer at the Wardroom party. Greer Garson was Churchill's favourite actress, and her popular film *Mrs Miniver*[2] was the first to be shown.

Life at sea, however, was not particularly easy and special arrangements had been made for baths and toilets for the girls. They took their meals in the Wardroom, and their laundry was done for them. They were even given their own batman but it seemed strange sending off all their clothes, even their underwear, on a mainly male battleship. Olive lost one of her 'smalls' so there was some embarrassment – but tracking them down in the system led her into the company of a young captain called Dan Hunt. One day she received the following:

NAVAL MESSAGE
TO: My sweet colleen
FROM: Daniel

I can see you are very busy this morning so I won't disturb you, tempting though it is to come and speak to you. I send you a silent kiss of greeting and I can see your brown eyes smiling.

I believe we both can understand what Wordsworth meant when he
wrote –

For I have learned
To look on nature, not as in the hour
Of thoughtless youth; but hearing sometimes [sic: oftentimes]
The still, sad music of humanity,
Nor harsh nor grating, though of ample power
To chasten and subdue. And I have felt
A presence that disturbs me with the joy
Of elevated thoughts: a sense sublime
Of something far more deeply interfused,
Whose dwelling is the light of setting suns,
And the round ocean and the living air,
And the blue sky, and in the mind of man:
A motion and a spirit, that impels
All thinking things, all objects of all thought,
And rolls through all things.[3]

Shall the rose petals [enclosed] be in token of all unspoken words?

Very dearly, Yours, Dan

This developed into a rather passionate though brief affair, made memorable by a particular incident. They arrived in Malta on 17 November and
were berthed in the Grand Harbour at Valetta. Malta itself was said to be
little more than a ruin, with piles of rubble and poverty and starvation
apparent. Olive was typing memos for Hollis who was visiting Churchill
on the island where, suffering from a bad cold, he was staying with
the Governor. There was a two-day delay, as Italian aircraft were near
Pantellaria and it was also felt that the Germans had got knowledge of
their trip. All the civilians were ordered below, but Olive and Dan climbed
up to a high place on *HMS Renown* and settled with a record player and
records, only to realise that the sounds of 'Bitter Sweet' rang out at night
over the silent harbour! Happily for both there was no reprimand.

To her future mother-in-law, Mrs Margerison, she later wrote:

On November 12th I embarked with the Prime Minister's party in
RENOWN. We put in at Gibraltar and Algiers, and were two days at
Malta. We had a wonderful time at Malta, which must have been the most
romantic place imaginable before the war. Even now, under a cloak of
darkness, it recaptures most of its old glamour and to go ashore at Malta

at night is rather like going back to another century, to the times of the Crusades. We arrived at dusk – 5.30 p.m. – and in accordance with custom the band of the Royal Marines in the ship played us into Grand Harbour. We had bathing parties and trips round the island and, while the Prime Minister was ashore, we had more or less the run of the ship. The band played at mealtimes and everything possible was done, throughout our stay in the ship, for our enjoyment. We had cocktail parties and dinner parties, and films after dinner every night. Perhaps I should add that we did work during the day! I was one of four civilian girls in the ship and we had a wonderful time.[4]

They arrived at Alexandria on 21 November, and the Cairo Conference was planned to last from 22 to 26 November. Disembarking in great heat, Olive and the rest of Hollis's party were driven to the airfield for the flight to Cairo in a very hot Dakota – the inside of which she felt reminiscent of an old tram. The Conference of the Staffs, preliminary to Teheran, was to take place a few miles from the Pyramids at the Mena House Hotel, which had been chosen as headquarters because of its distance from Cairo and therefore increased security. It was where the main body of the party were deposited, for the residents of the hotel had been evacuated to make way for this large gathering of delegates. Olive noticed the barbed wire fences all round the area, and they were surrounded with anti-aircraft guns, searchlights, pillboxes, gun emplacements, and fire-watch towers, and further precautions were taken especially with regard to parachutists. The US President, who arrived on the 22 November, the Prime Minister, and VIPs, were in villas nearby and the rest of the staffs in the hotel or at British clubs and army messes. When Lord Mountbatten spotted Brigadier Hollis Olive overheard him say: 'My dear Jo – so they've let you come on a conference at last!' She found herself billeted at first with the other girls from the War Cabinet Offices in the Junior Officers' Club, where her accommodation number was 33. In Mena House, where she worked and later moved to live, her delegate number was 22, her office number 59, and her phone number was 41. Everywhere was linked by an efficient transport service and security arrangements were endless; visitors were stopped and asked to show passes at several check posts however important they were. Olive's pass was serial number 147, valid only until 31 December 1943, and she carried a certificate of identity issued 'With the Authority of the British War Cabinet' indicating that she was an 'authorised member of the British Delegation, and [was] entitled to pass freely on the business of the Staff Conference'. She was also issued with an Entry Card, number 166, which was valid with her personal identity card for use inside the conference perimeter. Everyone had to be very careful.

The latest news was that in Italy the troops were fighting their way slowly north through rain and snow, and the Allies were bombing Germany with more and more aircraft, whilst the Russian advance was strong. Lady Ranfurly, who was in Cairo at the time, noted in her diary on 21 November that:

> The conference is assembling. Mr Churchill and his daughter, Sarah, are here and Sir John Dill from America and all the British staff. Generalissimo Chiang Kai-Shek arrived early and unheralded so no one was on the aerodrome to meet him. Lord Louis Mountbatten and General Carton de Wiart[5] came with him. There has been a scare that the Germans know of the conference and may try to break it up.[6]

Certainly conditions were most satisfactory as far as Olive and her colleagues were concerned, and everything seemed agreeably well organised, as she gratefully discovered from her copy of the *Delegates' Guide to Mena Conference, November 1943*.[7] Ranfurly also observed that at the Mena House Hotel the dining room was 'filled with sailors, soldiers and airmen, civil servants, interpreters, planners and staff of all kinds. The food and drink were superb.'[8] Delegates at the hotel were provided for the duration of the Conference with all they could need or want, including 22,000lb of meat, 78,000 eggs, 800lbs of turkey, 4,600lb of sugar, 5,000 tins of fruit, half a million cigarettes and 1,500 cigars.[9]

This meeting between President Roosevelt, Churchill, and Generalissimo Chiang Kai-Shek, was to have as its main subject the question of the Second Front; and then the situation in the Far East, China, Japan and the Pacific would be discussed. A joint declaration pledged continuation of the war against Japan until unconditional Japanese surrender, forswore territorial ambitions, and promised to strip Japan of all territory acquired since 1895. Korea was to receive independence 'in due course'. It was, therefore, a very full programme, with immense consequences, and the offices were always busy, with telephones constantly ringing. The secretaries were informed that the hotel and villas were staffed by civilian personnel whose security could not be guaranteed, so they were told to ensure that all secret documents in their charge were always kept in the custody of a responsible person or were securely locked away in the steel cupboards provided in the offices. Official papers must not be left loose in unoccupied offices, and they had to burn all unwanted or waste papers thoroughly in their own offices, as the only way to ensure that these were securely disposed of. Olive sensed that the atmosphere was very tense and Joan Bright commented: 'The five mixed up days in Cairo were very far from being days of united preparation for the first meeting of the "Big Three",' but it was clear that Churchill and Roosevelt would indeed be going to meet Stalin with important decisions having been made in Cairo.[10] Olive later observed:

> The Three Power Conference was only mooted at the start and as far as I knew was only confirmed after a few days in Cairo. It was only then I was personally told that it was taking place. One of the main contenders was President Roosevelt and it was uncertain whether he would be fit enough to make the trip.[11]

Olive discovered only at the last minute, and to her joy, that she would be going on to Teheran with Joan Bright, Betty Green, and Margaret Fairlie. They dashed out to the shops in Cairo for good quality make-up, which was even more difficult by this time to get in Britain, where it was rationed though still not couponed, and, on the Saturday morning of 27 November, they flew out to Teheran with Churchill, Roosevelt, and their staffs. Mountbatten meanwhile left for India and China with Chiang Kai-Shek and his wife, and others remained in Cairo. Olive thought it was a wonderful flight over astonishing country, with clear views of the colourful landscape. She later wrote to Neil's mother:

> …the General told me that he was taking me to Teheran. I just can't tell you how excited I was. It was thought at first that girls would not be allowed to go on the Stalin Conference.
>
> I survived all the rigours of the flight to Teheran, which took 8½ [hours] and was my first long flight. It was <u>so</u> interesting and I was particularly thrilled to see the Land of the Bible in its entirety. I had my eyes glued to the windows the whole time except when we were at an altitude of 16,000 feet going over the mountains and I hadn't the energy. We saw the Wilderness, the Dead Sea, Jericho, Jerusalem and Bethlehem, the Euphrates and the Tigris. At one time I was allowed into the Control Room with the pilots as we followed the oil pipeline up to Habbaniya.[12]

When they arrived at the airfield they were driven through ranks of guards and armoured cars to the British Legation compound, adjacent to

that of the Soviets. The Americans were a little further away. The delegation for Teheran was small and they worked in confined and difficult
circumstances. It was very warm during the day but extremely cold at
night, when they had only three or four hours' sleep. During the three
days of the conference the girls worked very hard, and in complete security; Olive played her part, as Hollis and Ismay pulled together minutes
of the meetings and extracted from them what was important to state
with clarity. As Joan Bright noted, the secretaries were 'professionals; they
remained calmly concentrated, pleasantly good-mannered and worked
together in friendly familiarity, never losing their own personalities or
their temper. They were aristocrats among stenographers, and it was a
joy to work with them.'[13] Later Olive wrote to Neil's mother:

> At Teheran we worked for three days and three nights. I have never worked
> so consistently hard in all my life. Teheran itself we all thought was the
> most filthy place. All the drains are open and run through the streets. The
> inhabitants carry out their ablutions, do their washing and wash their
> dishes, in public, usually seated on the street kerb. The sanitary arrange-
> ments are very primitive. We were billeted at the local Y.W.C.A. run by
> Americans. They had done their best to make it comfortable but if one
> wanted any privacy at all for washing one had to wash in a little stone
> outhouse which was very, very cold. There were baths, but there was no
> hot water. When one let the taps run there was a most appalling stench. In
> fact, it took us a week to get the smell of Teheran out of our clothes.
>
> We worked at the British Legation, starting at 9 a.m., and finishing
> usually the following morning about 3 a.m. It was always very cold at
> night and in the morning, when one would need hot water bottles, extra
> blankets and winter woollies. But at about mid-day it was so warm that
> one could sit in the garden in a summer dress.
>
> The food at the Y.W. was very indifferent. Bread was scarce and we
> usually had to go without it at breakfast. However, we were lucky with
> meals because both Generals gave us dinner parties at the Teheran Club
> and we usually managed to lunch there too.
>
> I was very sorry to miss the Jerusalem party which was given to the
> U.S. Chiefs of Staff by the British Chiefs of Staff. The General and I were
> to have gone but the Prime Minister stayed in Teheran another day and
> we had to stay with him.
>
> We really had rather a lovely day and felt quite consoled at the time for
> missing the Jerusalem party. We were very tired and there was not a lot of
> work so the General fared for himself all the morning and made me sleep.

He then took me to lunch and in the afternoon we had a car up to the
mountains with one of the P.M.'s secretaries. It was a superb day and the
mountains were beautiful; quite the most beautiful things about Teheran,
which is very grubby and tries, not very successfully, to be westernised.
The mountains looked as if they resented Teheran.[14]

The Teheran Conference lasted from 28 November to 1 December, and
was the first of the 'Three Power' conferences attended by Stalin.[15] It was
held mainly to strengthen the cooperation of the United States, Great
Britain, and Russia, and agreement was reached on the scope and timing
of operations against Germany, including plans for the Allied invasion of
France. Stalin reaffirmed his pledge to commit Soviet forces against Japan
after the defeat of Germany, and the final communiqué stressed the need
for cooperation through the United Nations in meeting the problems of
peace, whilst a separate protocol pledged the three powers to maintain
the independence of Iran.

Apart from the conference itself there were two other significant
events for Olive and the secretaries. One was a special ceremony at the
Soviet embassy, when Churchill presented the Sword of Stalingrad to
Stalin, to honour the people of Stalingrad.[16] The idea had apparently
come from George VI, who had been moved by the heroism of the
Russians in defending their city against the besieging German army,
and Olive had already seen the sword when it had been on display in
Westminster Abbey beforehand. The other big event was Churchill's
birthday party on 30 November. Seeing Stalin for real after all this time
was strange. She had seen many heroic pictures of him, where they
must have made him look taller than he actually was, for Olive found
him to be really quite small in stature, about five feet two or three, and
he wore shoes with built-up heels. But he made an impression, as she
later recalled:

I was in the Embassy and we knew Churchill would be given a birthday
party (It was his 69th birthday). We were allowed to be among the people
who welcomed Stalin and Roosevelt. Stalin, I thought at the time, was
really rather fun because he had twinkly eyes and he was obviously very
aware of the fact we were all there to see him. And I have seen him,
though not shaken hands with him. The PM had a bronchial problem. He
has often been criticised for slurring some of his words in his speeches,
but it was not the brandy. His favourite brandy, by the way, was Hine. It
was not always the brandy. He genuinely suffered. General Hollis suffered

from the same thing and they exchanged commiserations. I stayed on
with General Hollis and Churchill in Teheran, as he was not fit enough
to travel. Everyone else went on to Jerusalem. I formed part of Churchill's
entourage. There was also John Martin, later Sir John Martin. When he felt
recovered we set off to Cairo, and I went to Mena House.[17]

In fact they all returned to Cairo on 2 December, with Olive sitting
alongside Hollis and Anthony Eden in a Liberator. They remained working in the city until early on 9 December, and the girls appreciated not
only the greater comfort of their living quarters but also thoughts of
going home for Christmas. Plans for 'Operation Overlord' had been
strengthened and everyone anticipated much more hard work to be
done once they had returned to England and their Generals got into
the detailed planning of the forthcoming European invasion.

They left Cairo at the crack of dawn and took four hours to cross the
desert, travelling to Alexandria. There they embarked in the battleships
sailing to Malta, then on to England. *HMS London* was carrying the main
party, but Olive went with Hollis in *HMS Penelope*, as one of only seven
girls on board. According to Elizabeth Layton it was a 'joyful interlude'
in the round of duties, 'every minute of which seemed so peaceful and
happy that we might not have been at war at all'.[18] The girls were given
officers' cabins two together, and were wonderfully entertained by a
crew who told them all about the ship and her exploits. She was, they
said, unsinkable.

One day there was an invitation to the 'ladies' of *Penelope* to dine on
board *HMS Jervis* that evening. It entailed a hazardous transfer in rough
seas in a small boat from one to the other, which caused many squeals and
much fun for all concerned. Once arrived in the *Jervis* wardroom, Brandy
Alexander cocktails were served. The question was raised as to: 'Which
of you young ladies wears maroon trousers?' Olive piped up: 'I do!' To
the great amusement of the assembled company, the ship's logbook was
produced, and the day's entry read aloud: 'Pair of maroon trousers sighted
– bearing OH! OH! OH!' Everyone laughed at the recollection of the
party of civilian girls being winched merrily aboard *Jervis,* and they then
proceeded to enjoy a superb dinner and a splendid evening, before they
made an equally hazardous return trip to *Penelope*.

It took three days to reach Malta, and then *Penelope* went on to
Bizerta to await instructions. They were anchored there for the rest of
the week wondering what would happen next. No signal was received
from Churchill, so Hollis, as head of the Prime Minister's staff aboard,

went ashore for a whole day only to return with the news that he was very ill in Tunis and wanted Hollis to join him. Mrs Churchill was travelling out from England to be there too. Olive attended the conference in the Captain's cabin where it was decided that Hollis would leave *Penelope* immediately with Elizabeth Layton; Group Captain Earle, Joan Bright and Olive, with a number of WRENs would fly back to Gibraltar and then home to England. The farewell party on board *Penelope* that evening was a fine event, with the ship's band of the Royal Marines playing all their favourite melodies. This was especially poignant, for it was one of the last social evenings with civilians on board the most famous wartime battlecruiser which sailors had tagged the ship that refused to die. *Penelope* had been crippled three times by enemy action while serving in the Arctic and in the Mediterranean; but each time she was patched up and sent back into action. Her hull was riddled with shrapnel so many times that her crew nicknamed her *HMS Pepperpot*. Not long after, though, two German torpedoes smashed into her hull off the Anzio beachhead and she went to the bottom in seconds; a total of 369 officers and men perished.[19] One of Olive's most treasured possessions is a book about the ship, autographed by the officers whom she had got to know.

As they left *Penelope* the following morning, they were piped over the side – Olive almost literally, as she slipped from the top of the ladder into the arms of a rating below, who happily managed to catch her before she fell any further. The amusement of the crew lined up alongside ship did not alleviate her embarrassment nor anxiety. She lost the heel from a shoe and had to travel without it all the way to Gibraltar where she was able to retrieve part of her luggage and only then extract another pair of shoes. She later wrote to Neil's mother:

PENELOPE was to be the Rear Headquarters Ship for the Prime Minister who was flying from Cairo to Algiers, touching down at various points en route. But that, of course, was when he became very ill.

The rest of our party was in LONDON, a large cruiser in company with us until we reached Malta. We stayed at Malta for another two days and LONDON went on. Nobody knew what was happening and then, on the evening of our second day, we got orders to sail to Bizerta. We arrived at Bizerta on the Monday morning and were stooging around there for four days. Had it not been for the Prime Minister's illness we would have had a wonderful time there. In fact, we really did enjoy ourselves enormously. PENELOPE was thrilled to have girls on board – there were six WRNS, besides one of the P.M.'s stenographers and myself. We had a destroyer escort of JERVIS and PATHFINDER, and we had a wonderful party in JERVIS when we girls were dined in mess and danced afterwards in the wardroom.

Unfortunately, I was not feeling too well in PENELOPE. I had survived gyppy tummy and all the other illnesses which people seemed to get in Cairo. I was not really ill, but was just not up to the mark. We managed to go ashore for an afternoon which was <u>very</u> interesting. We wanted to walk over the hills, and so we hitch-hiked in American jeeps with some of the ship's officers. We saw German P.O.W.s and met lots of Italians who are now fighting with the British. You can imagine that we two civilian girls caused quite a sensation in what, a few months ago, was a vital battle zone. Bizerta itself is utterly devastated but it must have been very lovely before the war. The inhabitants are just beginning to return to the town and we saw them trailing back in donkey carts piled high with all their possessions. I was so pleased to be off the ship for a little while and felt so much better for the walking.

We quite thought that we were going to spend Christmas in PENELOPE and all the men were thrilled. They gave us a wonderful time and when they heard that we were leaving them the following morning they threw on the most monumental party for us. The royal marine band was laid on and we had dancing in the wardroom.

I managed to creep away by myself on deck for just a little while, because I had heard, while I was in Teheran, that Neil was going abroad, and I was wondering then where he was and whether he was in the vicinity. I was also sad because the trip, for me, was nearly over. I was to leave the ship the following morning with the General's two junior officers and fly home to England. The General was staying on with the Prime Minister in Tunisia and would be following in a few days time. He had given me the option of staying on but as I had not been well he said he would feel happier if I went home as conditions were not too good at the place where I would have to stay and there would be no comfort there at all.

It was a superb night, the moon was full, and I was trying to appreciate to the full how lucky I was. I had been given opportunities which were denied to millions of other girls. Here was I, in wartime, in a battlecruiser in the Mediterranean. The hatch of the wardroom was open and the light streamed out to the sky. One could hear the strains of INTERMEZZO, my dear INTERMEZZO, which Neil so often plays, being played by one of the officers, the laughter and tinkle of glasses and the water lapping against the side of the ship. Those men down below had no thought for tomorrow when the ship would return to her normal job – that of guarding the Mediterranean.

I was sad to be leaving PENELOPE but I wanted to get home, chiefly because I thought that perhaps Neil might still be there. Also my tummy was not feeling very happy and I really did want to be home for Christmas.[20]

After a day in Gibraltar there was an anxious overnight journey back to England in a Dakota. All of them were dressed in flying kit, which was very hot and uncomfortable. They had with them one exceptionally tall and substantial WREN, called Doreen Drax. There was not a flying kit to fit her, so she roared with laughter when she discovered that her flying trousers were simply much too short. Her good spirits enlivened the trip, which was very long and burdened with considerable apprehension. They heard the plane was running out of fuel whilst they were over enemy occupied territory, and the pilot stressed there was only enough for them to scrape over the English coast, with luck. Their welcome arrival at Portreath in Cornwall, on an early and very wet, windy morning, was therefore greeted with much relief, and they were offered trout for breakfast as guests of the RAF. Though the weather delayed them in Cornwall, they eventually caught the night train from Redruth, heading to London Paddington, and Olive finally reached home in East Croydon early on Sunday morning, 17 December. She carried an olivewood cigarette box, which had been presented to her, engraved 'MISS OLIVE CHRISTOPHER MENA CONFERENCE, NOVEMBER/DECEMBER 1943', along with her purchased 'loot' from Cairo, and all her luggage. There were no porters, no taxis, and no one to help, but she thought it was wonderful to be home again, just a few days before Christmas.

Olive planned to rest a little for the next week or so. She learned that Neil was either in Gibraltar or on his way there, and, somehow, the mere fact of her having been there so recently seemed to bring him nearer. She did not think, of course, that there was the remotest chance of her seeing him in the near future. Dan Hunt was also on her mind, as there had been a sort of promise that they might see each other sometime soon, and they did in fact manage to arrange a brief though rather strained encounter in London just before Christmas. It was not the same as it had been in the heady days in *HMS Renown,* and she felt the relationship should go no further – she was engaged to Neil, whom she longed to see, and her future was with him. Dan must become simply a friend.

She heard that Hollis had arrived home from Tunis a few days after her, but then he flew out to rejoin Churchill in Marrakech on Christmas Eve taking with him Elizabeth Layton and Brenda Hart, another of his secretaries. Olive told him that Neil was in Gibraltar, and, quite jokingly, said that, if there was the slightest indication of too much work for the others, he was to wire for her.

She spent a lazy time with her mother and sister Enid, rang her grandfather and Aunt Daisy, and then settled in to enjoy the festive season, feeling much better for the rest; but the break was not to last for long. On Boxing Day morning a cable arrived from Neil announcing his safe arrival in Gibraltar and she was ruminating in bed on the possibility of their meeting abroad at some time or other when the telephone rang. It was a call from the office telling her that Hollis had wired for her and she was to be ready to leave that night for somewhere with a warm climate! For security reasons she could not know exactly where. She was very excited, but nothing was ready; so she had to do the washing and ironing and get ready in a space of about six hours, with the help of her mother who was both thrilled and upset about her going, especially as she was flying in bad weather. Olive could say nothing about it to the rest of the family, who were simply told that she was unwell. She later recorded what happened:

- January 1944

EDITED VERSION OF A WRITTEN RECORD OF EVENTS IMMEDIATELY PRECEDING AND FOLLOWING THE "MARRAKECH" EPISODE. Typescript for General Hollis

On 12th November 1943 I embarked with the Prime Minister's party in RENOWN, as a member of the delegation travelling to the Middle East to attend the Cairo and Teheran Three Power Conferences.

I returned to London by air on 17th December 1943 with other members of our delegation, leaving Major-General Hollis in Tunis with Mr Churchill, who was recovering from a serious illness.

In the bleak winter days leading up to Christmas I learned, through my own "bush telegraph", that my fiancé, who had been posted overseas in my absence, was now in Gibraltar.

On Boxing Day morning I was luxuriating in bed, wondering whether I would ever achieve a trip to Gibraltar, when the telephone rang. It was a call from the Duty Officer at the War Cabinet Offices telling me that I had been summoned by General Hollis to join him as a matter of urgency and that I should be prepared for a few weeks in a warm climate.

I was to present myself at 8.00p.m. that evening at the Cabinet Offices. A car would collect me from my home [in Croydon].

On arrival, I was informed that I would be flying out to Marrakech from Lyneham Airfield, near Bristol, with Lord Beaverbrook[21] who had also been summoned to join the Prime Minister.

It was explained to me that because of the Christmas break there was a shortage of duty drivers and my driver was "new". Unfortunately, he was so new and nervous that he barely knew his way out of London, but I was able to steer him as far as Hungerford at which point we had to pause and I, as a civilian, thought it wiser that I should seek directions from THE BEAR at Hungerford, rather than an Army Duty Driver. On the pretext of requiring a visit to the "loo" and some cigarettes, I was able, diplomatically, to ask the Landlord if he could direct me to Lyneham!

Unfortunately, we arrived late at Lyneham, only to hear an aircraft taking off. Lord Beaverbrook's aircraft could not wait for me, and it was arranged for me to fly out in a Liberator of Ferry Command, destined for India. It would deliver me to Marrakech.

After a drink and a meal in the mess in front of a blazing log fire, I was presented with appropriate flying kit and told, apologetically, that I would have to travel in the bomb-bay but they would make it as comfortable as possible for me. [22]

The crew were Canadians and after "take-off" at 2.30a.m., they invited me up to the flight deck to join them in a game of "gin rummy" and also to share their rations.

I had already told the pilot, Captain Youell, who subsequently became famous as a result of some wartime exploits, that my fiancé was in Gibraltar, and he invited me to join him in the cockpit to see a magnificent dawn rise over Gibraltar.

We touched down in Marrakech at 1.15p.m. the following day and I was greeted by Group Captain Max Aitken, Lord Beaverbrook's son, and whisked off to report to General Hollis at the Hotel Mamounia.

Mr Jones, the General's Personal and Private secretary at that time and Brenda Hart, my co-secretary, were already there, having arrived a week previously.

Olive had tried to persuade the captain of the aircraft to touch down at Gibraltar so she could make contact with Neil, and she thought he would have done so but the weather was not too good and anyway she would not have been there very long. So they had a non-stop flight of ten hours, and, as she remarked later, she felt very important travelling out all by herself. The arrangements for her journey and reception at Marrakech were efficient, and a jeep came racing up to the aircraft as they touched down. When her legs appeared from the base of the bomber a voice said: 'AH – that's what we're waiting for!' and she was whistled off straight away to General Hollis, after being given a 'short snorter', which was a dollar note signed by all the crew.

Churchill and his private staff were established in a beautiful modern residence called the Villa Taylor in Marrakech. The Americans were their hosts and everything was done for their comfort. Hollis comments that after the austerity of wartime in England it almost seemed as if they were taking part in some fantastic film.[23] In the courtyard outside their office they could pick oranges which grew there in profusion. They drank Algerian wine and were entertained lavishly by the Americans. Hollis and his team were in the famous Mamounia Hotel. The accommodation was excellent, and Olive happily found herself in company with her friend Elizabeth Layton, who later wrote that the hotel was in a wonderful setting because they looked out on the beautiful Snow Atlas Mountains.[24] All day and night they could hear the faint beating of drums and far-off wailing; the days were hot and sunny, the nights chilly, clear and bright. When they arose in the early morning the sky would be still pitch-black, then pink clouds would appear and the sun would roll over the mountain ridge. Furnishings were colourful and Eastern, and everything seemed to be red and green or red and gold. They all worked hard – plans for the Anzio landings were being formulated – but there were occasional trips for picnics into the mountains and in some ways it felt like a holiday.

Olive was given a 'secret' booklet (copy no. 23 dated 27 December 1943) with 'Information on Marrakech and Taylor Villa' and a security instruction 'please retain your copy'. The contents included telephone numbers, general information, and a map. Apart from basic details about the city, a hundred and forty miles south of Casablanca, Olive learned that the European section was mostly French and that the Villa Taylor was located in the 'French Town'. Allied forces in the Marrakech area included US and French Air Force units, with other French armed forces. Command cars operated on a continuous shuttle between the Villa Taylor and the Mamounia Hotel, but everyone had to be provided with a pass if they needed to visit Villa Taylor. In fact many prominent figures visited the Villa during this time, and Hollis had all his meals there, appreciating its rather exotic atmosphere. He told Olive how, at one dinner, he was unexpectedly promoted. Everyone had settled at the table when suddenly Churchill rose and came round to where Hollis was seated. He placed in front of him a plate covered by a table napkin. 'Your hors d'oeuvres' he said quite simply, then returned to his seat. Under the napkin Hollis found lying on the plate the insignia of a Major General – cap badge, shoulder emblems and so forth.

On New Year's Eve the convalescent Churchill held a party at the Villa Taylor and invited everyone, whatever their rank or status, to see in 1944. At midnight they all gathered round a big bowl of punch and sang 'Auld Lang Syne'. Olive later recorded in a memo:

> We worked very consistently in magical surroundings in both the Mamounia Hotel and the Villa Taylor which was the home of the Duff Coopers and with whom the Churchills were staying.[25] There were several alleviations, notably a picnic trip to the foothills of the Atlas Mountains and on New Year's Eve I, with General Hollis and my colleagues and other Staff officers, was invited to join the Prime Minister and Mrs Churchill, Sarah, and their staff for drinks to celebrate the New Year. Also invited were Generals Montgomery[26] and Eisenhower, who were "passing through"! At midnight, we all joined hands and sang AULD LANG SYNE, followed by the Prime Minister complaining in stentorian voice – "Clemmie – there's a wasp in my punch"!
>
> The Prime Minister was now recovering well and following meetings to discuss Operation "SHINGLE" the minutes of which I typed, and were dictated to me at the typewriter by those attending the meetings, it was decided that preparations should be made for our return to England with the Prime Minister.

And she wrote to Neil's mother:

> No words of mine could adequately describe to you the beauty of Marrakech. The Villa where the Prime Minister was staying, and where we worked, is the loveliest place imaginable – everything one ever dreamed of and reads about in story books. I do wish you could see it – I know you would be quite rapturous – lovely courtyards and pools, orange trees, olive groves, roses, wisteria, bougainvillea, wild narcissus and violets. Tiled and mosaic floors, walls and ceilings. Lovely gay rugs and massive gaily-coloured leather pouffs, low tables and stools, in finely carved wood. In fact, the interior of the villa is an artist's dream and is the most romantic place. There is a tower to the villa with a room, which we called the "Love Room" at the top. It is the most beautiful room I have ever seen, with a

doorway leading on to the terrace where we used to laze in the sun and where the General worked and dictated when he wanted to be quiet. It was really not at all conducive to work and we found that the zest for official business tended to lag and we used to sit quite silently gazing at the mountains. The mountains are every conceivable colour from red to brown, green to blue, pink and mauve, sparkling, sweeping away into the distance and topped with snow, which, at night, can be seen, a thin white line across the deep, deep blue of the sky. In the foreground were deep, rich brown velvety foothills looking as if they were waiting to be stroked.

The colouring of Marrakech has to be seen to be believed. The soil is red; the buildings and walls, the latter being centuries old, and, indeed, some of the buildings are centuries old, are pink. Orange trees grow along the sidewalks. The gardens are a blaze of flowers and orange, grape fruit and lemon trees. The climate, at the time we were there, was like a late English spring, with a lovely nip in the air in the mornings. The sun shone brilliantly from about 8 a.m. onwards and the sky was a cloudless blue, except over the mountains, where the tops of the mountains mingled with wispy clouds.

I loved Marrakech and was so happy there. Signs of Master's rapid recovery manifested themselves more frequently every day and at the end of two weeks he was roaring around.

I must tell you that I was invited to a New Year party at the Villa and drank in 1944 with the Prime Minister, Mrs. Churchill and Sarah, Generals Eisenhower and Montgomery and my own general. I was nearly popping with excitement! They all made speeches and we all drank punch merrily and then we all joined hands and sang "Auld Lang Syne". The previous year I had been with Neil and Jimmie at the Watch Night service at St.-Martin-in-the-Fields. We had all travelled a long way since then![27]

Whilst she was overseas on this second trip Olive received several letters, filtering through to her in the diplomatic bag, two of which were special enough to give her pause for thought. The first, from Neil, was only too welcome and actually much more important to her than the second one, for she was now reassured that he was once again in good spirits. He did not, of course, know that she had left England again so soon:

Officers Mess RAOC
GIBRALTAR
27th December 1943

Hello Traveller!

I suppose that you have now arrived home again, with a head crammed full of fantastic memories, and a trunk full of silk stockings & Max Factor's beauty lotions. Damned shame in a way, because I can hardly describe the glories of the east to one so recently returned from even further afield.

How did it go, cherub? – I can almost sense the sizzle & bubble of excitement that must have gone on in your pretty head – of matters, State, & marvels, geographical. Second question which I must ask at once is whether you attended the official or semi-official parties which celebrated Teheran. The papers gave long & breath-taking accounts of the amount of drink consumed, the food that was cooked, the staff required to do the cooking, the transport required to bring the guests & the accommodation requisitioned to house the guests, until my head ached, & the veins stood out on my forehead. I had visions of a beautiful & sadly "biffed" Olivia, lying under the table, & reciting Betjeman, and of an even "tiddlier" Brigadier, giggling into a glass of port, & counting pink elephants. Out with it, woman! & tell me the worst.

What a long, long way there is between us, and how damn silly to go sun-bathing on Christmas day. Those are my main reactions to Gibraltar. They go together as thoughts because they are so diametrical in reason. The first reaction is so horribly serious & so unalterable, that so far I am unable to develop the idea. I cannot appreciate just now, what this separation means, & how it is to affect us. Sufficient to say that I miss you with the same shock & bewilderment that a man must feel who has walked a long way amongst mountains & suddenly finds that he is lost. Yet, although we are so very much apart, I can still sense you, & share your emotions. Bless you, my darling & insist on being happy.

My home is up a flight of jumbled, straggling stairs, through a little courtyard, heavily clouded in masses of yellow creepers, & up three steps to an always open door. The front of the house has six windows, framed in green lateen shutters, & the walls are of a pale creamy stucco. There is a balcony on the second floor & a little suntrap. Here one may sit, gazing across the brightly coloured roofs of the town to the harbour, & beyond to the blue fused haze which is Africa. The sky is an enormous expanse of blue, & the sun goes down like an amber bead into a sea of crazy, sparkling colours. We have an ancient piano, a bath with an Ascot heater, but only salt-water, a house staff of two senoras, one ancient & wrinkled, the other young and pretty. They do the chars, cook the food, make our beds, & leave us to clean our own shoes and buttons. I share this abode with two full Colonels. My own appointment is D.A.D.O.S. There is a spare bedroom & I shall expect you in three weeks time – don't be late.

May I apologise for the colour of this notepaper – also make a note of the fact that I love you. Give my salaams to all our friends, & send me a photograph. How long shall I keep this spare room for you?

Bless you, cherub.
Yours with true oriental dignity.
Neil

Little did Olive realise as she read this that she would, in fact, briefly and unexpectedly delight in being with Neil in these new surroundings in Gibraltar before too long.

The second special letter was from Dan Hunt. It prompted nostalgic feelings and happy memories of their days together on the battle-cruiser, but also invoked the unwelcome strain of their pre-Christmas meeting:

H.M.S.RENOWN
C/o GPO London
28th December 1943

My dear Olive,

I am most terribly sorry I have not written to you before. I know you will understand, for you know what it is to have so much to do in such a short time that there is just no time over at all and hardly enough to get any sleep.

Well it has been like that here since I got back on board, frantic preparations and chaos reigning all day long and most of the night.

This is the last chance I shall have of posting any letters for some time and when I do they will take a long time to reach home. My Mother will be able to tell you more if you do not already know.

Peter and Kennett are very well and were pleased to get your message. I do so wonder how you are getting on – have you taken over your new job – have the two gentlemen arrived back yet etc.

I have thought about you so often since our last meeting in town. We were fairly cheerful but I, for one, did not feel it really, as I don't know when I shall see you again.

Although we understand one another so wonderfully well and were so completely at ease and happy together, I feel that we really knew very little about each other. How could we, when our actual friendship has been so short and unusual.

We were ideal companions in a ship at sea; on walks through Malta's ruined streets or London's quiet roads at evening; drinking English tea by an English fireside; lunching in a London restaurant; playing a gramophone on the bridge of a battle cruiser. I love the way your eyes light up and smile at me sometimes, and the way you bend your head when you want to hear better what I am saying.

I shall never forget our first kiss – it just seemed to happen. Before I had realized at all your arms were round me – it was one of the simplest and happiest moments I have known. It always seemed so natural and it occurred too seldom. I think we were a little shy of each other when we met again, away from our ship, in London. I suppose that is not really surprising. I only hope the old mood will return next time we meet – if you have not forgotten all about me by then. Anyway please never forget Renown – she is so much more worthy of remembrance, for your precious life was in her hands for a short time and your trust was not betrayed.

Come and see her again one day, my dear, I feel in my bones – because she feels in her steel – that she likes you and wants you to come on board again.

Look in your Open Road and read two of my favourite poems "Sherwood" and "Old Homes" and then read "England" which expresses so well one's steadfast Love of our island.

I am feeling most terribly homesick – I always do – not so much for my own home as for my beloved country. I never tell my parents because it would only make them sad for me and until one has been away, as you have, one cannot really understand one's deepest love of England which grows and grows more and more each time one leaves her.

I am frightfully tired, so I really think I must go to bed now, we have a long sea trip ahead.

Goodbye, dear Heart, for the present – I will write again, as I promised, when I can.

Concerned with you all my thoughts are beautiful ones and you have brought something lovely into my life.

God bless you and keep you safely always,
Dan
Censor signed I.M.M.Hunt

Dan's sense of longing, his patriotism, and his obvious devotion to his ship impressed Olive, but she knew she would have to write one day and regretfully tell him that things could go no further.

Other letters tucked into the diplomatic bag were from friends back in the office who sent welcome news and gossip. She heard it was cold in London, they were envious of her, and she was asked specifically to pack up and bring home some sunshine and flowers. Various colleagues had received honours in the New Year List, including an MBE for a Barbara May, which made Betty Green, Jacquey D'Orville, and Joan Umney-Gray 'spit with rage'![28] The following letter came from Jacquey:

London
- January 1944
Wednesday.

Olive my dear,

Please forgive me for not writing before. It is simply beastly of me, and getting your lovely long letters made me feel such a pig. I <u>did</u> enjoy hearing all your news and so did everyone else. Your letters have gone the rounds and everyone I meet in the corridor says "<u>HAVE</u> you hear[d] about Olive's New Year party. Isn't it <u>wonderful</u>!"[29] I nearly passed out completely, and when I told mummy she was awfully thrilled. I'm terribly glad you're having a good time as it must have been rather chaotic to have to pack up again so soon. Your shoes, by the way, have not appeared yet, but we'll send them on as soon as they arrive. Your letters have gone on – and I took the one to Neil to George (Air Ministry George) as he has people flying to Gib. every day I think, and he said he would speed it on its way. Air Mail is apparently not possible. Then, of course, I had the frightful thought that perhaps he was no longer in Gib. but if not they will certainly post it on from there.

Life, as you may imagine, is pretty flat here at the moment, and I have very little to do. I am doing a day shift and get off pretty regularly at sixish, so there is nothing to complain of, except, of course, missing you all a lot. From my own selfish point of view, it will be simply grand seeing you all again. I shall expect a full and graphic account of your doings, so be prepared!

Betty is off on a week's leave at the moment and is going up to her sister at St. Anne's. Poor girl she has had practically no time off at all since we got back and had to start at the office the day after we returned. And none of us arrived home till very late – about midnight, so you can imagine how tired she was.

There have been one or two repercussions from Cairo, some amusing, some rather distressing. David is a bit worrying as I have had enormous numbers of air letters, and simply can't work up any enthusiasm to reply.

I just haven't a thing to say to him! Why is it that the people you don't want always write, and the others just don't give a damn!! I'm so sorry you weren't able to see Neil on the way and hope you have better luck coming back. It would be simply terrible not to see him when you are so comparatively near.

By the way, thanks awfully for the lucre. I had forgotten all about it (I still don't rightly remember how it came about) and am so sorry you have had to carry it about all this time.

We laughed so much over your description of the plane journey out. Betty and I wasted much official time trying to work out how on earth you managed under such difficult circumstances!!! We also enjoyed your letter to Margaret F. so much. She came in yesterday and we swopped letters and shrieked out our various bits of news till we were both quite hoarse.

Did I tell you that I had a letter from that dreadful Major Barsdorf's wife, saying could I come to tea and give her all the news. She had had a letter from him introducing me. I really don't want to much but I suppose it would mean a lot to her to get some first hand news of him. Mummy said she sounded simply sweet over the phone.

Simply must rush now as I've just collected two wretched Most Immediates and everyone's flapping.

Wish I could write you something exciting Olive, but you know how little gossip there is at moments like these. There is no one in the Office to gossip about! Love to everyone. I shall try to drop a line to Brenda. Love specially to the General and also to Jonah – it will be fun to see him again. So glad he's being decent. Lots of love Olive dear from

Jacquey

It was an enjoyably interesting, though hardworking, three weeks for Olive in Marrakech, where everyone observed the Prime Minister getting visibly stronger day by day. She recently recalled as follows:

Churchill was a man of great energy... but the PM [had become] extremely ill. Mrs Churchill and Sarah flew out from London – and it was decided he should go to Marrakech, to the Duff Coopers. They were part of the delegation [in Cairo] because he was Ambassador to Paris at the time, and so he was there representing the contingent involved with France. They were allocated a villa in Marrakech. I stayed at the Mamounia Hotel. You see it often on television in programmes like 'Wish You Were Here', and I say 'I Wish I Was'! We worked very hard. We didn't complain.

It was hard because it was demanding. We had to be available at any hour of the day or night. We were taking down minutes for there were meetings going on all the time.[30]

It was half way through January when the time came to depart because Churchill thought he ought to be back in London for the Anzio landing on 21 January.[31] They were flown to Gibraltar, to embark in the battleship *HMS King George V* in which the Churchill family was also travelling back to England. And it was here, on the brief touchdown at Gibraltar, that Olive joyfully made her brief but sweet encounter with Neil and was able to see him in his new surroundings. It was a meeting that would be treasured in both their memories for the next two years. She recorded later in a memo:

The Duff Coopers gave a farewell party for us the night before our departure (an abiding memory). The crews of the aircraft which were to fly us to Gibraltar the following day had been invited. In the course of the evening, General Hollis told me that he had done everything possible to enable me to contact my fiancé in Gibraltar, and Mr. Jones, his P.P.S. had instructions to help me.

We touched down in Gibraltar after a two hour flight and, contrary to our plans and expectations, Brenda Hart and I were whisked off in an Army car with an escort, destination the Rock Hotel. Anticipating problems about contacting my fiancé I asked the young Army Captain accompanying us if it would be difficult to contact the R.A.O. C. I told him that my fiancé was Major Neil Margerison, D.A.D.O.S. (AM) who had recently arrived in Gibraltar and he knew him!

He stopped the car at the nearest call box and telephoned Neil to tell him that I had arrived. Neil, who had been at lunch, was waiting for us as we drove up to the Mess. When we said "goodbye" in London, less than three months previously before I left for Cairo, neither of us thought we would meet again in Gibraltar.

Neil's Brigadier released him for the rest of the day and Neil suggested that we celebrated by having a drink in the Bristol grill. As we walked down the stairs to the Bar, suddenly there was a great cheer. It was from the crew of the Liberator who were now on their way back to England from India! It was a memorable reunion for me!

I had already been told that I must report back to the Rock Hotel in time to leave for the ship at 9.00p.m. Neil came up with me and met most of our party and was able to come down to the docks with us.

I sailed back to England with the Prime Minister, Mrs Churchill and Sarah, and General Hollis and my colleagues, in KING GEORGE V. Neil was allowed to the docks to see our departure and it was a very tense, white-faced fiancé who stood there, quite alone, and who, all too rapidly, became a shadow and then was lost in the darkness.

The ship was anchored well out of the harbour and got away immediately we embarked. After an eventful three-day trip, we arrived in England.

In a little under three months, I had travelled in three battleships, RENOWN, PENELOPE, and KING GEORGE V, and flown thousands of miles.

I had also twice celebrated "Saturday Night at Sea" in the company of Winston Churchill, first in RENOWN, on our way to the Middle East, and then in KING GEORGE V, when Mrs Churchill and Sarah were also present.

After their meeting Neil cheerfully wrote to Olive:

Officers Mess RAOC
GIBRALTAR
- January 1944

Hello Darling,

I have been standing outside my balcony. You sat there and drank lime-juice. I have been standing there at the foot of an enormous bridge that spans yourself & myself, trying to sense you in the darkness & tell you by thinking hard, how very much I love you. How much I long to kiss you, to hold you so warmly against me, nuzzle my nose into the soft warm parts of your throat, stare at your eyes, the silky white down of your cheeks, tease you, embrace you, frighten you with the intensity of my love. Then a ship's siren sounds – everything sounds unnatural. I feel utterly alone & marooned & I yearn for a bright light again. I step inside and pour myself a whiskey. One cannot commit the emotion of one's feelings to the tired medium of letter writing. I think I say more to you when I lean on my railings & stare towards you in the darkness?

Did you see me in Gibraltar? As the days pass, & a warm sunshine splashes the walls, stirring the dull flies & casting too strong shadows across my windows, I think of you in terms of darkness, cool plains & the intimacy of my dreams. Something which shares, & walks in step with, the deep secrecy of my ambitions – my very private thoughts. Let me repeat,

& don't accept it as a trite remark, that I love you. That I am "burnt up" with a longing for you, a respect for your courage, your character, & the trust in which you have placed one.

We shall go far, darling, as we said as we fell across the stairs on Morello's Ramp, "nothing normal happens"! Thank God for our abnormality & not because it is "nice to be different" but because we both feel the excitement of adventure, & because we both share the courage of experiment – Wordsworth's "genial sense of youth".

I am going to bed very shortly because I have too much to say to you, and because my sole contentment is to lie in the quiet of my room & think for long, long hours on the happy fortune of yourself & myself.

War divides us; it also heightens within us the urge to share whatever is fine & morally good in this world. I am one of the happiest mortals, because I have such an unfailing confidence both in you, & in our <u>mutual</u> success. War, or its echoes will shadow & inspire the whole of our lives. Before long it will occur again. By then we shall be married, shall have consummated & improved the enormous bond of ambition that lies between us. Until next time,

God bless you, darling, & apologies for being so foolishly serious.
Yours, always,
Neil

At the same time Neil recorded their encounter in a letter to his family:

…Olive suddenly arrived from the clouds together with a conglomeration of Cabinet officials. I was given the day off. It is impossible to describe the utter ecstasy of that day, the way we talked, the experiences shared, the horrible feeling of sadness when she left. I am, no doubt, in love, & very convinced that I shall make Olive my wife. Amongst other things she saw the New Year in with Mr Churchill & Generals Eisenhower & Montgomery! What a thing to tell one's children. …[32]

Some time after she arrived home Olive wrote a long letter to her future mother-in-law about these two exciting winter trips to the Middle East and North Africa, and she related the happy meeting with Neil and her mixed feelings of awe and pride in all she had experienced:

Croydon
12th February 1944

Dear Mrs. Margerison,

…I was very sorry to leave Marrakech but my departure was made more cheerful as the General had promised that he would do everything possible to contact Neil for me at Gibraltar. We touched down at Gib. After a two-hour flight and you can imagine how I felt as we landed on the rock? Was Neil there or had he gone away? I bobbed up and down and the General was very amused at me. To my horror, however, I was whistled away, with Brenda, from our party and was taken to the Rock Hotel. The General said he would 'phone Neil from Government House and would get him to me as soon as he could, but I didn't want to waste any time and I asked the officer who was with us if it would be difficult to contact the R.A.O.C. He replied that it would be easy and who did I want? I said "Major Margerison, DADOS (Am.)" and he knew him! He went straight off and 'phoned Neil telling him that I had arrived and Neil was waiting for us as we drove up the little street leading to his Mess. Poor Neil, he couldn't think of anything to say for quite ten minutes. Neither of us could. I just can't tell you how we felt. When we said good-bye in London before I left for Cairo, neither of us thought that we would meet again in Gibraltar.

There was so much to tell each other and we had a lovely day together. I liked Neil's mess and both the colonels there very much. I had tea and dinner at the Mess and stood on the balcony overlooking the harbour with Neil, gazing at his beloved Spanish hills.

While we were in the Bristol having some drinks the crew of the aircraft who had flown me out to Marrakech came in. They had been to India and back in the meantime and were so surprised to see me. They were very amusing about my flight with them and had Neil absolutely green with envy!

We had to be ready to leave the Rock Hotel for the ship at 9 o'clock and Neil came up with me and met most of the party. Unfortunately, he missed the General who was tied up at Government House. Neil was able to come down to the Docks with us, although I half regretted allowing him to come when the boat was drawing away from the docks and I was leaving him behind. It was a very tense, white-faced Neil who, all too rapidly, became a shadow and got lost in the darkness. Never will I forget that moment.

The ship which, for the moment, shall be nameless, was anchored well out of the harbour and got under way immediately we embarked. After a three-day trip which, socially, was again very eventful, we arrived in England. In a little under three months I had travelled in three battleships, been to a party in a destroyer and had flown 10,000 miles. On the trip home we had "Saturday Night at Sea" which was very impressive, as the Prime Minister and Mrs. Churchill came down to dine in the Wardroom and the ladies, in accordance with custom were "dined in Mess", the toast, or one of them being "To our wives and sweethearts, may they never meet". The senior WRNS officer replied "To our wives, sweethearts, husbands and boyfriends". It was a splendid occasion and one that I shall never forget. But then I have had so many "peak" moments, not the least of which was seeing Neil on the Rock.

I could fill a book with a description of all my experiences and emotional reactions to the events of the past three months.

…My supreme emotion on the trip out to Cairo in RENOWN was that of trying to appreciate how lucky I was. Whenever I managed to be alone on deck, which was not very often, I loved to stand in the bows, leaning on the rail, watching the wake and then turn and look up to the Bridge. The ship in which I was travelling was the most beautiful ship in the world and the only one of her class left and, what was more important and exciting, she was also carrying the greatest man England has ever known. But I could not appreciate it to the full at the time – one can only do that in retrospect and over a period of years.

Now I am left "mentally breathless" by all the excitement and experiences of the trip. I wish so much that Neil was in England.

I am sorry, for your sakes, that he was so gloomy while he was on leave. I knew he was miserable from the letter he wrote me which I received in Cairo after my return from Teheran. I must say I felt equally miserable at the prospect of not seeing him again, perhaps for years. But again, we were lucky.

Neil really is happy in Gibraltar. I do not think he will be bored there, except that there is not much scope for walking, but he has his painting, sketching, writing and dramatics and now sailing. But I expect he has told you all about it!

I would love to come up and see you in the summer if it can be arranged – perhaps Neil himself will be in England again by then.

I hope you won't be bored with this very long letter, and please forgive me for typing it – it is so much quicker. As you say, there is much that must remain 'verboten' for a time, but security objections have been waived on all the things I have told you.

I hope you are getting news of Alan and Jimmie through quickly. I'm sorry that all the boys are away at the same time, but let's hope they will be home soon.

Please remember me to your sister and Joan and Dr. and Mrs. Porteous.[33]

My love to you and Mr.Margerison. I would love to hear from you again when you have time.

Olive

Meanwhile, she and the other secretaries were run off their feet in the War Rooms. General Hollis was busy with endless meetings; Churchill and the War Cabinet were making decisions that would affect events in Europe; and the whole course of the war was about to change, with victory in sight.

(II) 1944 Quebec

Months and months of detailed planning had gone into the preparation of 'Operation Overlord', the Allied invasion of France, and, according to General Hollis, the early part of 1944 became a long period of 'dull slogging'.[34] England appeared dark and damp to those in the War Rooms who had enjoyed the contrasting sunshine and exotic atmosphere of Marrakech. Olive remembers it as a time of 'over, and over and over again', going through plans and agendas, rewriting memos and minutes of meetings, with endless filing. Preparations were pursued in detail; directions were being issued and duplicated for everyone involved, and Olive and her colleagues found they were working very hard simply to keep up with the reports and memos coming through from Hollis, who, as Secretary to the Chiefs of Staffs Committee, said he found little time for any form of relaxation with so much going on. From the earliest planning stages several of the girls knew the date of 'D-Day' – though of course they just kept that information to themselves. They all knew the Normandy landings were going to be the largest amphibian assault in history, and that the whole of Southern England was in the process of becoming a vast military camp.

On 22 January British and American forces landed at Anzio, on the western coast of Italy. In February, after dropping leaflets warning Italians to evacuate the area, the Allied air forces began to blitz an ancient monastery, the birthplace of the Benedictine Order, standing high above the town of Monte Cassino. It was finally destroyed on 15 February in what became a deeply controversial attack. German forces were spread out across the surrounding area, and there was mountain warfare at its harshest. Fighting went on for weeks until the monastery was eventually captured on 18 May: the desolation from the bombing and battle leaving behind the awesome horror of war, which was to have a profound effect upon Neil when he visited the area later in the year.[35]

By 22 May he was with the Allied forces in Italy, having flown in from Gibraltar, via Oran and Algiers. In a letter dated 25 May he told Olive he was in Italy but could not tell her exactly where, and he was rationed in letter cards, having only one a week, so he decided to send one to his family and one to her fortnightly for a while. She did not therefore hear much about what he was doing, though she followed the news of movements there as well as she could from work. Around this time his jeep got blown up and he was injured, lucky to be alive but effectively suffering from shell shock. He was hospitalized for three weeks, but did not tell Olive anything about it and she never would know the full details. He did, however, return to his unit and by 4 June was with the troops when Rome was liberated. Two days later everyone at home was busy monitoring the 'D-Day' landings and then they waited for news of the Allies' slow and difficult advance through northern France. Soviet forces were pushing closer towards Germany from the east, and Olive with her colleagues knew that Stalin aimed to establish Communist regimes and that Churchill and Roosevelt wanted to prevent this. So there was talk again of conferences, and Olive hoped she might be lucky once more.

She often had people complain that she never talked about her job, but, of course, it had been impossible to tell anyone about anything, and especially 'Overlord'. Her friend Evelyn Low pushed her and pushed her, but she resisted all the pressure. She remembers that when the Normandy landings happened Evelyn rang her up and said: 'I'll never forgive you for not telling me, your very best friend.' Olive replied that she was security bound, but Evelyn's bitter response was simply: 'Well that's it … end of friendship!' She calmed down, however, and said she would be in touch. And she did call again some days later, to say she had applied for a new job and was being sent to General Eisenhower's Headquarters in France so they would not see each other for a while.[36]

The Allies' presence in Europe meant not only the approaching end to war but also greater ease of communication, and from henceforth Olive and Neil's correspondence became much more frequent – Olive managing to keep more of Neil's letters than he did of hers. The excitement of events, the thrill of being on the winning side, and the expectation of an easier life once it was all over, led to deeper feelings for each other and relief that life would soon change for the better. His delighted response to the invasion of France reached her a couple of weeks later:

Italy
HQ AAI
CMF
14th June 1944

Hello darling,

My mind is a complete muddle at the moment. There are two reasons. Reason 1, received an enormous bumper of mail from you & home. I think it's all caught up to schedule, now. Anyhow I have been lying on my camp bed for the past hour reading letter after letter, registering news flash after news flash and generally wriggling with pleasure. Reason 11. Had a hell of a trip which I concluded yesterday & already exists in my mind as a muddle of mountains, long straight roads, bumpy twisted roads, roads with tarmacadam, roads with holes feet deep, roads beside the Adriatic, roads curling across the bottom corner of heaven, roads writhing in valleys – lots of ruddy roads...

I think I've been doing too much. Most things seem eclipsed here by the news of the Second Front. Wish I were there. God! What an experience, one loses all sense of the physical hazards in the sheer blind glory of it all; as a sense of sheer heroism it is abstractedly beautiful, as a thought of suffering it must be sheer & utter hell....

Your letter writing is the most happy bubbling effusion of high spirits I've ever read. It's quite fantastic. Like a little girl who has got a marvellous dolly, & has been given permission to describe it – only stopping for breath & with the most enormous blue eyes. Really, cherub, you're a wizard person!...

Now for Songs and the General's friend.[37] Certainly I will write to him but with absolutely nothing to offer him other than my ambitions, and nothing in my poor old napper. I'm not writing poetry at the moment, darling – simply because I cannot make up my mind about things. I've got all sorts of ideas, jottings scribbled down, sketches on envelopes & nothing besides...

Give my love to London and stand and have a "long think" for me into the Thames. Beware of dark corners, said she. I must close darling & find my bed. I wish I could hold you – if only for a moment. God bless and keep smiling.

All my love, Neil.

Italy
AAI CMF
6th July 1944

Hello,

Same wavelength, same bloke, different inside. I could almost find it in my heart to moan. You know – a real long fruity letter of sorrows and sins;

but to be frank and to the point. I have had dysentery, and came on deck this morning with glazed eyeballs and a tummy that still seemed to belong to someone else. The M.O. gave me the benefits of a new cure; tablets of the M & B family, called sulpha-something or something, which worked ruddy miracles but produced a most morbid outlook. I found myself looking for a length of rope; and eyeing my revolver with evil intent.

But, this morning, I shook hands with Pope Pius XII, in holy audience at the Vatican City and thus forgot my tummy except to ask myself halfway through the proceedings "what would happen if …?" I'm now feeling quite a hell of a fellow and proud of my morning's activities. Something to tell the cook's mother. His Holiness had an excellent stage manager. We stood in a long hall, massive in gold, festoons, enormous lamp pendants & tempera paintings. The focal point, an enormous throne of gold and red velvet reposing under a canopy of white silks and golden embroidery. Spot lights on the throne. Vatican Pikemen with funny hats – and suits of medieval-cut slashed with lacings of orange & blue, looking like figures from off a marmalade-jar label. (I can't remember which one). The hall packed with all sorts & conditions of allied soldiery, with Americans audibly to the fore. Enter the Pope, preceded by a retinue of men in gleaming helmets, gorgeous plumage, knee breeches & fal-de-lals, whilst the Pope is carried on a chair by six men, (& one who kept running about for a place), all dressed in red.

The Pope extended his blessing from side to side, beaming benevolently. Halfway down the Throne Room an American jumps on to a pillar and cries in best Bowery "Three Cheers for the Pope".[38] I recoil in embarrassment but the request is answered. I think wildly of Winchester Cathedral & a Johnny standing up thuswise & shouting "Three cheers for the Bish!" Well, the Pope finally climbs on to his real throne and speaks to us in English, French and Italian. He tells us of the war, stresses its horrors, and reminds us in the depths of our warmongering & despair not to forget God. He then speaks of "our dear ones at home" & promises to bless them for us. I think – quite like a big baby – of you, & my family, & lots more & thank him for an intimate secret shared. The shafts of sunlight pour in through the windows on to a black & white chequered floor of marble and coolness, & one or two of the faces round about become almost an inspiration, – particularly a tall, handsome pilot across the way with a D.F.C. & a chin like a crusader. The Pope then pronounces the blessing in Latin. He then stepped down from the throne & chatted to one or two. All the Officers were in front, & somehow he was suddenly in front of me, smiling. I took his hand, kissed the holy Ring, bowed, and said "Good morning, Sir". He asked me where I came from. I replied

"England". What part? "Lancashire". He grinned broadly and went on. I thought him a damn nice bloke, with an enormous personality and a terrific brain. I didn't like his little white hat.

When I turn the page I think of Cassino, because it is one of those sights which make one go sick inside until one feels ready to slink off, right into the middle of the biggest forest & talk out loud to the tree tops. It is a place about which one cannot speak to other people. If you meet a bloke who has seen it, one can express a mutual comment with the eyes alone. Politically, "it had to be". That we all know and acknowledge. I couldn't describe it because there is nothing left to describe – unless the passage of a bird across rubble, or the slime of a waterfilled crater are things one can feel & build atmosphere around.

Now you and your constant bubbles – every letter with a pop! – like a heritage of champagne.

You have got me doodling. I've got a glorious montage of you, gurgling about babies, thrilled as a father about your legacy, dancing along on a hoppity leg, suddenly flopping sick, deciding to have a flat, deciding not to have a flat, deciding to be solemn & spoiling it all with a laugh, being chased up road after road by flying bombs, tugging families from under the table, being tremendously happy, & tremendously busy. I say to you, very solemn-like, across a table, if you will, at Merries[39] perhaps, that I am simply glowing at this very moment in the sheer benison of your happiness. I can sense it, enjoy it, soak in it, – like having a very hot bath & and plenty hot left in the cistern. –Cherub, look back with me and beside me, at the misery we both have wrestled with. Think of those empty, hideous, unfriendly, darkened days when you cried & and I would swear until it hurt deep inside. Think, without inference, of what might have been. The condemnation of your marriage that might have been, the goodbye between us that proved you & I were not meant to say goodbye. Now we are warm in the unity of our very mutual happiness. You are, I know and sense it, changed completely from the dark, brooding, sultry creature who was. Were I never to see you again, I would be happy to know & have shared your triumph. As it is, I daren't stand any higher on my emotional tiptoe. I am away up, already, peering and squinting ahead into a future hellish obscure; but with an overwhelming confidence in both of us & a funny knowledge that we shall "make it". I wish you were really physically standing beside me now. I wish we were alone just long enough to sense the presence of "being & thinking together" – God, how I love you.

Bless you, Neil.

Shell shock still affected him and letters in the late summer and early autumn tell of both physical and mental distress, with a web of emotional contradictions and neuroses that led to visits with a psychiatrist:

Italy
AAI CMF
29th July 1944

Hello Cherub,

Large gap in my correspondence due to my being "under the weather". Have already attempted and subsequently rejected three efforts at a letter, because they all sounded so horribly depressing. Since I made up my mind never to write you a gloomy letter they didn't pass my personal censorship.

It's difficult to describe the ailment because it is so confoundedly complicated. Since leaving England I have at various odd times experienced a hardening, a tensioning of the face & neck muscles. It can best be described as a feeling as if my head had "stuck" in one position, or that my jaw was about to set. I have mentioned it to the odd doctor during my travels & on each occasion received a diagnosis of slight rheumatism. Recently I returned from fun and games up north, watching the fall of a new port. Shortly after my return, whilst working in the Office, I suddenly had an acute attack in which the old napper behaved most strangely. For the first time in my gay life I felt scared and beetled off to the M.D. Followed a long examination, shining of lights, temperature, saying "99" & so forth & an ultimate diagnosis of fibrocitis in very mild form. Otherwise the Margerison carcass was in fine fettle... but here comes the "rub" – the doc, who seemed very competent, said that my condition was complicated unduly by nervous disorders. We had a long talk in which he probed around in my mind, tweaking odd soft spots of worry, talking art, life in general, & also suicide! – a nice interview. As a result he said that I worried far too much, took too many problems & sensations into my mind, & that I could do with a long, mental relaxation. I pointed out that I was "made" that way, that I was grateful for my mental awareness & what the hell? The result of all this was an invitation that I should meet the command psychiatrist (trick cyclist), which interview takes place on Monday next. Doubtless we shall unearth something that I saw in the woodshed when I was four years old! Although I prefer to be flippant on this subject, I don't hesitate to confess to a growing mood of moroseness, ennui, distaste, distrust & disappointment (in large lumps) of the life we are all leading.

But I recognise all this as something which I can do my best to improve, either by writing about it, drawing it, or expressing it in film or some such medium. My efforts are of little consequence in the world, & probably this realisation frequently counters my enthusiasm to express these opinions. Friends out here all comment on the manner in which I have aged....

This all sounds very solemn, Olive. It isn't as bad as all that. I'm just going through a stage, I think. Mrs Hall's warning of "beware dark corners" seems mysteriously appropriate, and yet, out of this introspection I shall either build myself a strong, sober-minded character, or go utterly to little pieces. Call it idealism, which has habits of becoming a bit warped. I hope all this doesn't depress you – it doesn't depress me!

Dormans Park is a quiet, peaceful place. I like to think of you dawdling through the woods there, in the evening, maybe standing by the lake, or just peacefully walking....

Chin, chin, & keep smiling,
All my love, Neil.

Neil followed this letter with others written almost daily, though he had a move of station and had begun treatment for the nervous condition, which was evidently being taken seriously by the enlightened medical team in charge.[40] His psychiatrist had advised him to give up worrying and to relax, but he was deeply anxious about everything, including the doodlebugs over London and whether Olive would suffer.[41] Her temporary move out to Dormans Park thus came as a relief to him. He was very much on the defensive in this run of letters, worried that if he told Olive too much about his condition she would become convinced he was off to what he termed the "madhouse". A period of regular therapy, however, made him feel significantly better and he was more in control of what he called his "mental fruit salad". The mood swings disturbed him, but he was not always down. Here, for example, is a letter in which he responded cheerfully and lovingly to a (lost) letter from Olive:

Italy
AFHQ CMF
8th August 1944

Hello cherub,
    Just received your last letter dated the 2nd of Aug. in which you sound "down in the dumps". Bad show that, Fotheringay! I know how utterly

miserable you must get at times, how work has a nasty habit of snowing one under, and just how utterly remote one feels (on occasions) from other people. If I were home again, I think I could cheer you up. As it is, never lose sight of the fact that constantly I am thinking about you, admiring your efforts and planning as best as I can, for a future shared with you. Just how much I love you, and you, me, is shown in your last letter, when you suspect me of having "curled up in dark corners". My subsequent correspondence tells you just how true was your hunch, and instances that peculiar form of mental telepathy which spans the long distances between us. Frequently, during the day, I can sort of look up at you & see you, wherever you may be, catching a sense of how you are feeling & in a way "willing" my love for you across the skies. Your feeling I should come home and tell you I didn't want to marry you is a waste of mental breath, & represents my mood before I think I fell in love with you. It couldn't happen now. If it happened I should lose not only you, but life. The thought & ambition it creates are my greatest mainstay out here. In fact recently that was the one thing that kept me sane. Even the old "trick cyclist" smiled when I began to race over the question of you, doodle bombs, not seeing you, wanting you; "all the things you are". I also know that if I were home, quietly with you, all my present conflicts & emotions would become smoothed out. I sometimes tremble in sheer emotion when I think of the power we hold for each other, & I sometimes recapture that great flood of strength, happiness and utter loveliness which seemed to surge between us whenever we held each other close. I used to love also the pride I always experienced, & the determination which was inspired when I would catch you off your guard, looking 'orribly solemn & somehow so very "little girlish" with a frown on your face and a bother on your mind. It always made me want to burst out in a great laugh of confidence, because I always felt so very capable of sorting your worries out & giving you the help you needed. No, Olive, never worry any more about that, rather seize hold of it as a formidable compensation for all the other worries that this world offers…

How far is peace away, cherub, & how on earth are we ever going to catch up on the things we have been unable to do during the last five years?…

Well cherub, all my love. God bless you. Keep looking up, & looking ahead. Think of all the things we are going to do together, all those precious moments of quietness & completeness we shall share together, all the fights we shall have, the tears & the great laughs. Keep your sense of will, and sure as God made little artichokes, we will make the grade.

I love you,
Salaams, Salaams, Me.

On 14 August Allied troops landed on the French southern coast between the ports of Toulon and Cannes, but the letters from Neil did not register events happening not so far from him in Italy. Rather, he became increasingly preoccupied with marriage and the future, and what he might do once he was demobilised. Although he had become an expert in armaments, and was highly regarded in this field, beyond his art schooling he had no particular training, did not have a degree, and felt totally unprepared for civilian life. On 18 August he wrote:

...Where are we going for our honeymoon?... I would like to escape from people & be really lazy, interspersed with sudden furious activity like climbing a mountain or riding fifty miles on a camel! Very difficult – I think you'd better choose?

Do you know that I haven't got any clothes. I don't mean that I'm writing in the "altogether" whilst my batman finds out who has swiped my large valise – but I mean peace-time clothes. I don't think you've ever seen me in mufti have you. ... I hope that there is still no ban on turn-ups, pockets & things by the time I have finished my work in the Victory procession.

Back in the office Olive received these letters with pleasure, but also with a certain degree of anxiety. She was feverishly writing back, thinking about how she might help Neil find employment, and longing for the day when they would meet:

London
14th August 1944
TOP SECRET AND PERSONAL
EYES ONLY

My darling,
When I knew the trend of events I decided that the obvious thing to do was to scrap the two letters I wrote to you from Blackburn last week and ask permission to send this out to you by bag.

There is so much to tell you, but the priority subject is you. Your two letters worried me, my poppet, and, having been re-directed by the office, arrived simultaneously with the letters to your Mama and Papa.

Your Mother and I had a long pow-wow about "doddering old cranks" and formed ourselves into an "Admiration for Neil Society" which, sober-sides, is going to pay first-class dividends. I know exactly what is worrying you and you know I said in my last letter that I felt you had been retiring into dark corners because I had been feeling so depressed about you.

I know it is easy to say "Take life more easily" but I <u>do</u> advocate it. I do think you are much too intense – I have told you that before. But I love you for what you are. You worry far too much about things which you cannot alter – all sorts of things – but its going to be a long and tedious job changing human nature and your best contribution is to live your life according to your own particular creed, which I know to be an excellent one. Don't create worries and troubles for yourself – there are plenty in store for you without throwing in numerous additional ones.

You have your own post-war problems to solve. I know <u>you</u> are going to make out – I hope <u>we</u> shall make out. I have enormous confidence in you, and, because of you, and what you have made me and can make me, I have enormous confidence in myself. Think of what we have both done, individually, and then think of the combination of effort, controlled and directed towards the supreme goal – achievement, which in itself, because of what we are, will create happiness, happiness for us and others. I want us to achieve a family, united, happy, and with a solid background. I often wonder now about people who say they find life dull and boring. There is always so much to do now. Children are interesting and I want to be interesting to them. Neil, have you ever thought how wonderful life could be for us even if we had a very little money. Am I being stupid or over-optimistic? Do you not think that our inner resources are such that we shall be able to cope with all the trials and misfortunes that may befall us?

Therefore, if the "doddering old crank" will consent to having me for a wife, I guess I can cope with him as a husband.

I was so terribly glad to have your letter, darling, saying that you were feeling better. You are so sane and balanced and I know you will get the right angle on things.

Your Mother said "Neil is the most gifted of our three sons" and your Father agreed. So you see, your Mother and Father have confidence in you and your Mother and I have supreme confidence in you. Every time I talk to Leslie and Benjie they say, "Olive, we're so looking forward to the time when Gerry can come in with us". In short, most people think you're the cat's pyjamas and you must have done <u>something</u> to deserve their respect and admiration.

I had an amusing, interesting and lovely holiday in Blackburn and enjoyed every minute of it. I saw Aunty Mary, Joan, May Baron, Ethel and Walter Marsden (whose home I liked very much) – Christine Marsden, Auntie Gertie and Uncle Fred Howarth. Mrs. May and Mrs. Mary Holden and Tommy, Jenny, Elsie Ormerod and David (bless his heart). Mrs Geddie and Uncle Tom Cobley and all. It was a round of gaiety and to walk down town for coffee with your Mother was like going in a royal procession. I felt very sad at leaving and didn't want to come home.

Despite all warnings about travel I had an excellent journey up to Blackburn, travelling first class and with two other people in the compartment. Your Father was at the station to meet me. Jimmie was playing tennis with Tommy Holden but materialised for tea. Jimmie is longer, thinner and older and at times ridiculously like you – much more so than Alan I think. It was grand to see Jimmie again and more and more I like the idea of having him for a brother-in-law! I missed Mary, unfortunately, but your Mother and Father think she's the tops.

As a matter of interest I think I'll tell you about my departure from Blackburn but you must promise not to breathe another word about it. I almost burst into tears. Your Mother, having bidden me a very affectionate farewell, your Father completely eclipsed it. He came to the station to see me off and when established in the train I made all the right noises and was quite honest when I said that I felt quite sad about leaving them. I really had had a lovely holiday. Anyway, your Father smiled and shook hands and said, "Well, you'll be coming again of course. There's nothing more to be said, is there?" I said "No" and then, as he was going, he shook hands again and said "Will you kiss me goodbye, bless you". Your mother and Father have been absolute pets, Neil, and I grew very fond of them.

Your Father was so amusing and I saw them rather as you would be seeing them; viewing them detachedly, as it were. Your Father always would insist on doing the washing up and would stand at the sink with black apron tied round his waist while he whistled arias, argued with your Mother about the "boys" and dangerously wielding a washing up mop. With a clatter a cup would fall into the sink and your Mother would say "For goodness sake, Jim, don't break all the dishes". Poor Father, with a giggle, would reply, "Well, I'm doing my best, honey" and then, with a glance at the clock – "I've gotta go, Annie" at which he would dry his hands, grab hat and dash out of the door. But he 'got into a row' when he dropped half a meat pie into my tea! Eee, he did too! Darling, it was fun and I enjoyed every minute of it.

We saw "A Canterbury Tale" with Jenny Holden and enjoyed it immensely. The photography was terrific and the production was superb.

Incidentally, did you know that I'm going to meet Noel Coward and did I tell you that Wing Cdr. K. de G.[42] was so impressed with your letter that he hardly knows how to answer it? He mentioned it again this evening. I also persuaded your Papa that it would be a good idea if he let me have some of his music for the Wing Commander.

Another thing that I meant to say to you ages ago was that you should be over here now. Guess you'll be finding plenty of material for your writing in Italy, but there's an awful lot in England with flying bombs around. The people are terrific.

Dormans and the woods, peace and quiet, the earthy musky smell of the early morning, the birds and flowers and those heavenly moments when I can lose myself and be far, far away from the world – those moments when I am nearest to you and yet long for you desperately.

Neil, I want to talk to you, to talk and talk and walk and walk with you. I've so much to tell you. There is no one quite like you. You're everything I want and need.

I feel quite mentally rather than physically stimulated by my leave. I feel I could achieve almost anything now. But I was so tired before I went away. I had time to think, to read, to talk and be interested in things that had nothing to do with the war. It was sheer joy to be with and to talk to people whose minds were not wholly preoccupied with the war. I liked to listen to Blackburn people talking about post-war planning, to hear their views on the war and to listen to your mother and father talking. By jove, your Mother can talk. We were at the Marsdens' one evening and the conversation veered around to education. My poppet, your Mamma had us all very enthralled for nearly an hour. I enjoyed listening to her so much and all the time I could see Walter Marsden thinking, "Now this is the woman to have on our Education Committee". I think your Father senses it too because he said to me later in the evening – "Annie's not well and when she leaves school, if she's not careful, she'll find herself roped into activities which will be too much for her". All the same, your Mother ought to have a say in the very vital controversy on Education. She has the right ideas.

It's nearly 2.a.m. and I've hardly breathed a word. I left Jacquey to clear up while I finished your letter. She has gone to bed and I'm almost there.

I wish I were in Italy now. It won't be long before you're home.

I must have told you about John Pinsent and I meeting. I've written and told him that Jimmie is in England so I expect he'll be contacting him.

I slept in your bed and read your books and dodged 'Daddy Long Legs', saw the view from your bedroom window, shrouded in mist, and then clear, crystal clear. I saw Darwen Tower and Billinge Hill, Pendle Hill from Wilpshire, Longridge Fell and Stoneyhurst College, I loved your Aunty Mary, adored Joan, liked May Baron <u>very</u> much and basked in the warm hospitality which was extended to me wherever I went. I loved everyone, in fact. I was amused when the eiderdown kept slipping off the bed and remembered how you had warned me about it before. It has black tapes sewn on the corners now. Perhaps it had when you were at home before. I helped Jimmie pack for Hereford and we had lots of fun. Your Father told me about the toilet paper which is made in Fred Howarth's mill, showed me the large store in the cupboard which, he said with a chortle, would last for years. When he roared downstairs with two long streamers of it floating behind him I thought how amused you and Alan and Jimmie would be if you could see him. He was using it to wrap up dyes for someone who was keen on fishing and wanted to dye feathers to catch the fish. All fun, my sweet, but you mustn't tell him I told you – I wouldn't like him to feel hurt.

By the way, they are thrilled with your watercolour of Algeciras – so was I.

I repeat, I think Neil D. Margerison, Major, R.A.O.C. 134025 is the 'tops'.

Lots of love from the old "ball and chain"! Keep Smiling. I'll write again soon.

Olive was busy at work, fully occupied as personal assistant to Hollis with whom she was now on excellent terms. His wife, Rosemary, was treating her almost as a daughter or niece, and it became clear that as a couple they were taking a genuine, personal interest in the future of both Olive and her fiancé. For the moment, though, all focus was on Europe, for, by this time, most of Italy was in Allied hands and troops were moving quickly northwards. On 24 August the US army entered Paris and it seemed the outcome of the war was no longer in doubt; but the Allies still needed to consider the period when Germany had been defeated and Japan had not. It was decided that a second conference would be held in Quebec, between 12 and 16 September, for Churchill and Roosevelt to decide the final phases of the war strategy in north-west Europe and the Mediterranean and to concert plans for the overthrow of Japan.[43] Mackenzie King would again act as the participating host.[44]

It was with great delight that Olive heard she would go to the conference with Hollis, and she was thrilled to receive a handsome clothing allowance of fifty pounds with coupons. Aunt Daisy supplemented this with a cheque of another fifty pounds, so she felt richer than she had ever been in her life. Bearing in mind her salary was six pounds a week, out of which she had to pay for a weekly ten-shilling season ticket for the train, this seemed a mighty sum. She toured the shops to see the new Dereta and Windsmoor garments, and ended up buying an expensive Dorville suit in Dickens and Jones. There had been some discussion in Government about the pay given to these special secretaries, in terms of: 'Did the young ladies earn enough for them NOT to be vulnerable to spying?' But Olive and the others felt they were well treated and the dress allowance more than generous. The money that her aunt gave her in fact enabled her to shop also in Quebec with Jacquey, for some make-up, a blouse, and a two-piece dress suit, in blue crepe, for the Roosevelt reception. (At the time, she did think of it for her wedding to come, but in fact wore something else). And they were to buy nylon stockings there – so many, enough for family and friends, and all the girls in the office. Olive cheerfully packed twenty pairs to be shared out once she got home.

Preparations at the office were hectic and the secretaries were kept busy right up until the last moment. By chance, Olive's old friend Bill Sutherland was leaving for Canada, having been invalided out of the army. He wanted to see her sometime in the next three weeks before he departed and left a message suggesting they meet at the Berkeley Buttery. When she heard that he had called, Olive could unfortunately do nothing about it, as she was herself leaving for Canada that very night, and had all her luggage waiting at the office.[45]

Churchill embarked in the *Queen Mary*, which had been stripped of all its luxuries and was being used as a troop ship for American soldiers taken to and from Europe. The Chiefs of Staff accompanied him, with their teams, and the voyage lasted five days. For the girls it was very exciting, although conditions were relatively austere, but the trip was lightened by different deck games such as a makeshift 'Atlanta Park Race Meeting 1944', with a Cairo Steeplechase, the Teheran Hurdles, and the Cunningham Cup, six 'horses' running in each and given names like 'Smart Alick', 'Flutter' and 'Water Wings'![46] Olive particularly enjoyed the evening when, with Hollis and her colleagues Jacquey and Sylvia, they were joined by the three Chiefs of Staff for dinner. Sir Alan Brooke, Chief of the Imperial General Staff, talked at length about his favourite leisure activity, bird watching.

On 10 September they reached Halifax, Nova Scotia, where the Governor General's train awaited. Canadian Mounted Police were present

in full regalia while the luggage was unloaded from the ship and a huge
crowd gathered. Olive was close by when Churchill and his wife stood
on the station platform waiting for the train. The crowd surged forward,
and whilst Churchill stood on the observation platform at the back of
the train, he joined in with the crowd singing 'God Save the King' and
'Oh Canada', which Olive found most stirring. Avoiding stating the
exact location, the *Montreal Gazette* reported:

> An East Coast Port, September 10. – Grinning delightedly behind a big
> cigar, Prime Minister Winston Churchill stepped ashore from a big trans-
> port this afternoon and with Mrs Churchill left an hour later for Quebec
> to confer with President Roosevelt.
>
> A tumultuous crowd of hundreds cheered the Empire war leader and
> his wife as they waited on the observation platform of their special train,
> and the smiling Churchill led them in song after song up until the train
> pulled out.
>
> With the Churchills came a group of high British military, naval and
> air officers. Two special trains were required to carry the full personnel of
> the conferees and their advisers.
>
> Mr. and Mrs. Churchill were cheered by the crowd, who began gather-
> ing at waterfront vantage points when the big ship carrying him moved
> slowly up the harbor. Time after time the throng called the Churchills
> out of their car.
>
> A V-for-victory sign or a genial wave of his cheroot was the Prime
> Minister's acknowledgement of the welcome. Mrs. Churchill smiled,
> waved and sang lustily.
>
> The Prime Minister, as is his custom when he travels by water, wore
> the semi-naval Trinity House uniform, dark blue with gold buttons. His
> wife wore a grey tailored travelling suit, topped by a flowered turban of
> grey and red.
>
> As the couple left the big liner, cheers of hundreds of service men
> lined along her rail and perched high up in her rigging sped them on
> their way. Churchill acknowledged the farewell of his fellow voyagers
> with the V sign.[47]

Olive, Sylvia Arnold and Jo Sturdee shared a train compartment on the
same train as Churchill and his party and they enjoyed the journey from
Halifax to Quebec, which all three remember as 'great fun with lots of
laughs'. Moving from the austerity of the *Queen Mary* to the luxury
of the Canadian National Pacific Railway was almost overwhelming

for they were served quantities of food they had not seen for years in war-torn Britain.[48] Along the whole route to Quebec there were cars lined up, with crowds waiting and hundreds of people waving, hoping for a glimpse of the Premier. After three days they finally steamed into Wolfe's Cove where, again, there were crowds waiting to greet Churchill. He was driven straight to the Citadel, the Governor General's residence, whilst the delegates went on to the Chateau Frontenac hotel to start preparations for the conference. The Prime Minister's entourage was small, but the main body of delegates was vast, with all the Chiefs of Staff taking their own teams, and there were lots of clerks, secretaries, and typists. Joan Bright had found herself in charge of all the British administrative arrangements and had been determined that her girls should be well served, and that, like the more senior members of the delegation, they would all have a card bearing their office and room number, an official pass and a telephone directory.[49] All day long meetings had to be prepared and recorded, and there was drafting of papers and staff discussions, as if still in London. The girls worked long hours, hardly seeing the light of day, and Olive was particularly grateful for the company of her co-secretary, Jacquey D'Orville.

Neil did not discover that Olive had gone to Canada until some time later, but he did get to hear about her shopping extravagance – without realising she had been provided with a generous clothes allowance. He also wondered whether she was in Quebec with Churchill:

Italy
AFHQ CMF
10th September 1944

Dearest you,

I wondered what was the matter with you – now I know. Bitten savagely in the midriff by a Bugs Squander!! What the jingling bells do you mean by spending "nearly £40 or £50" on a new suit which "looks grey until you examine it"? If I were within striking distance I would deal with you my poppett. It represents almost 1/6th of my total assets, and I quiver like a wobbling jelly to contemplate such shocking waste.

Seriously, I am very pleased, but that's only between you & me and the lodger. I well remember the days when you used to be unhappy because your wardrobe consisted of nothing but 'essentials'. I wanted to take you into the slickest shop in the West End and buy you something perfect. You would never let me. Now comes the swing of the pendulum and I only wish I could be there to admire, approve and go "on parade" with you. Sometimes you remind me of a tiny little girl such is your happiness & enthusiasm.

I read that Churchill is in Quebec, & I fall to wondering whether you are also there, basking in the aroma of his political cigars? Next letter is awaited anxiously. You ask me what my plans are when the war is over. It's a difficult one to answer, depending entirely upon the whim of War Office. When the European war ends, there will still be a "show down" in the Far East and also countless armies of occupation. Presumably, and regrettably, I expect I shall be hauled in to one or other of these shows. If it is the Far East, I can't do much except repair my 'skeeta net & fall in. If it is an Army of Occupation, I shall make enquiries about bringing wives out. If it is allowed, then I intend to beetle home, grab you as fast as I can grab you, see a parson or some other "authorised person", and take you back with me... You must realise that I cannot specify details, although I allow myself to indulge periodically in the most romantic day-dreams of "you-ing & me-ing". It's one of those things that keeps one straight & level, and enthusiastic about the future...

Whichever way one looks at that "after-the-war" period, it is difficult to visualise anything other than intense readjustment ... what we intend to do is not a gamble; rather are we grasping that which is basic & common to us both, and preparing to develop it. We have precious little to lose and everything to gain. Our problem of circumstance is shared with everyone else who has been involved in the war; & we, I know, are better quali-fied than most to overcome it. If I didn't think this, I assure you that life would not hold very much more for me. Were I to lose you, I can think of very little that would be left to me. That is not an exaggeration. Perhaps someday I can tell you just how much that meant to me recently, and how very near I came to – perhaps, again, let's forget it.

All my love, darling, and keep smiling. Neil.
PS. I love you.

The objective of the Second Quebec Conference was to consider such matters as the Allied Zone of occupation in Germany, finance and the post-war period, and the war against Japan. Elizabeth Layton thought it did not have the 'glitter and magnitude' of the First Quebec Conference, and she found Quebec itself still suffering from the events of the visit the year before, when extensive buying had taken place, and the shops were relatively empty. For Olive, and the others who had not been there in 1943, it all seemed very glamorous, and they were bowled over by the luxury of the hotel and its rich provision – 'Food, of which one sometimes dreamed'.[50] Olive was at the Mackenzie King reception, for which they had needed the new outfits and where she met Mrs Roosevelt. The table decorations were ice carvings, which she had never seen before, even though she had been involved with her grandfather's large catering business; and there were huge fruit baskets filled with fresh peaches. It was a great banquet, and, thrilled by it all, Olive wrote to Neil on headed, illustrated notepaper:

Canada
Chateau Frontenac
Quebec
Saturday 16th September 1944

Hello, Candleends![51]

I'm bursting with excitement, and am liable to bubble over any moment now. Neil, I'm enjoying myself so much. I adore Canada, and we have got to come here again one day. I want you to see it. I wish you could be here now to share all the thrill and excitement.

The speed with which your letters get around the world is amazing. The very long letter written on 2nd September and sent to England reached me in Quebec on the 12th!

The X on the left of the picture at the top is where I work – the X on the right is where I sleep and my bedroom, which I share with Jacquey, overlooks Quebec City. The Office window overlooks the river to Levis which one can reach by ferry (or "fatty puff").

The view at night from my room is heavenly. A sea of lights, with lighted trains sliding across the sky. Quebec is quite the noisiest city I know. Guns fire, river boats boo, taxis squeak impertinently, bicycle bells tinkle incessantly, church bells ring, motor klaxons shriek, trains whistle, pneumatic drills brrr-brrr, and three times a day the band plays "God Save the King", "O Canada" and "Star Spangled Banner" in rapid succession. Nearly always there is a sort of holiday atmosphere, and despite the work, which is pretty hellish, I rather feel that I'm on 'vacation' as they say in these parts. I'm having a wonderful time and am enjoying it all enormously.

All over again I experienced the thrill of setting foot in a new country in particularly exciting circumstances, the cheers and roars of the crowd, the sunshine, with the red uniforms of the very attractive "Mounties" contributing to the general colour scheme. The exciting and interesting train journey, with iced melon, lemon and lots of sugar, and tea with <u>real</u> cream in a simply wonderful train – quite the most wonderful train I've ever travelled in. Sylvia was with me on the special train and we popped with excitement all the time. We saw the President and Prime Minister meet and on Wednesday night Mr. Mackenzie King gave a reception to the Delegation at which Mrs. Roosevelt and Mrs. Churchill were present. I was so thrilled to see Mrs. Roosevelt and to be presented to her – I thought she was a darling. She is so jolly and I think she must be great fun to be with. I think she is very attractive.

I've done some shopping of course and have got some things for your Mother.

What fun to think that we might be able to meet at the Morgue soon.[52] I've bought the Horlicks and Phospherine tablets in anticipation. (I must say, to anyone not "in the know" that sounds rather naughty).

I seem to be up on you still, my poppet. I can't remember how many countries you've been to, but I've been to France, Africa, Egypt, Persia and Canada. What fun when we can go places together – even if we go in cargo boats or work our passages!

My wander bug is growing awful fast. Please don't go and get yourself slung off to Burma or some frightful place. I suppose that's being selfish, isn't it!

Anyway, my darling, gotta go now. Will write a long, long letter to you on my way home and post it as soon as I arrive. All the "scandal" however will have to be kept in cold storage until you come home.

God bless you – I'm loving you very much. O

The conference lasted a week, and the most important decision made was that Roosevelt and Churchill together approved the European Advisory Commission's scheme for the division of defeated Germany into US, British, and Soviet Zones of Occupation (the south-west, the north-west, and the east, respectively). Also, a radical plan, elaborated by Henry Morgenthau, Jr.,[53] was discussed, the aim being to turn Germany 'into a country primarily agricultural and pastoral' without 'war-making industries'. Advisers, however, did not give full approval for this and arrangements for the Allies' final plans for Germany were not confirmed. The conference did establish Britain's right to share in the war against Japan, where there were over 150,000 British internees and prisoners, and it also strengthened the situation for the Allies in Italy, where it was decided to retain troops. Impoverished Britain still needed American assistance in Europe, and Churchill was concerned to keep as many US troops as possible there rather than see them depart for the Far East. Olive and her colleagues typed up the Anglo-American agreement, which was of great significance, to convene conferences to discuss and organise the permanent structure of the United Nations as a peace-keeping organisation and to set up a world monetary organisation as well.[54]

The British delegation finally returned to England in the *Queen Mary*, sailing from New York on Wednesday, 20 September. A special train collected the party in Quebec, took them speedily there, and, once safely home, Olive wrote several letters to Neil about the trip:

London
28th September 1944
Home again

My supreme emotion at this moment is my love for you and the thrill of being once more in England surrounded by all the things which you know and which we have shared.

Of course while I was away there was all the thrill and novelty of being in a new and lovely country but I was lonely – just a little – and wanted you <u>very very much</u>.

Darling – I really had a wonderful trip. You know, of course, that our transport was the Queen Mary – it was announced on the radio. As Secretary to the General I had a super cabin to myself with my own bathroom on the Main Deck – annexed to the General's Suite. (Jacquey said she was going to sleep in the bath to keep things decent!) I was told that the fare alone for a suite such as the one we had would be roughly £300 to £400 in peacetime. It was absolute luxury and I enjoyed every minute of the voyages. We travelled by train from Quebec to Montreal and then on to New York. Wow! New York is just terrific and Broadway is just what its cracked up to be – lights, lights, lights. The Empire State Building at night, and then again in the morning, its top immersed in cloud – part of a grey and toothy skyline as we slid down harbour past the Statue of Liberty and out to sea. All very exciting and interesting and I wished so much that you were there to share it. Perhaps we will share it one day. More letters on way.

God bless you always, Olive.

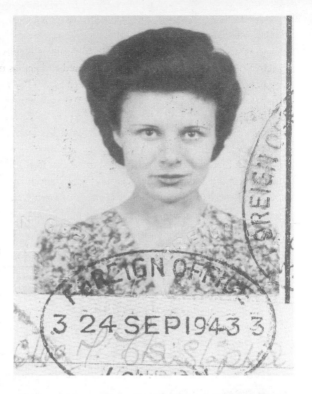

Right: 1. Olive
Christopher, passport
photograph, 1943.

Below: 2. Winston
Churchill as Prime
Minister, 1940–1945,
at his seat in the
Cabinet Room
at Number 10,
Downing Street.

Above: 3. Neil Margerison, 1943.

Left: 4. Herbert, Margaret and Olive Christopher, 1920.

PASS
No. 504

C.W.R.

On presentation of this Pass the holder

Miss O. Christopher

is authorised to enter the C.W.R. on official duty.

E. E. Bridges .

1st March 1944.

Date of Issue

5. Cabinet War Rooms Pass.

6. Cabinet War Rooms Typing Pool in Room 60A.

Above: 7. The Big Three at Teheran, November 1943.

Left: 8. Canadian National Luncheon menu.

LUNCHEON

Iced Celery Hearts	Queen Olives
Potage Andalouse	Celery-Bouillon en Tasse

Fried Scallops Ayoll Sauce

Cold Boiled Gaspe Salmon Vert-Pre

Capon à la Bourgeoise

Roast Sirloin of Beef Yorkshire Pudding

Potatoes Persillees	Cream Whip Potatoes

Potatoes Rissolées

Swiss Chard	Broccoli à L'Hollandaise

Chicory Salad

Bread	Rolls	Bran Muffins

Cherry Tart	Croutes au Madere
Montreal Melon	Cantaloupe Sundae
Cheese	Fruit

Tea	Coffee	Milk

QUEBEC CONFERENCE
OFFICE PASS
CONFERENCE ROOM

The bearer *Miss Christopher* whose signature appears hereon, is permitted to enter the Conference Rooms and all Offices during the progress of the Conference. **1944**

S. T. WOOD,
Commissioner, R. C. M. Police.

PASS No.

B 93

SIGNATURE OF HOLDER

Above: 9. Quebec Conference Pass.

Right: 10. Chateau Frontenac dinner menu.

DINNER

| Chilled Apple Juice | Supreme of Fruit |
| Celery and Radishes | Stuffed Egg à la Russe |

— — —

Jellied Essence of Tomato
Consommé with Vermicelli   Cream of Asparagus, Argenteuil

— — —

Fried Fresh Long Island Scallops, Tartar Sauce
Fresh Vegetable Combination with Poached Egg
Vol-au-Vent of Sweetbread, Toulouse
Grilled Small Steak, Béarnaise
Roast Stuffed Valcartier Turkey with Cranberry Sauce
Cold Chicken and Ham with Waldorf Salad

— — —

Fresh Green Peas   Creamed Succotash
Pont Neuf or Duchess Potatoes

— — —

Chateau Salad, French Dressing

— — —

Maple Eclair   Frozen Charlotte Pudding   Coupe Amandine
Deep Fresh Plum Pie   Canadian Apple   Oka Cheese

— — —

Tea   Coffee   Milk

CHATEAU FRONTENAC
Quebec   September 16th, 1944

Canadian Pacific Hotels

Saturday – 16th Sept.

CHATEAU FRONTENAC
QUEBEC

Hello, Candleends!

I'm bursting with excitement, and am liable to bubble over any moment now. Neil, I'm enjoying myself so much. I adore Canada, and we have got to come here again one day. I want you to see it. I wish you could be here now to share all the thrill and excitement.

The speed with which your letters get around the world is amazing. The very long letter written on 2nd September and sent to England reached me in Quebec on the 12th!

The X on the left of the picture at the top is where I work – the X on the right is where I sleep and my bedroom which I share with Jacquey, overlooks Quebec City. The Office window overlooks the river to Levis which one can reach by ferry (or "fatty puff").

The view at night from my room is heavenly. A sea of lights, with lighted trains sliding across the sky. Quebec is quite the noisiest city I know. Guns fire, river boats boo, taxis squeak impertinently, bicycle bells tinkle incessantly, church bells ring, motor klaxons shriek, trains whistle, pneumatic drills brrr-brrr, and three times a day the band plays "God Save the King", "O Canada" and "Star Spangled Banner" in rapid succession. Nearly always there is a sort of holiday atmosphere, and despite the work, which is pretty hellish, I rather feel that I'm on 'vacation' as they say in these parts. I'm having a wonderful time and am enjoying it all enormously.

All over again I experienced the thrill of setting foot in a new country in particularly exciting circumstance the cheers and roars of the crowd, the sunshine, with the

Left: 11. Letter from Olive (16 September 1944).

Below: 12. Olive with General Hollis and Maggie Sutherland at Lake Beauport, Quebec, September 1944.

Right: 13. Letter from Neil (4 October 1944).

Below: 14 Berlin/ Potsdam Conference. Olive with General Hollis, Maggie Sutherland and Joan Umney-Gray.

Berlin Conference
of the Three Allied Powers

1945

29. 8. 45.

These roses were from
my garden - and I
made them to-night.

I'm in a silly,
sentimental mood and
I want you to have
them for I hope I've
put in some very good
spade work for us this
evening.

God bless you - I
love you. Mike.

CABLE (C AND W) WIRELESS LIMITED
"Via Imperial"

OFFICE OF ISSUE

Circuit. Clerk's Name. Time Received.

NLT 0414

C W

MOA430   SO   23   3

ELT   OLIVE   CHRISTOPHER   ROOM   52A   OFFICES   OF

CABINET   GREAT   GEORGE   STREET   LDN   -

GRANTED   FLYING   LIAP   FOR   28   DAYS   HOME   THIS

MONTH   NEIL   -   MARGERISON   *

52A   28   *

Opposite above: 15. Berlin/Potsdam Conference Pass.

Opposite below left: 16. The Reichstag, Berlin (22 July 1945).

Opposite below right: 17. Letter from Olive (29 August 1945).

Above: 18. Telegram from Neil (5 November 1945).

Right: 19. Warrant for MBE.

BUCKINGHAM PALACE.

I greatly regret that I am
unable to give you personally the
award which you have so well earned.

I now send it to you with
my congratulations and my best
wishes for your future happiness.

George R.I.

Olive Margaret, Mrs. Margerison,
M.B.E.

Left: 20. Letter from
Buckingham Palace, signed by
King George VI.

Below: 21. Olive and Neil.
Wedding at Patcham, Sussex (15
December 1945).

The following long letter was written in three airmail instalments:

London
29th September 1944

Here I am on the wire again, my little chickadee. I've just been talking to Blackburn 7963 and had pow-wow with your Mamma and then your Papa who announced he was 66 yesterday and I didn't know. He said he had lots of books to read, bless his heart. I sent him from Quebec a book on the history of Quebec and I also have another book for him called a "Quebec Sketch book" which is rather fun – it has some attractive "washes" in it. On second thoughts I think I'll keep it for you and our grandchildren. I have one or two interesting heirlooms for them already. Did I tell you about the copy of the New Testament, bound in olive wood which I have. It came from the Garden of Gethsemane. And the olive wood cigarette box with "MISS OLIVE CHRISTOPHER MENA CONFERENCE, NOVEMBER/DECEMBER 1943" engraved in silver on it. I have scores of menus of all the gorgeous meals I've had in the Queen Mary, Canadian National Railways, Canadian Pacific Railways and the Chateau Frontenac. Absolute heaven, and I pine for the sliced fresh peaches and cream and lashings of sugar and coffee with cream which I had for breakfast every morning. The delicious chicken sandwiches, iced pineapple juice and a peach which I nearly always had for lunch, and the simply wonderful dinner every night. Oh dear! I am missing it all. We had a riotous dinner one night when, to start with, about four people appeared to serve us and suddenly no one materialised at all. We waited 30 minutes and when, finally, we registered a protest, we were informed amidst many giggles from a very young waiter, that our waitress "Felt tired and had gone home". All very silly and certainly amusing.

I told you that I sent you a very grand letter on Chateau Frontenac notepaper with a Canadian stamp from Quebec. I do hope it arrives. I wanted to write you long, long letters while I was there but what with work, shopping and parties life was crammed full and all I could do was to "cable my love for you across the skies" every night from my bedroom window. The sky, as I think I told you, was always a blaze of myriads of lights and always there was a train to be seen, sliding like a glow-worm across the sky.

Did I tell you about Mr. Mackenzie King's reception and my being presented to Mrs. Roosevelt, with a few hundred other people. I was so thrilled because I didn't know she was going to be there, and, having wended my way rather shyly and nervously up a line of celebrities I was suddenly confronted with Mrs. Roosevelt I almost collapsed on the spot. She is a darling and I liked her very much. She asked me if I'd been to America and hoped that I was enjoying my stay in Quebec and then I was handed on, after I'd made all the right noises, to Mrs. Churchill, Mrs. Mackenzie King (and Mister) and the Countess of Athlone. All terrific fun and if you haven't already seen me on the news reel, look out for me sitting at dinner with the General. All East Grinstead spotted me apparently and Mother and Enid rushed in excitedly saying that they had seen me twice – once at the reception and once at Wolfe's Cove, Quebec as the President and Prime Minister drove away upon our arrival. In the film of the reception I should be almost at the bottom of the screen in the left-hand corner and the General is on my right and Colonel Price on my left.

I wish you would come home soon – I'm sure I'll never be able to keep all the lovely things I bought until you come home. I bought a heavenly hyacinth blue crepe suit with three quarter length sleeves – I like it so much and it's superbly cut. Please come home soon, I want to wear it so much and I'm trying to keep it. I know I shall capitulate before long. I bought 20 pairs of silk stockings, gave 12 pairs away and have kept 8 pairs for myself – I shall be canonised almost any moment now. A man I know in Washington who heard I was coming on the conference brought me a set of handmade underwear and an attractive georgette blouse (white with lots of lace and frills down the front). He wouldn't let me pay him for them and said he would send me some stockings from time to time. I bought two more sets of underwear and another blouse in Quebec and then I concentrated on perfume, face creams, etc., and all sorts of lovely things that one had not seen in London for years. I bought a complete set of creams, powders, bath powder and toilet cologne to save and one complete set to use now. I bought 3 bottles of perfume for myself and the General gave me one bottle for doing his shopping for him. The rest of the stuff I bought I gave away and it was a major achievement getting my loot home – I had to buy a new suitcase.

It was such fun to watch Enid with all the things I had brought for her. She was prancing around, each finger painted with a different coloured nail polish, wearing stockings, pyjamas and blouses in rapid succession. Mother registered rather less emotion and pleasure, but I think was equally pleased. Part of the pleasure of coming home was to watch everyone's reactions to the presents one had bought them. More in next letter.

God bless you, darling, O.

London

29th September 1944

Still London – same date (next instalment)

This letter writing in serial form is decidedly wearing and even more tiresome to receive, I imagine. What I meant to tell you before was that I have sent your Mother some stockings and announced to her this evening that they were on their way. They're the right size too. I have lots more to tell you about the actual trip. I couldn't tell you before, but on our way out, the first night in the ship, Jacquey and I were having dinner with the General and Colonel Price and the three C.O.S. bore down upon us and joined us for dinner. C.I.G.S. sat himself next to me and he's a poppet. I liked him very much. I like them all. Jacquey and I were petrified when they appeared and asked if they might join us and all our fellow trippers were both astonished and amused to see us dining in such exalted company. We had too much work to do on the way out. We embarked at 1p.m. and a meeting was called at 2.30 and so it went on, more or less until the Conference was over. We had 28 meetings in five days and I was on duty from 8a.m., working three nights until 4a.m. with 2 hours off for lunch, most of which was spent shopping and, in the evening, from about 6.30 until 10. It was fairly easy to get away then as there was no work for me until after dinner when I had to get all the General's papers ready for the Conferences the following day. I missed a couple of tricks but he was very kind about it and said it didn't matter a fishcake! Actually, I don't work awfully well in double harness and, whilst Beer is an absolute dear, I didn't work with him frightfully well. I always work much better by myself. Anyway, we surfaced and sank back with relief on the Saturday afternoon when everyone departed for their fishing or whatever it was they did. I worked the whole of Saturday afternoon and evening and all day Sunday clearing up and on the Monday I had a day off. The General took Maggie Sutherland and me up to the Lakes for the day.⁵⁵ I've discovered a marvellous place for our honeymoon. We must go to the Lake Beauport Hotel in the Laurentian Mountains. Wonderful swimming, boating, walking and climbing. Heavenly climate, superb scenery and <u>very</u> romantic. We had a picnic lunch after a lovely walk and a climb, debated about having a swim and decided against it, returned to the car and drove back, almost to Quebec, out over the enormous bridge to the Isle d'Orleans, around the island, with its enchanting villages and apple orchards, back over the bridge and up to Montmorency Falls, said to be higher than Niagara, so high that I had an attack of vertigo and nearly fell off the top, while I was watching tiny rainbows reflected on the showers of snowy spray by the sun – fascinating and reminiscent of you as being something you would have loved. Back to the Hotel for delicious tea, a sleep, a bath and changing for drinks, dinner and dancing afterwards. Oh, I did enjoy myself. We left Quebec at 8a.m. the following morning for New York, stopping at Montreal. An interesting journey, particularly when we crossed over the border into the United States. From then on the scenery was magnificent. We travelled right along the shore of Lake Champlain which is 131 miles long and it took 2½ hours. The Lake resorts are fascinating with their attractive wooden and log bungalows. We stopped at Troy, where we got out and at Albany, and then we rolled along the river and into Grand Central Station, New York.

To be in New York was so exciting, but I've told you all about that. Unfortunately we didn't have much time there and we weren't able to do anything exciting except a rapid sightsee which included a drive down Broadway and up Fifth Avenue. New York harbour is terrific. One can touch the Queen Mary almost from the street. She was right up alongside. By jove, she's terrific too. When we arrived at Halifax and I had walked down the gangplank, I ran over to the side to see what an ocean liner looked like really from alongside and all the troops roared and cheered. I thought they were cheering me, but the General said he thought they were probably cheering the P.M. who could be seen addressing the crowds from the observation car on his train. Did I tell you that Sylvia and I travelled in the special train from Halifax to Quebec with the P.M.'s party? – absolute luxury, and so exciting. The people certainly knew we had arrived. Hundreds and hundreds of people were lined up at the stations en route and as the train stopped they all rushed up roaring, cheering and shouting for the P.M. They waved to us and we waved back and I almost burst into tears with excitement until the General said I must come in because I would be worn out with excitement and I had some work to do, so I had to sit quietly in the lounge, yes, lounge, in a train, until it was time to have drinks before dinner and a John Collins arrived which tasted of onions – horrible, but the compensation was a sumptuous dinner – I have the menu as a souvenir.

Coming home in the ship the P.M. was very kind to us and we had hardly any work to do. We spent most of the day sunbathing on the sports deck, or reading in the sitting room with the portholes open. To be cont'd.

More in next letter.

Lovely to be able to tell you I love you 3 times in one night. O.

London,
29th September 1944
3rd Instalment

As I was saying, the days were spent lazing on the return journey and about 5.30 I would begin leisurely to change, have a luxurious bath and be dressed in time for a cocktail party at 6.30. The first night the General gave a cocktail party, the two following nights General Ismay gave cocktail parties and the fourth night Mrs. Churchill gave a semi-private cocktail party to which all the high-ups and their Secretaries were invited. I would inform you that we had dozens of other invitations for drinks in various people's cabins and we usually managed to fit in two or three parties before dinner. After dinner there was a "free for all" every night in my General's sitting room to which lots of people came and we played all sorts of silly party games like Hunt the Slipper, Priest of the Parish and Penny, etc.[56] It really was riotous. We very rarely got to bed before 2a.m. or 2.30, making allowances for the clock gaining an hour each night. It was such fun and I so wish that you could have been there. I know you would have enjoyed every minute of it. Everyone was such fun and there were no discordant notes.

I seem to have committed the dreadful crime of overdoing the superlatives in these letters, but I hope I'm forgiven – I'm afraid I was carried away by my enthusiasm.

Your letters came through in record time – the very long letter, describing the interior of your tent and which reduced me to hysterics, was written on the 2nd Sept., posted on the 3rd, reached me in Quebec on Monday, 11th Sept. It had done the round trip from Italy to England and then out to Canada in 9 days – it's a record isn't it?! Your other letters reached me very quickly too.

An Air Mail letter came through to me in 6 days, reaching me in Quebec on the afternoon of the 7th day (that sounds a little biblical).

It was lovely to be back at Dormans again. Because of you I love the autumn; all the delicious earthy, leafy smells, the morning frost and the evening mist give me a nostalgia for you and all the things we used to do together. A year ago tomorrow I went down to Bramley when you were making the film with Bladon Peake,[57] to say good-bye to you before I left for Moscow.[58] And on November 12th last year I sailed for Cairo. It has all gone so quickly.

Have you heard about the lights being on in London? – don't get excited! It's just about as black as it possibly could be and the Wing Commander said that the blackest night of all was the night they were supposed to be on for the first time. When we stopped at Monckton on our way to Quebec some Canadians rushed up to us and said "The lights are going on in London, Hooray, hooray". We hurrahed and roared and cheered and laughed and danced. Well, it was fun. But the trains, my love, have proper lights again, and one feels that one can now navigate the innumerable tunnels on the cuckoo line to Dormans in reasonable comfort. I loathed being plunged into complete darkness while a train crawls slowly through a tunnel.

I want to live at Dormans and I want to live at the Brackens, particularly. I could grow roots there Neil. I don't want the house to go out of the family, as I suppose it will. I want it to belong to me. I love the trees, the birds, the squirrels, which are much in evidence now, and the frogs. I love to wander through the woods and plunge into the deep undergrowth and then stand quietly listening for the woodpecker. Once I was standing in the bracken and I looked down – there was a partridge; I had thoroughly scared him and the poor little thing was too scared to move an inch. We have lots of magpies in the woods too. They haunt a particular tree and make a hell of a row. I love the smell of the wood fire and the pine cones which we are burning, the soft lights of the dining room and my own little room – very little, about 12ft. long and about 10ft. square, I should think on the ground floor, with a casement window. Just outside the window is a lovely hydrangea bush. I have the curtains drawn and the window open at night and I can lie in bed and watch the patterns of the trees and leaves against the sky; I can hear that silence of the countryside, the faint patter of insects, leaves stirred by the breeze, the whisper of the trees as they sway slowly through the night, the croaking of the frogs, the seclusion and comfort of my own little room in a house I love. My supreme emotion there every night is my nearness to God and you.

You have been so near to me today, so near that I would not have been surprised to hear your voice on the telephone.

In short, my darling, I love you.

God bless you always and take care of yourself. Olive.

Meanwhile, Neil's letters became more pre-occupied with the distance between them, made greater by the comparatively exotic lifestyle Olive had been leading, and the pressures on him to find something to do once he was out of the army. Demobilisation would not happen all at once for everyone, because forces were still needed in the occupied zones, and in the Far East, and there would be unemployment problems if too many were released at the same time. Neil was anxious to know how the government's policy on this would work out and which 'batch' he might find himself in:

Italy
AFHQ CMF
16th September 1944

Dear "OMC",

I don't know whether to try visualising you sitting in the gloom of Whitehall, the firelight of "Brackens" or the frosts of Quebec – maybe you are "just sitting" and deserve some freak address such as Carroll loved – "c/o ALICE'S RIGHT FOOT" or something of the sort....

Apart from the odd day off, work continues with an emphasised monotony as the war draws nearer to its end, and people allow themselves the luxury of post-war dreamings.

In my last airmail letter to you I discussed my plans after the war. There is little point in repeating them here, except to say we are all very much in the dark as to our ultimate fate as soldiers. The soldier's newssheets make frequent reference to a Government policy which is already approved & ready to set in motion. Is it so? Was the matter discussed in Parliament? Was it ever recorded in White Paper form? Or is it one of those mysteries which was whispered in the sanctity of a Conference Room and which we must therefore be told nothing about? If there is any "popular literature" of a reliable nature on the subject I would gladly like to read it, in order that I may develop my plans. The subject of demobilisation is occupying more time in barrack room discussions than any other subject. It is amusing how everyone has got his own little plan whereby he intends to by-pass the slow-moving column of official procedure. I too, have my ideas, but so far have refused to put complete reliance on them... my prospects are 'average', and I cannot expect some fairy-godmother to tap me lovingly on the napper with her wand, and transport me back to Berkeley Square or Ilkley Moor! Still, what could be pleasanter than living with you in some charming Italian villa for a year or even two?

...All my love cherub. I wish the war would hurry up & end quickly. Chin chin & keep smiling. Neil.

Italy
AFHQ CMF
26th September 1944

Dear Far-away,

This letter may be considered as a special treat 'cos it's in excess of your "ration" of airmail letter cards. I happened to scrounge this one when the owner had his back turned... I'm writing this at close on 2400 hrs, so don't be alarmed if it reads badly.

Well, have the lights gone out yet in your new city or are you still either toiling or giving vent to a spot of "natural spirits"? I wrote home the other day bemoaning my post-war fate & stating that whereas the average bloke will return to his love & astonish her with highly-coloured accounts of life overseas, I (like Jo Soap) will be required to sit quietly in a corner & say "Yes, Olive", or "Really, cherub!" or something, whilst her ladyship indulges in a description of Teheran, Cairo, the blue mountains behind Marrakech, the waywardness of "Gib", the frosty spires of Quebec – to say nothing of strange flights in aircraft, & gay "goings-on" aboad H.M. Ships!! Still, my poppett, I think you're the cat's pyjamas & between you & me, I will be a very interested listener.

Are you ever going to settle down again after all this jumping around? Or has it kindled a flame of adventure (or whatever the novelists call it), in your maidenly bosom (or whatever the novelists call that!). It's a little bit different in my case, because it is one thing to visit a place, & quite another kettle of fish, to stay in a place. Seriously I do think that the matter of adjustment to physical environment is an important thing. There is, I am sure, some strange primordial relation of man to his background, as strong in us as in any other animal. Remember how you used to take a set dislike to places at home? – The Morgue, Chisholm Road, Piccadilly, bits of Baker Street, etc., – strange too, how commonly alike were our respective "hunches"....

Now I haven't got much room left and I had promised myself plenty of space to tell you how much I love you. The night before last was a night when I simply could not sleep for thinking about you. Once over I dozed off, & woke with a start, thinking you were there beside me. Finally, I got up & stuck on some boots and lit a fag and went out. I walked up and down our pathway for hours with an immense feeling of funny "softness" & "wanting for you" tumbling about in my brain. All the stars could do was to wink at me, whilst I talked aloud & told them about you. Which boiling it down means I love you – millions & millions of true, fine, happy times. I hope you're smiling – wherever you are.

Goodnight and bless you. Neil.

Italy
AFHQ CMF
1ˢᵗ October 1944

...I wish I knew how long I was likely to remain in the Army. It colours nearly everyone's thoughts at the moment. It is impossible to really plan ahead. I suppose you are similarly inquisitive, as the days tick away and the papers indulge in lively discussions of post-war "this" and post-war "that". Still we must be patient & at the same time <u>very</u> grateful for our situation, & the fact that we are alive & in "one piece"....

Have they turned any more lights on in London yet? The last letter from home described gleefully the relaxation of blackout restrictions & the comparative fairy-light gaiety of the town. Surely they have done something to improve the lighting on that fearsome Croydon line where one sat amidst silly pools of flickering light & relied on your seventh sense to get out at the right station?...

I'm getting restless cherub, and anxious to be back with you again. There's so much time to make up, so many very important things to tackle, so much "you" that I want to wink at, pull faces at, scowl at, grin at, and work with.

I love you, darling. Neil.

With the pressures in the office a little less stressful Olive began to write more regularly from Sussex, where she now went on off-duty weekends. She enjoyed the poems and songs Neil sent to her and tried to find ways in which they might get published, or lead to future employment. She also liked him to know that her own intellectual energies were being realised:

Dormans Park
3ʳᵈ October 1944
I still haven't answered all your letters properly.

Dear Jo Soap,

You're all around me tonight. I had a wonderful letter from you yesterday and another one this morning and now I must answer <u>all</u> your letters properly that I had during the trip and since. A letter from you, the one with the poetry, was waiting for me when I arrived at Quebec. I read it twice and then put it away to read again when I arrived home amidst things familiar and things that I love. Darling, I like 'The Appy 'Un Way – it's typical of you – I think it's good. "Dark Corners" is you, of course and because it's you I love it – it's an expression of something that is by now familiar to us both. Yes, I think it's good, too. No. 3 on 'MAIZE' again is typical of you and I like its colour. I like "Freckles on a beam of sunshine, husks of gold and gleams of grain" – "Peasantry and bells of evening". I have been trying to judge them impersonally, as it were – all very difficult! But, having done so, and allowing for a little natural bias and pride, they're good, and with a particular appeal – or I'm no judge!

I am writing to your Father this week and will let him have them. I shall also stir him up about his music.

Then came your next extraordinary mail letter (very long) – the one which arrived so quickly. Neil, I'm so glad you didn't buy me any perfume. I adore it, of course, but as I was almost bathing in it at Quebec it would have been a most regrettable waste. Are you keeping the bracelet until you come home? Perhaps it would be better if you kept it in case it gets lost. I envy you your shopping expedition and wish I could have shared it, or that you could have shared all my expeditions in Quebec. I have one or two things for you, but I think I shall save them because you will only have to carry them around with you which will be a nuisance, and they are things I want you to keep.

You asked me for a description of my new bedroom. I gave a brief account in my last letter – here are some embellishments. In front of me as I lie in bed is a fairly tall chest of drawers (that sounds funny ha-ha to me!). On top, in succession are Will Shakespeare, And So To Bath, Oxford Book Of English Verse, Lewis Carroll, Kenneth Grahame, The Moon Is Down, Dante's Paradiso by Laurence Binyon, Mount Helicon, the Christopher Robin Book, Matthew Arnold, A Shorter Pepys, Ruskin's Time and Tide, Wordsworth's Sonnets, Emerson, Omar, E.V. Lucas's Essays, Newbolt, Milton, Voltaire, Herbert Spencer, Browning, Open Road, and Between The Thunder And The Sun by Vincent Sheean. In between Matthew Arnold and a Shorter Pepys is a large blue woolly horse with a bright pink mane which I bought for your godson Richard and which will be sent to him this week. On top of the books is my new red hat, a box of Chesterfield cigarettes, two cigars, my gloves, a "Sketchbook of Quebec" and a very rude but amusing and well-written French book called Clochemerle, which, incidentally, is Enid's and which was given to her as a 21st birthday present. Have you read it? I can recommend it. It's very rude, but so well written and I'm sure you'll appreciate it. I haven't recovered from my unpacking yet, so I must confess to being very untidy still.

In front of the books are two pairs of <u>washed</u> silk stockings, my sunglasses, a bottle of ink, a clock, an aluminium soap box, a clothes brush, a new powder puff, a new box of Max Factor powder, a gold pencil, my watch and my silver Marrakech bracelet; hooked on to the back of the chest against the wall is my lizard skin handled umbrella.

Next to the chest on the left hand side are four suitcases, on top of which is the famous zip leather bag! The bottom suitcase is blue, the next one is the famous fawn leather suede hidecase. On top of that is a new case I bought in Quebec for two dollars 75. It looks rather like grey and black tweed with black and white stripes alternately on either side. Right on top is a small brown suitcase. Next to the suitcases is my brown sportsbag standing up on one end. Next to the sportsbag in the corner is a somewhat ancient washstand with even more ancient and unused appurtenances of doubtful ancestry. Beside the washstand and a little in front of it is a casement window under which, on a very wet night the frogs can be heard croaking. I've already described the view through the window and the large hydrangea bush. This side of the window and immediately on my left is my dressing table which, indeed, is a sight to behold since my return from Canada and the United States (said she very grandly). It has two small shelves on either side. On the top left hand shelf are a bottle of Cutex cameo coloured nail polish and a bottle of polish remover. On the next shelf underneath is a box of heavenly Richard Hudnut "debut" face powder and an <u>enormous</u> jar of Harriet Hubbard Ayer Luxuria face cream. On the top right hand shelf is a jar of Innoxa foundation cream. On the next shelf is a bottle of Lentheric TWEED brilliantine (lovely). On the main top of the dressing table are Peggy Sage "Clover" nail polish, another large bottle of polish remover, a bottle of Revlon SHY nail polish, an enormous box of Helena Rubenstein "HEAVEN SENT" bath powder, a box of Elizabeth Arden face powder, some Dorothy Gray foundation make-up film, and a bottle of Dorothy Gray texture lotion.

Continued in next instalment but before I go – I love you. Olive.

Italy
AFHQ CMF
4th October 1944

HELLO YOU!!⁵⁹

After a long and irksome silence, the mail arrived this morning and contained four airgraph letters and a very elaborate-looking letter written

from the "Chateau Frontenac-Quebec". I was so thrilled to bits by the
excellence of your writings and overwhelmed by the "posh" form of notepaper that I decided to have a go myself – hence the unusual heading to
this letter. I assure you that I do not use it on <u>all</u> my correspondence. I read
your news with the same attitude that one adopts when reading "Alice in
Wonderland" – it all sounded so utterly fantastic. I half expected to come
across a "P.S.", saying "I have sent you two Red Indians and a head of bison
by parcel post". When I came across a casual reference to 'walking down
Broadway' I damn nearly subsided with a contented gurgle beneath the
desk. You are a lucky blighter, cherub, & to say that I am <u>green</u> with envy
inadequately describes my reactions. One thing you simply <u>must</u> realise
is, that you will NOW WRITE A BOOK; perhaps some fine day I may
be allowed to illustrate it. Your experiences are outstanding whether you
accept them simply as a travel record, or whether you can go much higher
and relate them historically to the progress of the war and as evidence of a
group of nations establishing what we all hope to be the basis of a new and
better order. Yours is the rare opportunity of meeting these peoples, seeing
their cities, watching their enthusiasms, noting the conduct and attitude of
our own representatives, being able to describe it all in terms of intimate
example & detail which in time implies history. Hell! I wish I could see
you & help. There's nothing I would like more than to settle down in a
deep chair by the fireside, and listen to your story. I wonder how long it
will be before the Embarkation Officer shouts the magic order "Pick up
your monkeys and parrots and prepare to go aboard!"…

    You seem to be wrapping the atmosphere of Dormans around you like
a warm travelling rug. Your description of the woods there, the antics
of the odd blackbird and the quiet vapours sleeping amongst the trees
are very alive in your letters and delightful to read. You are a pleasant
creature. Don't think me silly but when we first met I got a very strong
impression about you as of a person whom life had hurt – and hurt badly.
The result had been a hardening of your emotion, a tight nervous grasp
on your little bundle of emotions which insisted on choking back any
attempt at happiness. Not that you didn't want happiness but that you were
frightened of being hurt again. As I began to know you, you seemed to
venture little smiles of confidence in our friendship, and you didn't hang
on so viciously to that tight bundle of worries. When we decided not see
each other again, your face seemed to say quite plainly, "I told you so"
– you had risked, and been hurt again. It's difficult to describe what <u>has</u>
happened since then, but I know from your letters and your continual
bubbles of merriment that at long last you have let go, and are preening

yourself, peacock-fashion, in the confidence of a new existence. Believe me, cherub – hang on to that confidence and get firmly into your napper that I will never, never, never give you the chance to say "I told you so" again. Don't be afraid of sensations, go on loving Dormans, and life, in your own fashion & with confidence....

I'm glad you're back again. God bless you and remember that I love you. Neil.

Italy
AFHQ CMF
13th October 1944

...There is so much to write about which involves time and the opportunity for reflection. That is not possible in wartime. So frequently these days I get the poetry or the writing bug in my brain, I hate the call of "work", and desire nothing better but to clear off to quiet places and work things out. It has been like that with Cassino. The first time I saw it, the war had only just moved on & the emotion created in my mind was honestly & truthfully enormous. Never have I wanted to write about a place so intensely before. I went away tumbling ideas over in my brain. I sat down and tried umpteen times. Every effort was a flop; it did not "express" the place – maybe it defies expression. I have seen the place many times since. Rain and mud, burning sun & the activity of weeds and workmen have altered it; turned it back to nature, dulled the sharp jagged rents of blast, and washed it in a grey monochrome of quietness and simple desolation. The undefinable spark of utter tragedy that dwelt there has been nipped out and I have <u>not</u> sung my song. Somebody <u>must</u> describe it; nobody has done so, unless some modern Brooke or Sassoon is still trundling around in the forward areas with the effort scribbled on a bit of paper and a twinkle in his eye. I hope so. Sometimes I think I am losing my grip, and slipping away from the standard of self-education which I try to impose ... nothing can bring us peace but ourselves... and the triumph of principles...

Neil.

In a quite different mode, Olive wrote the following letter to Mrs. Margerison, reworking the pleasures of her Canadian visit:

London

24th October 1944

Dear Mrs Margerison,

I have put myself out of commission and divorced myself from work for the afternoon in order to write to you. Please forgive me for not having written you before but since my return it has been so difficult to find enough time, without interruptions, to write you a really long letter. As I told you, I have been carrying a half-written letter around with me for days and when I brought it out today it looked so tatty that I felt I must really start all over again.

It did not occur to me until one day last week that you might think I was in Moscow. I happened to mention to Mother that I had not written to you and she said you would probably think I was careering around the world again. Whereupon I thought I had better telephone you but of course you were out.

I had a wonderful time on the Quebec trip but the glowing stories of the Moscow Conference make me wish that I had been able to go on it instead of to Quebec. I know I've been terribly lucky and I mustn't be greedy, but they all had such a wonderful time and such interesting experiences that I'm green with envy. When I heard that they were going to Naples I almost wept! But even had I been able to see Neil I would only have had an hour or so with him. Betty, one of my best friends here, remembered his surname, which was very clever of her. She searched the A.F.H.Q. telephone directory and got through to his Office, but he was out. Anyway, apparently the whole of A.F.H.Q. were searching for Neil and located him after about two hours. His call finally got through to Betty and they had a long chat. He sent lots of messages. When Betty got back and told me she had talked to Neil I was so thrilled and felt I simply must ring you right away and tell you.

I wish you could see all the caviar, vodka and champagne which is lying around the Office!

We would have gone to Moscow had the General not been ill. We all caught chills on the return journey from Quebec as we were switched from almost tropical heat to the chill of autumn very suddenly and one was lazing on deck in shorts sunbathing in the morning and in the late afternoon one would have to don one's winter woollies. The General contracted bronchitis and was away for several days. He did not feel well enough to travel, particularly as they were to do some very concentrated flying, so someone else went in his place.

It was probably just as well that I didn't go because I developed a chill and bad cold and had to stay away from the Office. Since then we have had three other people away in our Office and I've been at the Office since last Friday. I feel like part of the furniture now and, in fact, feel tired and irritated with having to be here all the time. But I go home to-morrow afternoon until Thursday afternoon. This sounds a terrific hard luck story doesn't it! Next week I go back to normal duties again and then I hope to have two or three days' leave which I think I shall spend sleeping.

The night I returned from Blackburn I was told that there was going to be another Conference and that my name was down on the list. I was very thrilled, of course, but not as excited as I was when we went to Cairo. As you know, we crossed in the QUEEN MARY – a very calm and enjoyable crossing both ways. Going out we were working practically the whole time, but we managed to cram in a few parties. Coming back the P.M. was very kind to us and we did practically no work. Life was a round of deck tennis, lazing in the sun on the sports deck, and, in the evenings, a round of cocktail parties, dinner parties, etc. We were usually invited to two or three parties every night and it was really rather a strain trying to attend them all! The after-dinner parties were usually fun. We would nearly always gather in someone's sitting room and play all sorts of silly party games like "Penny", "Priest of the Parish", "Hunt the Slipper", etc.

Needless to say, the food was marvellous and I will not tantalise you with details, but I can't resist telling you that in Quebec I used to have sliced fresh peaches, lashings of cream and sugar and coffee every morning for my breakfast. But our most exciting meals were in the Prime Minister's special train from Halifax to Quebec. As General Ismay and General Hollis had to work during the train journey – lasting 21 hours – Sylvia and I had to travel with them in the special train. It was such fun and so exciting and interesting. The population had news of the Prime Minister's arrival and enormous crowds were waiting to greet him and at the stations en route, where we stopped for fuel and to change engines, etc., hundreds of people stormed the train and roared and cheered. The P.M. would come out to the observation car and speak to them. There seemed to be upturned faces at all the stations as we went through and the Prime Minister was given a riotous welcome. We were having dinner when we arrived at Monckton and we were told that we could go on to the platform for a short while. As we stepped down from the train some Canadians rushed up to us shouting "The lights are going on in London". Everyone cheered and laughed and felt quite ridiculously emotional. (Their illusions would be quite shattered if they could see London – it is just as black as ever!) But it was exciting at the time.

Sylvia and I were thrilled with Canadian trains and gurgled happily when we were confronted with the splendid array in the "Ladies' Room" (as compared with our own scruffy trains!) Pale green marble washbasins, pale green pile carpet and curtains to match. All the towels, glasses etc., were sterilised. The coloured stewards on the train were charming. Of course, I'm not forgetting that we were in a "special" train, but even going to New York in just an ordinary train we had a very comfortable trip.

We arrived in Quebec the following morning and Sylvia and I alighted from the "wrong" side of the train to find ourselves amidst the Prime Minister's and President's party. We saw them meet and drive away together and got ourselves filmed – so everyone has told us since. We did not know we were being filmed but our respective parents saw us and so did everyone else apparently. We were also filmed again at Mackenzie King's reception and they said we were very easily recognisable. I haven't seen the films myself.

Jacquey and I shared a bedroom in the Chateau Frontenac. It overlooked the St. Lawrence towards the island of Levis. At night it was wonderful to look out of our window and see all the lights winking at us, lighted trains sliding like glow-worms across the sky, the lights of cars winding their way down the hills opposite. I think I may have told you that the band played outside the Chateau four times a day – "Star-spangled Banner", "O Canada" and "God save the King" in rapid succession – we're still humming then even now!

Fortunately, we arrived at the Chateau before our office equipment and the first thing Jacquey and I did was to dash out and do some shopping. Again, I won't tantalise you with details, but we both bought new dresses, blouses, undies, stockings, perfume and lots of other exciting things that we haven't seen in England for years. Of course, I spent an enormous amount of money but it was well worth it and such fun being able to go into a shop without having to worry about coupons and rationing, etc. I'm so thrilled with my dress which I've only worn once – at Mackenzie King's reception, when, incidentally, we were presented to Mrs. Roosevelt. It is a hyacinth blue moss crepe suit, superbly cut, with three-quarter length sleeves. I only bought one dress – I thought it was better to buy just one good one. Now, of course, I'm hankering to wear it again. I wish I could have bought more stockings – they are the sort of thing one wants to give everybody. Tell Mr. Margerison that I honestly didn't think about "silk socks". Very stupid of me. I wish I had thought of buying them, but I'm afraid I thought only in terms of "silk stockings".

I was very lucky because a friend of mine in Washington heard that I was coming out to Quebec and brought me some handmade undies and an attractive white georgette blouse trimmed with heavy white lace. I was so thrilled.

You are probably wondering whether we did any work in Quebec. We had 8 meetings in five days and were on duty from 8a.m. to 3.30 or 4a.m. the following morning. I used to have two hours for shopping in the middle of the day, foregoing my lunch, and I used to go off duty from 6p.m. or 9.30 or 10p.m. every evening. There was dancing every night at the Chateau but I was only able to go twice.

The Conference ended on the Saturday and we all had a night off. The General gave a cocktail party – we had a terrific dinner party and danced afterwards. The Sunday and Monday were to be holidays and we split our own office into two parties, three of us going out for each day. We had a most wonderful drive up to the Laurentian Mountains, stopping at Lake Beauport for a picnic lunch and a swim. It was breathtakingly lovely and the country was magnificent. We drove back to Orleans and around the island, back over the St. Lawrence and up to Montmorency Falls. It was fascinating to watch the tiny rainbows dancing over the falls as the sun shone on to the water. We stood on a tiny little platform at the top of the falls and I nearly fell over the top – I just cannot bear heights.

I travelled back in the Queen Mary in comfort and luxury with a cabin to myself and my own bathroom. I was told that the single fare for my cabin in peacetime would be about £170 to £200. But I felt rather guilty about it when I saw all the troops herded together below deck. I felt so sorry for them.

The social highlight of the return trip for me was a cocktail party given by Mrs. Churchill. The Chiefs of Staff, General Ismay and my own General all gave parties of course. In fact I'm quite blasé about parties now – we had so many – almost too many.

Going out, Jacquey, Sylvia and I had dinner with the three Chiefs of Staff and our own general – much to the amusement of our fellow travellers, as the three chiefs asked if they might join us at our table. Jacquey and I were petrified at first but they were very kind and charming and we had an amusing dinner.

Our journey to New York lasted fourteen hours – I thought it would be much longer. The country from Quebec until we crossed the border was relatively dull – rather flat and uninteresting. Montreal is very attractive but we were only there about an hour. Immediately we crossed the border the country became magnificent – vast fir forests sweeping away into the distance, tree-covered mountains, terrific gorges, waterfalls, lakes – Oh! It was all so lovely. We slid around the shore of Lake Champlain, which is

131 miles long. It took us 2½ hours. We arrived at Grand Central Station, New York at 9.30p.m., spent the night in New York and left the following morning at 7.30. Of course, we did not see very much of New York but we did manage to walk down Broadway and Fifth Avenue. We were told that there was a "dim-out" in New York, but the lights were brighter there than anything we have ever had in London. Broadway was just as one sees it on the films and one wanted to squeal with delight at all the lights, the people and the gaiety. I had my eyes glued to the grey toothy skyline as we slid down river in the morning, and I wondered if I would ever see it again. The top of the Empire State Building was immersed in cloud. I waved to the Statue of Liberty and then subsided to unpack.

I'm sure I've forgotten lots of little things about the trip – anyway, to describe it <u>all</u> in detail would cover pages and pages. It would be such fun to see you again and talk to you all. I won't be able to have a long leave before Christmas but I was wondering if I could come up and see you again early in the New Year which, after all, is not so very long hence! I enjoyed my holiday so much, and it was every bit as interesting and enjoyable, in a different sort of way, as going to Quebec. I'm tired of being with people who think war, talk war. I can't tell you just how refreshing and restful my stay in Blackburn was.

I'm longing now to go home, even though it will only be for a few hours.

I wrote Neil a grand, long letter from Quebec on Chateau Frontenac notepaper. He was quite overwhelmed and responded with his own effort at illuminated headings! I think it is clever and amusing. I must remember to show it to you one day.

Neil seems to be very much better now and, of course, this tour he is doing should make life a little more interesting for him. He writes me wonderful letters and is being much more philosophical about life these days. I'm not sure how to take the statement that he "hopes to be home sometime soon". I'm scared to take it too literally.

Has Mr. Margerison done anything about his music because <u>I</u> haven't forgotten about it?

Is Jimmy better now – I do hope so – and I hope you are both well. I can imagine that a vast amount of your time is spent "skivvying" but I suppose it is a relief to be home again and to be able to relax a little when you feel like it.

Please give my love to everyone – Aunty Mary and Joan, and all the kind people who made my stay in Blackburn so enjoyable – it will be such fun to see you all again.

There is still a lot to tell you but I must return to my desk now as I have lots of work to do before dinner.

My fondest love to you both,
Olive

Neil has sent me some poems which I will copy and send to Mr. Margerison. Please forgive this badly typed letter.

In late October Neil was posted briefly to Egypt, from where he wrote to Olive telling her about a surprise telephone call from her colleague, Betty Green, who was in Italy before he left:

Egypt
GHQ Cairo
24th October 1944

…here am I, large as life, and twice as natural doing my best to reduce the travel lead which you hold at present. I left Italy at 3a.m. on Friday. The previous evening I was preparing for a very early bed when I received a strange message asking me to get in touch with a Lady something or other, or a "Miss Green". The second name sounded vaguely familiar. I approached the phone with suspicion, because figs don't grow on olive trees, & I thought maybe the whole thing was a hoax. I was completely flabbergasted to recognise a familiar voice, which rang a bell in the misty corridors of Whitehall, and the comings and goings of one "Miss Christopher". It was great to hear Betty's (?) voice, and to hear all the latest news of your doings. We chattered very busily for about 20 mins., only to be cut off in the middle of the conversation, and then reconnected. I heard more about your activities in Canada, the outrageous extravagance of buying cosmetics, the London doodle-bugs, how you were, and how you were looking. I was honestly tickled pink! – I was asked if I had any messages for you. I sent you all my love – I can't give you anything more than all of me? – & I wished very, very much that you had come to Italy & not Betty. Is that selfish of me? There seems to be some fate about the whole thing because if Betty had delayed till morning, I should have been gone…

Tomorrow I shall find where you stayed in Cairo, and look for your name in the visitors' book… I wish I could send you a cardboard box full of sunshine. London must be full of fogs just now. I shan't get any mail until I get back to Italy, so this must be a one-sided conversation for the moment.

All my love, cherub, and keep your fingers crossed. Salaams, salaams.
Neil.

This letter from Cairo prompted envious recollections on the part of
Olive:

London
1st November 1944

Hello, Poppet!

A wonderful letter from you today, as a result of which I've worked
myself into a frenzy of longing for Cairo. How I envied Betty when I
knew she was going there again and how I envied you when I heard that
you were going. I think that Cairo was spoilt for me by the conference
for I left it last year thinking that I did not mind very much if I were
never to see it again. Now I would give anything to go back there. Isn't
there an old Egyptian saying – "He who drinks the waters of the Nile
will always return to Egypt"! Neil – isn't there something about the East
that gets under one's skin? The smell of it is revolting, it is hot, dusty and
relentless, but when one has left it it is not of the unpleasant things that
one looks back upon. Just the things you mentioned in your letter gave
me a push along the trail of my longing to return – the hustle and bustle
of the streets, honking of horns, the rattle of trams filled to the brim with
funny men in red tarbushes and dirty flannel nighties, the shops (my dear
Groppi's yum! yum!), the indefinable something which I can only describe
as a deep, mystic undercurrent and of which one is more poignantly aware
at night. The lights of Cairo, the drive into the cold night air along the
road to Mena and the Pyramids. Is "Auberge des Pyramides" still there
and did you go there to dance? Did you smell the horrible smell on the
way to Mena and were you fascinated by the dromedaries and the men
in dirty flannel nighties indecently displaying brown bony knees riding
bicycles and the little boys riding donkeys – not in the usual fashion, but
sitting well back on the haunches of the poor animal and hanging on to
its tail. And then Mena House and the Pyramids in the moonlight. I've
forgotten all about the rats (four legged ones) in my bedroom at Mena
– I can only think of the deep, deep blue of the desert night and Mena
and the Pyramids, the buzz of Cairo in the distance, the calls of birds and
animals, the chatter of natives and the occasional honking of a horn. Oh,
darling, I would give anything to go back there again. Please can we go
there one day?

I wish you <u>could</u> get a decent job in Cairo that would keep you there long enough to make it worth while my wangling a job there. The General said today that the thing to do is to find a man who wants a P.A. and then persuade him that he wants me. Cairo and you – la! la! The combination would be heaven. It's just a fledgling of an idea but I've been dreaming on it all the evening.

Talking of heaven – Maggie Sutherland was asked on her way out in the ship if she could advance any theory for her being there. We were at lunch one day and Maggie was so obviously enjoying herself. Maggie's theory was that she had been "killed by a buzz bomb and this was heaven"!

What fun your going to Malta! Did you have to stay on the airfield all the time? I know those tin seats! Aren't they hot too – did you go in a Dakota? Could you smell Valetta and did you see Grand Harbour – that sure is some place at night. Did you fly over Alexandria? Have I really seen all those places and have I really sailed down the Mediterranean in RENOWN? It all seems like a beautiful dream now. But I must stop this blubbering.

Neil, if I thought that you could get a job in Cairo and that I could come out to you I would be wild with excitement. More than anything else I want to be with you. I miss you terribly and these last two weeks I have been blind and deaf to almost everything else except my love and my longing for you. It eclipses everything I have ever known before, and my comforts now are my trees and woods, my own little room and my books. As I told you, last week I was denied all those things through having to be at the Office and I was so glad to get home on Saturday night. Before I went to bed I stood on the balcony of the drawing room and watched the moon having fun with the trees.

We have had lots of wind and rain and the way the acorns bounce on the roof in the night is quite terrifying. One bounced into my room one night. You talk about the Slough of Despond, darling – you should see the pathway through our woods. Poor Mother fell flat on her tummy one night last week and tottered home covered in mud from head to foot.

Mrs Hall and I went for a long walk in the rain on Sunday morning and picked lots of leaves and berries. I enjoyed it so much.

Still lots to tell you – will write again tomorrow. Must go to bed now – it's 1a.m.

Did Andrew tell you that Colonel Day married again a month or so ago?

God bless you, darling, O.

Dormans Park
11th November 1944

Neil darling,

A very "funny peculiar" me tonight – have been for the last ten days.
Sorry, Carruthers! I've been wallowing in dark corners or as Mrs Hall
described it on Sunday I've been "shrouded in a dark, dark leaky cloak
in which there was not the tiniest slit through which I could see". How
right she was – she's a wonderful woman and I'm very fond of her – she
is fond of us too and always sends her love to you. I do so hope she is
right about you coming home soon.

I've torn a hole in the cloak, my sweet - and it will be in shreds in a
few days. Tonight was my first proper glimpse of my woods and fields in
the daylight for 10 days. I spent the whole of last week at the office getting
home one night to sleep. Margaret was on leave and Jacquey's mother was
ill – so she had to stay away. Altogether life was grim.

This evening I walked slowly from the station through the woods shuf-
fling the leaves. Saw an owl sitting on a piece of fencing looking so solemn
that I had to laugh at it – and suddenly everything came alive again.

There is a vast amount to tell you and two more letters will follow
this tomorrow.

I'm green with envy of Betty and was <u>thrilled</u> that she was able to talk
to you. (More about this later)!

John Pinsent rang me on Sunday and I'm seeing him next week.

Spent a night with Ulla and Andrew short while back.

Letter from Oscar which I'm quite unable to read!

Just had a bath and wish you were here – I want to snuggle into your
arms.

I love you.

Give my love to Cairo. Maybe we'll see it together one day. Olive.

Dormans Park
11th November 1944

As I was saying – I love you and wish we were married and could be
together – the latter being <u>very</u> important because then, maybe, I could
do something about these "dark corners"!

Our marriage is supremely important and, like you, I am impatient for
it – although we are so close to each other now that it seems as if we
<u>are</u> already married.

My darling – I always know when you are feeling miserable and at those times I champ and rage at the circumstances which are separating us. Then I take myself off for a walk and try to tell you amidst the woods on God's good earth and in that silence of the country how much I love you. Or sometimes I take myself off to bed early and lose myself in the darkness – trying to find you. Sometimes I do find you and bring you back with me.

Please Neil, remember always that I love you.

I'm writing this by the fire and I am going into East Grinstead on the bus, to post it. I shall walk back. Mother is away and Enid is ill in bed today. I'm still loving it very much here but it will be fun to have Auntie back – she returns next Sunday.

Try and come home soon – or is that a forlorn hope? I'm missing you very much.

God bless you, Olive.

Neil returned to Italy in mid-November, by which time the Allies had cleared the road to Florence. Primarily on his mind, however, when he wrote to Olive was the space between them:

Italy
AFHQ CMF
16th November 1944

Dearest you,

Behind your letters I sensed an urgency of some emotion difficult to define. Behind them too, a feeling of sadness quietly in tune with Autumn & the passing of the year. That sounds pedantic? – but I am not good at expressing myself. Your mood suggests loneliness and that you are tired. Your last letter was more cheerful to <u>me</u> because you had managed leave, and had got away from the mad scramble of the office. I feel so damnably helpless, & at the same time so frantically anxious to help you and make you smile more. All I can say is not enough; the only thing that can really help is to see you again. I wish this were possible. The longer we are apart, the greater the test of faith, & the more insistent are the temptations of despondency and quick gain. Gradually one finds oneself utterly alone, utterly quiet and brilliantly aware of the unvarnished facts of one's own predicament. We have both reached this state & we are both in a position where we cannot offer support other than letter-writing. The main problem is therefore faced alone. For myself, I seem to acquire an ever-increasing confidence in my isolation. My daily experiences reiterate my faith. It is miserable to watch the months toppling by, the war dragging itself over another year-end, the remoteness of the people I like or love, but somehow these things no longer worry me so much; they only stress the need to hang on to principles, basic things which the war <u>cannot</u> change. My love for you is amongst my principles. At times it is literally the only thing that has "kept me going". It is all yours to use – remember that when you watch the leaves falling, and the gold of November sunsets through the woods at home. Pretend that I walk beside you – I think I know the way.

Neil

London
21st November 1944

My darling,

I've just made myself an enormous mug of cocoa – it being 10p.m. and cocoa time. Usually Maggie makes it as she considers it beneath the dignity of the General's secretary to make cocoa, but unfortunately Mags has gone off duty early tonight and I'm alone. The General has been ill, as I probably told you, and he is now convalescing so life for us at the Office is pretty slow right now.

I returned from my leave today and it will take me at least two or three days to get revved up again. It's fun missing work for a week but it's absolute hell picking up the threads again especially when one has to answer the 'phone and make all the right noises. I really don't like doing this job in double harness – I'm much more efficient when I'm on it all the time. But to be here the whole time would be literally killing and I've no notion for you to find a wreck of a woman when you return.

How right you are, darling, when you say that we are both reluctant bystanders. You have been away nearly a year and it is over a year since I said good-bye to you, except, of course, for the Gibraltar interlude which now seems like a wonderful dream. But, who knows, I may descend upon you amidst the palace and the tents one day. Betty did, so there is hope for me I guess. Somehow, despite distance, we seem to become imbued with each other's moods. It is extraordinary. Only the day I received your last letter I was thinking how heavily time was dragging on – wishing and longing for your homecoming - wondering how long it would be before we could be together again – thinking of all the things we could be doing – wishing, too, that you could share the lovely home and all the delightful things that I have now. It would be wonderful and, darling, you would enjoy Dormans so much.

How many of our pleasures are sensual – nearly all of them – in fact I think nearly all of mine are. Even the knowledge of God is a combination of the spirit and the senses. I am nearer to God when I am in the country, in the midst of nature, or can see the sky, the stars and the moon from my bedroom window. The sense of wellbeing, derived from the feeling of being near to God, gives me a spiritual uplift which makes me think that I am a very lucky girl, but that I'm not as nice or good as I should be. That life is pretty good for me, but there are lots of things I can do to make life happier for other people, with a resultant inner happiness for myself. I think there is something to be said for Pantheism if it gives one that spiritual uplift which is a part of one's creed. I do not see how anyone could deny that the Universe, or Creation, is God.

Why did I start this? I'd almost forgotten. For four days last week Mother was away and I realised then how much I would enjoy having my own home and making it beautiful. I walked into the room late one afternoon when the last of the afternoon sun was seeping through in shafts of light. There was an enormous log fire crackling happily, and reflecting on the oak panelling and polished wood. On the table I had stood an enormous amber glass bowl filled with large shaggy bronze and yellow chrysanthe-mums. It looked so lovely and I stood there letting the light and colour, the beauty of it surge through me. It only needed you to complete the picture and my happiness would have been complete! I hope we have enough money to have a very beautiful home, but however small it is I shall make it as lovely and as charming as I can. Neil, we shall have such fun planning our home. I'm sure we shall squabble because we shall each want to have a very large share in the planning and decoration. Even if we have very little money, which seems more than probable, we shall have just as much fun making the most of what we have got. What would be fun would be for us to be able to potter around the world for a while, but, for your information and, if necessary, consolation, I don't anticipate any difficulty in my settling down in England if we have to! As long as we are together and you are happy then I shall be happy. You see, I love you. (I'm sorry, I forgot I've told you that before).

You have so often said that I must write a book. Maybe I will, one day, but not until you can be with me.

I wish you could have come walking or "biking" with me this week. The weather has been absolutely ruddy and most of the field are under water, but we have had one or two dry spells with cold biting winds that make one's cheeks tingle and make one thirsty and hungry. Most mornings I went walking and most afternoons I went out on my bike in Ye Famous Maroone Slackes. I pedalled "there" happily, but was not so enchanted at the prospect of pedalling back. However, I usually managed to get back in time for tea, which I drank curled up by the fire. As I had people down to stay, nearly every night, by that time I had either to go and meet them or start to prepare dinner. About 6p.m. or 6.30 I would stand myself a glass of sherry and have another one when the guest or guests arrived. I usually achieved dinner by 8p.m. and after dinner most nights we played cards. Enid enjoyed all this enormously. She looks very well and happy despite the long train journey and the ungodly hour that she has to get up every morning.

Coming home in the evening now, the musky, earthy smell of the woods, the whiffs of wood smoke are absolute Heaven and always then I think of Rupert Brooke's "These I have loved". I'm still faithful to him, as I told Jimmie, who always teases me about him. He said he will always remember my rendering of "The Hill" in the lounge at the Morgue.

John and I chose your Christmas present when he was in Town and I will send it out to you by this same route. I have also bought you your Christmas present. Both should reach you easily before Christmas.

Darling, how sweet of you to think of sending me shoes from Cairo. They would have been very welcome and, for future reference, I take size 6½ in Cairo shoes. I still have two pairs, one a trifle worn, which I bought there last year.

I can imagine that you would not be at home in a "Frippery" shop and am so glad that you did not buy me stockings as I have plenty. Dress material, a trifle less expensive, was a good idea too and if you do see any exciting nighties and "things" in your peregrinations, I take size "34" bust (getting down to the grim details!). I have got several things "put by" for my trousseau and I periodically take them out and have a good old gloat. I'm going to try and find a decent fur coat with my next allowance of coupons.

I gather that Cairo is having precisely the same effect upon you that it had upon me. I found it oppressive, almost, and most certainly overwhelming. I couldn't grasp it and I left it thinking that I would not mind if I never saw it again. Now I would give anything to go back there again. I hope we return together to "Drink the waters of the Nile".

Did I tell you what John said when he came to stay? We were curled up in front of the fire talking. There was a brief silence and then he said:

"You know, Olive, I'm most awfully pleased that you and I get on so well together – it would be a frightfully bad show if my best friend's wife hated me"! Isn't he sweet? I feel so much older than John sometimes and almost always want to mother him. I'm very fond of him and he is a most refreshing person to be with.

I told you that I spent last Friday at the General's home at Haywards Heath. I'm awfully fond of him, as you know. He has been very good and kind to me and I was so thrilled to meet his wife whom I liked enormously – you would like her too. I do want you to meet the General, darling. He's always teasing me about my "boy friend trouble" and he thinks you must be a "jolly decent chap" because you do such beautiful handwriting.

Yes, I'm happy enough – I miss you terribly and would be happier if I were <u>with</u> you. I live for your letters and, Neil, I <u>will</u> always remember that you love me, as you must always remember that I love you. It is relatively easy to be faithful to someone when you love them, but I think it is rather different for a man and <u>I do understand</u>, sweet. If ever I find myself in danger of being attracted to someone, and I'm fairly susceptible, there is always you – you are there <u>all</u> the time. It's fun really to love, and be loved, for the first time in one's life. I want you to come home soon – I want you and need you very much. Your letters tell me how you feel about things and, apart from letters, I think we feel our need of each other. I feel your need of me, and I wish I could do something about it. I know it is not entirely physical – it is the mere fact of being together.

Darling, does the photograph make you laugh? It's an absolute shocker of me. Actually I was snapped at a bad moment – the sun was bang in my eyes and, as you will see, I was not really "comfortably seated". I look as though I'm "hanging on" which, in fact, I was. It's wonderful of the General and its pretty good of Maggie. Sorry it's such a bad one of me, poppet, but thought you might like to have it. It was taken at Lake Beauport in the Laurentian Mountains, Quebec Province. Our little WAAC driver took it and sent it over. Sylvia managed to get us copies.

I had my photograph done ages ago, as I probably told you but I wouldn't dream of sending it to you. The general saw it and he said when I'm photographed I become "some strange woman – you're reasonably good looking, but I've never known anyone photograph so badly". All very sad. I will have another shot at getting a reasonable picture of myself for you.

Must go now, my sweet, it's nearly 1a.m. and this letter writing has been punctuated with several stops for chit-chat. Jacquey has been to a party at the Mayfair and has been telling me all about it.

I was in Cairo this time last year – wish I were there now (with you).

God bless you – you're very important.
Olive.

Italy
AFHQ CMF
6th December 1944

Dearest you,

Life is somewhat intense at the moment… yours truly has been given the task of running two jobs for a while…

Something you said in a recent letter [lost] has set me puzzling "…it was just that a succession of events made life very difficult for a while & I wanted you with me. Will tell you about it someday … everything is more or less plain sailing now…" and again "…The past year holds a long story and one day I will tell it to you. I cannot be more explicit…" Can you give me even a little clue so that I may work out the answer – or is it something so involved or so difficult to express that I must be just very patient?

I love you, darling – keep smiling.
Neil

Olive was obviously not able to share with Neil all the details and excitements of work with General Hollis nor the social life that went with it, but she was at this time also committed to family matters. When her grandfather died in April 1944 Aunt Daisy had decided to sell 'Brackens', and, with the proceeds, buy two houses in Brighton, one for herself in Dyke Road and the other in Redhill Drive for Olive's mother, in trust for Olive and Enid. This would mean upheavals for everyone, and thus their last Christmas at Dormans Park had an elegiac feel to it. In the New Year Olive wrote again to Neil:

Dormans Park
5th January 1945

Dear Will-o'-the-Wisp,

How did you know I wanted a bracelet just like that? Bless you, sweet, I was enchanted with it. I bought an almost identical one in Teheran for Enid and when I got home I wished I had bought one for myself. Darling, you're a wizard and I'm thrilled with the handbag which arrived yesterday – I'm so proud of my new possessions and am dying to flaunt them. I wanted a new handbag so much and they are terribly expensive over here. My poor old Marrakech one is getting tatty now and creaks with protest every time I bear down upon it.

Neil, you must think I've been negligent in not writing you about old man Eisenstein,[60] but really I've had quite a pother, though one wouldn't have thought so, finding out about him. I've badgered Foyles, Times book club, every place I could think of and then Andrew finally hit upon the idea of ringing the Librarian at the British Film Institute. Abracadabra – Eisenstein has written one book, published by Faber & Faber called FILM SENSE. Faber's address is 24, Russell Square, London, W.C.2. Sorry I've been so long about this.

Wot else have a got to tell you. I'm sitting on one of the little wooden seats by the fire, an enormous log fire, typing this. Nellie is sitting opposite me on the other seat.

She has never seen a typewriter before, wonder of wonders, and she's fascinated by this silly thing sitting on my knee. She reminds me of a member of the audience on the Centre Court at Wimbledon. Her eyes are following the carriage backwards and forwards and her funny little face is quite expressive. I think she is somewhat overcome by the fact that I can type with the thing on my knee.

Neil, I know if I live with Auntie much longer I shall become one of them there bloated, very bloated, plutocrats. I'm waited on hand and foot, literally. If I let them they would clean my shoes. Nora and Nellie really do us proud and, much as I like being waited on, I don't like it all the time, and now and then life is so good I almost feel as if I'm being smothered. I'm not ungrateful – I'll never be that and I'll never take things for granted. I guess there will be times in the future when life won't be so good and I shall have to bask in the happiness, and pangs, of pleasant memories. Nellie asked me just now, or rather she said – "I don't know what to give you for a wedding present, Olive". She is 85 and I think she has the idea that she won't live to see me married. Bless her heart, I adore her. Just think – she has been in the family since she was 14 – she could write a saga about us, as a family, I guess. Imagine knowing Grandpa as a little boy, nursing daddy when he was a few weeks old, knowing all the family, the bad ones (in the majority, I'm afraid) the good ones and the indifferent, all the births, weddings and funerals and she says she wants to see Enid and me married. It would be lovely to have her there. She would be so thrilled.

I've not heard from you since two days before Christmas, poppet. I guess you're alright because Enid had her letter from you written on Christmas Day. But I get worried in case you're not well – I know always when you aren't feeling so good and I get afraid of your losing weight. I wish I could feed you on creamy milk and Horlicks and look after you. You're very precious.

Nellie wanted to see your photograph just now and when I looked at it myself I felt just a little tearful and wished you were home with me. It's almost a year since we were together and as the months pass the longing for you and my love for you grow more intense. You are the only thing that really matters – you are the pinpoint of my little universe and it all evolves around you. All my thoughts, hopes and aspirations are centred in you. Are you glad, or sorry? Perhaps I'm silly, but anyway I can't help it. I'm living for the moment when I shall hear your voice on the telephone and when I can be wrapped in your arms for a long, long time.

I needed an anchor, those years ago when we met, and I knew that I could find my fulfilment in you. If it could not be you then it would be nobody else. Never doubt my love for you.

We have seen a wonderful house at Brighton – on a hill, darling! It is a detached house, with a meadow at the side, and we can walk out of the gate on to the Downs. Aunty is giving Mother £3,000 with which Mother is buying the house. Aunty said Enid and I would be having the money eventually, so we might as well have the benefit of some of it now. I do hope we get the house. It is very attractive and I think you would like it – and lovely – to be able to live on a hill! The other house we bought was in a pretty bad state and repairs and decorations would have cost us £1,000 so we decided to sell it- and sold it at a profit of £5! More in next letter.

Heigh ho for now. Remember that I always love you.
What is your <u>news</u>! I can't bear the suspense much longer!

As the winter of early 1945 turned into spring, Olive was occupied helping both her mother and aunt resettle on the Sussex coast. In the office there was talk of conferences, but for the time being the plans did not include General Hollis, so she could not anticipate another trip abroad for a while. Neil, however, heard on the grapevine that Churchill would be in Malta at the end of January and he optimistically made arrangements in an attempt to see her there.

(III) 1945 Berlin/Potsdam

The Allies' final plans for Germany had yet to be confirmed, and it was decided that another 'Three Power' conference was necessary. They had not met since Moscow back in October, since when the Red Army had established a new government in Hungary and had entered Warsaw. In the Far East, the British 14th Army were in a new offensive in Burma, and the Western Allied forces in Europe pushed east, aiming for the River Rhine and trying to reach Berlin before the Russians. Stalin would not travel far from Moscow, but it was too cold to meet there, so they agreed Yalta, on the Black Sea. Churchill and Roosevelt had a preparatory four-day meeting in Malta beginning 30 January 1945, and then joined Stalin in the Crimea on 4 February.[61] Hollis did not, however, attend this conference and he and Olive remained in London.

Neil was in Caserta and assumed, wrongly as it turned out, that Olive would be passing through Malta as a delegate with Hollis on the way to or from Yalta. He got himself transferred, primarily in the hope of seeing her but officially for an inspection of ammunition – which was not entirely spurious. Messages spun across the wires, and, on their way back, Betty Green who was with Lord Ismay, staying with Hermione, Lady Ranfurly, informed her hostess that she had just received the news that her friend Olive Christopher's fiancé was nearby. Lady Ranfurly immediately cried: 'We must try to get in touch with him' and Neil was invited, through his connection with Olive, into the Delegation Area. From all reports he was welcomed enthusiastically – not least by Betty Green and Sylvia Arnold who gave him news of Olive. He thus met many of her friends, but not, of course, Olive herself. With much frustration he sent off the following:

Malta
AFHQ CMF
31st January 1945

Dear Olive,

For once the gods have thought fit to frown, and thus I find myself shaking hands with Sylvia & not yourself. I have metaphorically kicked myself all round this blessed island; days of waiting, waiting & wondering, a brief glimpse of Joan Bright in the distance, a pessimistic enquiry from Betty Shepherd, & a final miserable confirmation that I had "had it". Viewed philosophically, I have no right to expect meeting you, I just happened to be sent here on a routine job from Italy, & having completed it, to go home again. I worked myself up into a lather of optimism, quite unjustified & very foolishly. Two days ago I felt suicidal – now "his lordship" smiles again.

At the worst it has been grand meeting Sylvia & having a chance to talk about you, find out what you were doing, how you looked, whether you are well, in fact merely to hear someone talk to me about you – ordinary everyday chatter, but somehow producing an enormous "kick" for me. Now I know that you persist in working too hard (which seems a characteristic by now, rather than a compulsion), that you have had a cold, but are better, that your leg has given trouble but is now improved, & that your recent elevation in appointment is a serious & exacting 'bisney'.

Sylvia shyly remarks that I "look thinner"; – she may elaborate the criticism in a letter to you. Therefore I ask you not to worry about it. I am not fit yet but am considerably improved from last summer & "mending" all the time. My nerves are the only snag, but there again they are getting better & it is a long business. It resulted recently in my colonel telling me that I was not sufficiently recovered to be considered for Far East postings – thus there are mixed blessings. I have been posted from Allied Force HQ, & will be assuming my new appointment on returning to Italy. I cannot tell you my new address yet.

No more news now cherub, except to remind you how very much I love you. The last few days seem to have made things even more realistic & urgent. To meet a common friend bridges so many gaps of memory & places you on a more realistic & tangible footing – almost as though we had met again & touched hands. God bless you darling & keep smiling.

Yours always
Neil.

The Yalta Conference lasted a week. In glorious sunshine beside the Black Sea, in a very recently restored environment,[62] Churchill, Roosevelt and Stalin agreed their final plans for the defeat of Germany and its unconditional surrender. Arrangements for the zones of occupation were strengthened and conditions were made for Russia's secret entry in the war against Japan. Amongst other agreements, one was also reached on reorganising the Polish government (supported by Stalin) on a more democratic basis. A date was also set for a United Nations Conference in San Francisco in late April.

Meanwhile, back in London, V2s continued to harass the city but life in Olive's office was relatively quiet – though she felt green with envy that her friends had met Neil and she had missed out:

London
9th February 1945
Workhouse
Letter No. I

Bless you, my darling.

Now I'm way up on top of a great big bubble – instantaneous reaction from the desolation and misery of last week. Seriously – I am feeling so very much better – result of an easy time this last fortnight with all the lassies and lads away. Jacquey, General and I have been riding calm waters and everything simmered down after the great departure. I know I was miserable when I wrote my last letter to you – or maybe the one before that and the low mental and physical state was due mainly to lack of sleep and a heavy cold.

Unfortunately the bag containing your letter via Sylvia was delayed and did not arrive in time for me to get a reply back to you by the same route. Just in case Margaret Le Sueur saw you again on her return I enclosed a letter for her to give to you but, of course, you left just a day or so after them. I did not give it to Sylvia because I thought it would be much more likely that Margaret would be seeing you.

I gather you went over big with my female colleagues. How you survived the impact of so many goodlooking girls I just can't imagine. I suppose, on this 'do' the percentage of goodlooking girls was quite small. All the real goodlookers had been left behind (said she!). Anyway, I want to know what you think about all the people I work with. Don't you think they're a grand crowd. I do and I'm terribly fond of them. They have all contributed in some way towards helping me to survive this long period of your absence. Of Sylvia and Noreen I'm particularly fond. They are great friends of mine and I guess I'll always know them. Don't you think Sylvia is a poppet? We all adore her here and I would say she is easily the most popular girl in the office. Yes, she did tell me you looked thinner and she has been terribly good. I've had four letters from her telling me almost everything – how you looked, what you said, what you did, the party at the Savoy, the photographs, how you had cut a picture of a girl out of a magazine who looked like me – all sorts of things. But she says that there is still a lot to tell me and she is dying to get back and give me all the news.

Funny you should know Betty Shepherd better than I do now. I had not met her until I went to Quebec and then I saw very little of her because she went around with a different crowd from us. I think she is rather nice and certainly pretty. I just can't tell you how pleased I am that you have met everyone – it seems almost as if you're part of the office now. Poor Junior! I gather you only met him 'at a distance' and having seen him in a duffle coat, also more than "squeakered" as he is rather fond of saying, I can well understand that he would be an object of mirth. He's 28, a frightful snob, is an awful old woman at times and when he's out on the make can be terribly, terribly charming. I have no great love for him. He was one of the people who helped to make things difficult for me when I first got promoted.

What did you think of Margaret Le Sueur – the girl with the lovely red hair? I can never make up my mind whether I like her or not. I never feel quite sure of her – it's almost as if she were two people, one of whom I don't like at all and even find slightly repellent. Very naughty of me, perhaps, and I try to sublimate it but it rears its ugly head now and then. Anyway, as you met her at a party you were probably not with her long enough to be able to say whether or not you liked her. She is my opposite number on this job and has not been on a trip before. That's why she went with the Group Captain. My dee-ar Group Captain. He's a go-getter that man. Very capable, great fun on a party, extremely likeable (I'm very fond of him) but is he hell to work with!

Did you see J.B.?[Joan Bright] I mean did you see her to talk to? How odd it must have seemed to you suddenly to be planted in the midst of a place with hosts of familiar faces around you. I suppose it was interesting for you to find yourself in the midst of a Conference venue. Now you'll know what it's like when I go on a Conference.

Darling, all this week I've been saying "if only I had gone"! And I felt so miz about it when I knew but, as you say, meeting a mutual friend bridges a gap and it's lovely to know that you have met lots of my friends. Wendy's boss was there in place of mine.[63] Did you see much of Wendy? She's very clever, writes extraordinarily well, and is extremely amusing.

The news about the commission you have given Betty Shepherd, my poppet, gives me an enormous fillip. Supplies are getting lower and lower as a result of one or two misfortunes and I was getting awful worried. It's so sweet of you, darling, and very thoughtful.

In my next letter there is a piece of news which will interest you enormously.

LOV ME. Olive.

Dormans Park
9ᵗʰ February 1945

I told you about the diamond double clip brooch Aunty gave me ostensibly for my birthday! Now she has given me the material for a new coat. It was some that Grandpa bought at the beginning of the war. She doesn't want it and has given it to me – for my birthday. She is just so generous it is almost embarrassing. You just can't refuse - even if you wanted to. She gets so hurt.[64]

When we were turning out a cupboard the other week we found a box with a lot of soap in it. I had been conserving my soap ration for you but Aunty presented me with eight tablets of soap and told me to send them to you from her. Then I thought you might want a razor, so I asked the General if he could get me one for you, and he said he had a new, unused one which he would bring up. He wouldn't let me pay for it so what is a girl to do? I was going to send you a parcel from me, but I thought I'd better confess to the soap and the razor. Wot I have bought for you is a bottle of very good hair lotion – good for bald heads – and some books. "I Planted Trees" by Richard St. Barber which was reviewed in the Times. It had a terrific write-up and has some excellent photographs of trees from all over the world. He was at one time head of the Forestry Commission and describes his peregrinations all over the world in his search for trees. The other book is called "Rhetoric And English Composition" by Sir Herbert Grierson. I had already bought it for you and then Andrew told me it was marvellous, so I was more than pleased with my choice.

I will send the soap, hairoil, razor and books in separate parcels as soon as I know your new address. I wanted you to have all these things for your birthday, but they won't arrive in time. I'm also sending you some more Black Russians. If there is anything else you want please let me know.

I'm pleased about Alan and May Baron. I liked her very much and I think she will be an ideal wife for him. She adores him, of course, but I don't think she will let Alan have too much of his own way. I'm certain that he loves her and I'm delighted for both of them. I've never been able to imagine the girl Alan would marry – for that matter I've not been able to imagine him married at all and I think May will be good for him. I like her better than Ida. Joan is very fond of May too. Incidentally, I adore Joan. I think she's a darling and if she would like to I want her to come and stay with us in the summer at Brighton. I think you will like our new house.

I'm going up to Blackburn on leave just as soon as the lassies get back and are settled down again. I shall try and fix some leave about the middle of March I think. I'm so looking forward to seeing everyone again. How sweet of Uncle Fred Howarth to write to you about me. I must say I liked him and Auntie Gertie enormously. I liked everyone so much that I was just bursting with goodfellowship and affection for everyone and everything when I came back. Your father writes me the sweetest letters. Had a letter from your mother this week. She misses you very much – she misses you all, but I always feel that you and she are more akin than Alan and Jimmie are.

I'll take a bet that Sylvia told you the story of Foot, Foot-Foot and Foot-Foot-Foot! I hope she remembered all the funny stories I've told her from time to time.

It's the General's birthday today and he has gone to a party so I'm all alone here tonight. I shall go to bed early – after I have sucked my orange! Such fun having oranges decorating the table after all this time.

Did I tell you Evelyn is in Paris with SHAEF? She is having a wonderful time. She is in uniform – American – and life, I gather, is pretty good for her right now.

Do you remember the girl who wrote to me and told me I was always chasing shadows? She has just moved to Brighton with her husband and small son so before long I shall renew my acquaintance with her. Everyone is going to Brighton to live. Leslie said he and Benjie have been down there looking for a house this week.

I promise I'll have my photograph done but you know how I hate it and Sylvia probably told you that the one I had done for you was not a success.

Before I go – I'm so very pleased darling, that, although you didn't see me, you were able to see people from home – particularly Sylvia and Betty Shepherd (of whom I gather you saw more than the others). As Betty told you, we don't know each other very well, but she'll probably be coming home soon; or maybe I'll get a trip to Wash.[ington] and will get to know her better. Those few days must have made an enormous difference to you and I'm glad you enjoyed them.

Finally (and irrevocably) I love you very much. Olive.

Winter moved into spring and it became clear that, with the decline of German resistance, the war in Europe was indeed nearly over. Everyone was tired and sought for peace and a return to normality. Occupied with trying to get Neil fixed up in employment, Olive did not hear from him for a while. Then in April she discovered that the British forces were mounting a new offensive in northern Italy and assumed he must be involved. On 12 April came news from the United States that Vice-President Truman[65] had become President after the sudden death of Roosevelt, and then, a day later, news of the liberation of Belsen and Buchenwald.[66] Olive had some time off so travelled north to visit her future in-laws, and at last received the following, in which Neil was more forthcoming than usual about his activities:

Italy
HQ 3 DIST CMF
18th April 1945

Hello cherub,

Doubtless you must be worrying by now as to why I haven't written. In fact I have just arrived back from a rather hectic session in Bari. It was broadcast on the wireless & reported in our own newspapers, so that for once in a while I can tell you about it without causing breach of security. We have experienced one of the worst ammunition explosions of the campaign, involving an ammunition ship which blew up in Bari Docks. Casualties amongst civilians alone exceeded 750 dead & 100 wounded. I am responsible for all ammunition matters within that particular area & consequently had to get over there "pretty damn quick". The following ten days have been extremely hectic as I had to act as Technical Adviser to the Court of Enquiry convened to investigate the explosion and at the same time organise ammunition clearance & disposal throughout the dock area. I will not weary you with the rather gruesome detail except to say that I am thankful that it is almost over, & that the lads worked magnificently despite mob hysteria…

I gather that the trip north was a success, & you certainly seem to have "got around". According to the family bulletin, you appear to have scored bulls-eyes for charm & whatnot wherever you went. I only hope that all this social "dashing around" didn't prevent you from getting the rest that you needed, & that you have returned into harness feeling really fit & well? If I had been there we wouldn't have done anything "sociable" – rather would it have been a period of enjoying the countryside, getting plenty of fresh air & exercise, coupled with lazy "talky" evenings by a private fireside, with Horlicks, dressing-gowns & early bedtime. Still, I don't think it will be very long now before we shall be together again, doing the things we love and catching up on the days that have slipped away.

Now, my poppett, how far is the end away? When do I start drawing marriage allowances – will officers be allowed to have their wives with them during the Army of Occupation – are you a mason – are you hoarding beer for my return – have you any ideas about us for the immediate future, because I think that the war has reached a stage when we can begin to wallow in the luxury of our private post-war plans, and the arrangement of some fixed policy. In other words, how quickly can we get married – "your early comments would be appreciated". I refuse to go on loving one letter per week, one glow of memory, one thought that the war must end soon. We have been elusive far too long my poppett, and I am impatient for a chance to start flirting with you & of making you the happiest of mortals. You've not the sausage of an idea my poppett as to how much I love you, & how much I long to see you.

Neil

The weeks of April and May 1945 were packed with historic events which filled the press and newsreels, but they are hardly referred to in Olive's and Neil's correspondence. By the time his next letter arrived in early May, Mussolini[67] had been executed by Communist partisans and German forces in Italy had surrendered to the Allies. On 1 May German radio announced Hitler's suicide, and a day later the commander of German troops in Berlin surrendered.[68] Neil could not have been unaware of all this, but, because of censorship, neither he nor Olive had been used – nor were able – to write about events in the wider world. Not unexpectedly, therefore, his letters were still focussed almost entirely on their relationship and coming home, and he was as ever profoundly concerned about his future means and prospects:

Italy
HQ 3 DIST CMF
3rd May 1945

Dearest Toots,

...I often wonder if you fully appreciate the proposed circumstances under which we are contemplating matrimony & of the extent to which we are compelled to rely on good fortune. I refer now to the subject of income & the intended source thereof. Remember that before the war I was a young man of 21, working and studying as hard as possible to catch up with my late start in the field of Arts. At that time I had no fixed idea of how I was to apply, or how I was to canalise, my efforts. On the one hand was a dour sober-headed father who advocated playing for security in what he considers to be the most precarious livelihood in existence. On the other hand my 'umble self with a vague idea of what I wanted to become but with the view that I should continue my studies until the idea crystallised into something more factual... Came the war and with it the setting aside of all the things held dear to me... Heart must be reconciled inevitably to circumstance & although in my case I loathe the restrictions & implications of the term "security", it would be unfair to you that I should marry you without being able to support you at a "reasonable level"... A job will have as its financial premium a salary of approximately £400–£500 per annum...

(a) Initially and before I marry you, I must be assured of a job. I don't mind personally if the salary is as low as £300 per annum, providing it represents a start along the right channels.

(b) Secondly, and after we are married, we must acknowledge the gamble of my getting back my pre-war efficiency, and of my ability to develop that ability.

Arising out of (a) above, if this assurance is given, even whilst I am in the Army then I see no reason why we should not marry as soon as King George permits. This may take the form either of a leave to U.K. during the coming summer, or of a suitable opportunity whilst I am in the Army of Occupation. I am in Release Group 25 which prevents my being sent to the Far East, & should ensure my release within 12 months from cessation of hostilities...

I'm sorry if this reads like a private Atlantic Charter; I don't wish to trespass on sentiment, but we know each other so very well, that we can stand a little "deglamourisation"...

Tales of U.K. are very disheartening... you may be interested in one or two common opinions from chaps who have returned from U.K. leave:

(i) London has lost its manners. People fight and shove one anywhere, fail to pay proper respect to the "fairer" sex.

(ii) ATS Military Police are the cat's whiskers.

(iii) Considerable evidence of drunkenness, loose living & the like amongst young girls of 17 & 18.

(iv) Remarks at (iii) above are further coupled with a marked partiality for Yanks (include. coloured troops). One sees the English Tommy walking around by himself whilst women go "in a big way" for the Yanks.

(v) People in England don't understand the conditions which have prevailed in Italy. They think we have been disgustingly slow about the job, & that any propaganda regarding difficult terrain & bad weather are an official excuse for our procrastinations.

(vi) Chaps who served in the Desert are no longer remembered with sufficient gratefulness. Chaps serving in Italy are "good time boys" or "D.D.D.s" (Day Day Dodgers). Chaps who have returned from overseas service in the Med. (4½ years) take a back place to the chaps who are serving in France & receiving leave every six months.

(vii) England has had a battering, & London people are a tribute to the Empire.

(viii) Conditions at home are far better than one is led to believe.

(ix) Military installations in U.K. are grossly overstaffed in comparison with similar layouts in Italy.

(x) Too many "good time soldiers" are dodging the column.

(xi) (War Office visitors only). The War Office has no practical sense of overseas problems.

Despite all this, they all agree that England is a good place, & that the sooner we invade it, the better!!

Well, apart from the above, I have nothing further to report, except to say that I still think you are the cat's pyjamas, and that the sooner I get home, the better. I'm given to believe that I may be home by Christmastime, so keep your fingers crossed, & be a good girl.

All my love, darling,
Neil.

On Tuesday 8 May, *The Manchester Guardian* headlined "VICTORY IN EUROPE: PROCLAMATION TO-DAY" and noted that the Prime Minister would make an announcement at 3p.m. and the King would speak at 9.[69] The war had ended on 4 May, Germany had capitulated without condition at Reims on 7 May, and victory was to be announced simultaneously in London, Washington, and Moscow. Olive learnt that both 8 and 9 May would be public holidays.

In fact she spent the whole of VE Day itself in the office with General Hollis and the rest. They ate lunch on the premises and there were drinks in the canteen, and they went up onto the Treasury roof when

Churchill was being applauded below. Around three o'clock Churchill's voice came over amplifiers announcing that Germany had surrendered and hostilities would end at midnight. They knew there was mass euphoria in the jubilant crowds filling Whitehall, the Mall, Trafalgar Square, and towns and cities all over Britain. Later, with Jacquey and a couple of other colleagues, Olive decided to go out and mingle. Flags flew from all the buildings; shop windows were stuffed with red, white and blue cloths, and flowers were everywhere. Planes flew overhead, and streamers, ticker tape and paper poured from windows. They got down to Parliament Square, and went on to Buckingham Palace where they just managed to see the royal family. As evening wore on church bells were rung, floodlights took the place of blackout, and Big Ben's tower shone brightly for the first time for years. Olive, like everyone in the War Rooms, was very tired, and overwhelmed by all the lights and excitement. There was an incredible atmosphere, a joyful time for all. And then, shortly afterwards, she was delighted to receive the following:

MISS O. M. CHRISTOPHER
OFFICES OF THE WAR CABINET AND MINISTER OF DEFENCE

At the end of the war in Europe we should like to send to all members of the staff of the Offices of the War Cabinet and the minister of defence a special message of thanks for their untiring services during nearly six years of war.

The work of this Office in war-time has necessarily involved long and irregular hours; and on top of these many of you have had to endure the dangers and discomforts of enemy air attack. Through all these trials and tribulations you have carried on with undiminished efficiency, with cheerfulness, and in a spirit of helpful co-operation beyond all praise. You have proved yourselves a grand team.

Best wishes to you all and many thanks.

Edward Bridges
Hastings Ismay

Great George Street, S. W. 1.
11th MAY 1945.

Neil sent her this celebration of the recent monumental events:

Italy
HQ3 DIST CMF
10th May 1945

Dearest 'Ermintrude,

And so the Herrenvolk have had enough, and the Big Bad Wolf presumably dead. Happy days!

I cannot claim any sense of mild jubilation, but rather a feeling of enormous relief and thankfulness that the end has come, and that I am in a reasonable state of health. The Italians have shown little enthusiasm for rejoicing − except on the evening that peace rumours started. I was in Naples at the time, motoring solo down the Corso Umberto. The air suddenly filled with papers & streamers, wild Americans threw the contents of their stationary cupboards to the four winds, the bottom of my jeep was covered in minute sheets & streamers of toilet rolls, and the seemingly millions of ragged street urchins shouted and whooped amongst the mess. On the following day we were confined to office and barracks with occasional pauses to listen to Winston C. and Alex, and Cunningham and Uncle Tom Cobley and all. In the mess that evening the wines member produced 36 bottles of White Horse whiskey specially accumulated over long months for this particular occasion. Hatches were raised, and the whole crowd became very "boss-eyed". I crept into bed at 2a.m., after serenading my colonel on a guitar whilst he slept on the counter of the bar. Streets were deserted.

The following day was an official holiday. At 10.30a.m. we all attended Church Parade, dressed like soldiers. The ceremony was conducted by the side of a little goldfish pond in the grounds of our HQ. The General said all the right things, two violins and a piano (with the back off) constituted our orchestra, and we sang hymns with great vigour. The padre spoke extremely well, and I found myself becoming very sentimental, and rather cheeky in the fact that I was British. We finished off with a spirited rendering of God Save the King, lots of salutes, heel-bashing and sharp orders. That service concluded official business for the day. Accordingly two types and self acquired transport and beetled off to a quaint Italian restaurant down by the water-front...In the evening we returned to the mess, had a special dinner with each course named after a notability (melon glacé à Churchill)... and in the early hours a merry party of old desert rats decided to have a brew-up in traditional Desert style, & we were treated to the unique experience of five war veterans crouched round a wood fire in one of the main thoroughfares boiling tea in an upturned petrol can.

The following day we were back to almost normal, but feeling very "war weary".

Now that the tumult has died down, it seems very strange to realise that we have finished with things like Op orders and Battle plans; that the whole procedure must now be reversed, and that things like ammunition expenditure have ceased to exist. Ordnance responsibilities feature very prominently in the work ahead... Release Plans and demobilisation papers are read with deep concentration, and one comes across the odd chap sitting quietly at his desk with a far-away look in his eyes, and a photograph of his missus propped in front of him.

Now that the European show is over, can you not wangle a liaison trip to Italy? You would have the most wonderful time of your life – I promise you. I have an enormous appetite, an aching heart, and my own car. I also know the countryside, can speak enough Italian, and am on top of my job. Do your best, beautiful, otherwise I shall burst into flames. Surely you can vamp Generals, or has he got wise to the wiles of the Christopher?

Be good and remember that I love you.
Salaams, Salaams.
Neil.

Italy
HQ3 DIST CMF
21st May 1945

Dearest Erminstrude,

I have a spot of news for you. I was ushered in to the presence of my boss, who shook me warmly by the hand, said that he had been talking to my general, and that despite my age, they had decided to make me a Lieut. Colonel. The job will involve my departure from Italy nearer home, it may even include a brief but passionate visit to one of our lesser known colonies – namely, England...

I feel the need desperately to be with you & to talk all sorts of things over together. The remainder of this year is going to crawl along – just so long as we are away from each other. Keep smiling, cherub, and be patient just a little while longer. I love you, right down to the soles of my boots.

Salaams, Salaams,
Neil.

His promotion would of course mean extra pay till demobilisation, but more importantly it meant a new posting which was as yet uncertain. Olive's fear was that he might be whisked off to the Far East after all, but fortunately this was not the case. At the beginning of July he motored up from Rome in an 8 cwt. truck, spending a night in Venice, and then moved on to Klagenfurt in southern Austria. He was there to supervise explosives and the destruction of enemy munitions, and then to oversee the rehabilitation of the coalmines after the Russian departure. All future correspondence would come from Austria, and he still did not know exactly when he would come home, but he held on to the possibility that he and Olive might meet in Vienna in late July.

Following the signed declaration in Berlin, the Allies assumed supreme authority in Germany on 5 June, and 27 June saw the signing of the United Nations Charter. A final tripartite conference was felt necessary, and the Allies decided on Potsdam in Germany as the place to clarify and implement earlier agreements made at Yalta. It was codenamed 'Terminal'. Churchill, Truman and Stalin would meet on 17 July in the beautiful Cecilienhof Palace, which had belonged to Kaiser Wilhelm II, on the outskirts of Potsdam. The problems discussed would be mainly political and concern the future of Germany and Poland, the delimitation of frontiers, the terms for Japan's surrender, and a variety of economic, financial, and social questions. Churchill invited Clement Attlee, the Deputy Prime Minister, to accompany him, as an observer more than as a full participant.[70] The country went to the polls on 5 July for a General Election – the first such poll for nearly ten years – but the results were postponed for three weeks by voting procedure for the Armed Forces abroad. The conference would therefore begin before the results came through, and Churchill and Attlee would have to return to London for them.

As General Hollis was part of the British delegation Olive accompanied him as his personal assistant, and, after the requisite shopping for suitable conference clothing, they flew out on 15 July, expecting to be away for three weeks. She carried her official 'Allied Expeditionary Force Permit', which stated: 'The bearer of this permit has the permission of the Supreme Commander Allied Expeditionary Force to enter the Zone of the Allied Forces in N.W.EUROPE', and it was valid from 3 July for three months. She was to work closely with the other secretaries, Maggie Sutherland and Joan Umney-Gray,[71] and they were kept immensely busy typing and filing the papers, minutes and reports for all the meetings Hollis prepared and attended. There was little time to get out, though when they did they noticed that Potsdam was devastated, and that the Soviets had planted red flowers in the shape of a large red star in the gardens of the Cecilienhof. [72]

The British Victory Parade in Berlin on 21 July was an understandably memorable event, and everyone seemed to be there. Olive received a four-page programme which informed her of the troops taking part and the order of March Past, with exact timings of when things would happen. At ten in the morning the Prime Minister accompanied by the Commander-in-Chief arrived at the Saluting Base. They were met by GOC British Troops Berlin, and there was a salute by guns of the 3rd Regiment Royal Horse Artillery. At 10.05 the Prime Minister, accompanied by Distinguished Visitors, drove around and inspected the parade. At 10.30 he returned to the Saluting Base and the March Past began, lasting more than half an hour before he departed. Olive was so excited by all this, but most of all she loved the Band of the Royal Marines (Chatham Division) playing the joyful tunes which always stirred everyone's heart.

Halfway through the conference the Election results were to be declared and Churchill and most of his staff returned to England to await the result. This provided a small breathing space for those left behind and Hollis decided to profit with a little sightseeing. He took the girls and some others off to tour Berlin, and they visited the ruined Reichstag[73] and Chancellery building, where they entered Hitler's study.[74] This was a place Olive had seen when younger, in pictures and newsreels of Hitler receiving people there. It was a huge room, perhaps forty to fifty feet long, and people had been marched in to face Hitler at his huge red marble desk at the other end. Now that desk was smashed and bits of it were lying all over the floor. Everyone picked up small pieces to carry away, and Olive's seemed a grim souvenir weighing down her small bag. The following is a long letter written during this short break by Olive to her colleague back in London:

Germany
Potsdam
23rd July 1945

My dear Jacquey,

I'm sure that all the other girls, who seem to be excellent correspondents, have told you almost everything about TERMINAL and, therefore, there doesn't seem to be very much to tell you except to give you my own impressions.

From my standpoint, and I think, General Hollis's, it has been a good Conference. Despite Maggie's few days in hospital, work has gone smoothly, there have been one or two major flaps, and it has been nothing like as hectic for us as Quebec and Cairo. That is probably due to the fact there are not the distractions of shopping, sightseeing, etc. One is confined to the conference compound except for the odd trips to Berlin when work has eased off and invitations to local Officers' Messes etc., for parties and dances. There have, of course, been the usual official functions, such as a cocktail party given by Sir Edward Bridges and General Ismay.

My first real night off was last Friday when the officers of the local Signals corps gave a dance to which Betty, Wendy, Johnnie and I went, with a few more of the girls from here.[75] It was terrific. They presented us with flowers on arrival, the evening was flowing with champagne, I had a marvellous dancing partner who was very good fun and we danced till 3a.m. I enjoyed myself enormously.

Earlier in the week I had dinner with the General, George Mallaby and Rosalind Petrie. The Band of the Royal Marines "beat the retreat" in Kaiserstrasse and as we were walking down C.C.O. joined us. I wished so much that you had been there! It was very impressive, too, to hear our National anthem played in a German street and then to hear reveille.

Betty has probably told you about the dance at UfA film studios and the party with Bill Cunningham – yes, that was the night Teddy Ablett was with us. He's a pretty poor type and I don't like him. We found ourselves in a most attractive boathouse on the side of the lake at one time in the evening. It really was most romantic, but of course, one had to be with the right person!

The highlight of the trip for me was the British Victory parade in Berlin on Saturday morning. We had been to the dance the night before and didn't get to bed until 3.30a.m. We had to be up again at 7a.m. to go to Berlin. Very difficult!

The Parade was so thrilling, Jacquey. It was a terrific experience to be standing in devastated Berlin watching all our famous Generals and Field Marshals, the Prime Minister and all the leaders of our Government taking the salute on the Charlottenburger Chaussee where, so many times in years past, have been held demonstrations of the "Nazi Might". Particularly amusing was an inspection of the Parade by the Prime Minister and "distinguished visitors" who made somewhat slow progress in "half-tracks" – a kind of open tank. Half a dozen or so people piled into each vehicle and General Hollis was among them. I do so wish you could have seen him. He caught sight of Maggie and me waving to him and looked very pleased with himself. He gave us a very jaunty salute. General Ismay looked as though he might have caught a glimpse of Betty who was with us in her red suit. He was having a jolly good look anyway. They all looked, and said they felt rather as though they were in tumbrels on their way to the guillotine. General Hollis said it was quite an ordeal.

We had all the troops around us and they were grand lads. I felt so sorry for them because they had wandered into our enclosure and had an excellent "stand", but they were moved away by the M.Ps. I felt very mean about it because one felt they had played so great a part in the Victory and they deserved special front line "stands". However, they seemed fairly happy about it and were very interested in all of us. Of the Parade, the 7th Armoured Division ("Desert Rats") were the most interesting. After them I liked the Navy and the Army and the Royal Marine band. After the Parade we got in a traffic jam with the 7th Armoured Division – an amusing experience!

Yesterday afternoon the General took Maggie, Margaret Rose and me into Berlin. Victor Nares, whom you may know, was our guide, and an excellent one too.[76] We drove through the outskirts of Berlin which, except for a portion of the south, is a complete and utter ruin down the Charlottenburger Chaussee to the Tiergarten. We stopped at the Franco-Prussian Victory memorial, climbed to the top and had a marvellous view over Berlin. After that we went to the Reichstag outside which there were crowds of Germans and Russians, wounded soldiers, etc., all trying to catch a glimpse of the British sightseers. Outside the Reichstag is the Black Market where the famous bartering is conducted. They will barter anything for soap, cigarettes, chocolate, and any little thing that will contribute to their comfort. I believe one or two people have managed to secure excellent cameras.

We went round the Reichstag which, of course, is just a ruin and then we drove on down the Unter de Linden to Wilhemstrasse and the Chancellery which by far was the most interesting. As you have read in the paper, bits of Hitler's desk are great souvenirs and we have all got them.[77] We also managed to get some medals.

I have seen so much in the short time that we have been here and an hour or so in Berlin is not long enough in which to register everything. It certainly gives one to think and I would like to spend perhaps a whole day there alone, without having to talk to anyone.

It gave me a great thrill to watch General Hollis walking down the vast, vast entrance hall of the Chancellery. It is a terrific length and very high. The floor is of marble, although you wouldn't recognise it now. At the end are the enormous doors leading to Hitler's own room. There is also a vast reception room which was once white and gold with two great chandeliers of white and silver and crystal. They must have been magnificent and are shaped like a Christmas tree. Now the floor is covered with plaster, broken furniture and torn furnishings. The ceiling no longer exists – all that is left is a mass of twisted iron with great holes through which one can see the Red flag waving in the distance. Both chandeliers are down and if one stands very quietly and listens one can hear the plop, plop of water dripping through. A slight breeze makes a piece of paper flap and a bit of plaster falls off the wall. That was where the people who planned our destruction lived and worked.

Nothing you or I have ever before seen is anything like the devastation in Berlin. As for the people – don't believe all you read and see in the papers. In a photograph they may look reasonably glamorous but the women generally are dirty, badly dressed, some with shoes, some without – all without stockings. I saw one woman with her feet bandaged walking along without any shoes. A number of the girls have smart sandals, but they usually have tatty dresses, untidy hair and are generally scruffy. Several of them have glamorous hats and the prostitutes are quite well-dressed and very much in evidence. When I say well-dressed, I mean compared with the average German woman we have seen who is almost invariably pushing a handcart piled with belongings and a child sleeping on top. How these people exist in Berlin, I just do not know. There is very little food. There is no milk for the children. A large number of the people have a sort of headquarters in the city because they are afraid to leave it in case a prisoner-of-war relative comes home and won't know where they are. There is no post and no form of contact at all. In the morning a large number of them can be seen trudging out of the city and down the autobahns into the country where they can scrounge a few vegetables and some fruit. In the evening they may be seen trudging back again. There is no transport except what the Russians and Americans choose to give them. A lot of them have bicycles but most of them walk. A large number of them, girls particularly, are just "on the road" with their few possessions. They have nowhere to go. They have been turned out by the Russians and are fast becoming "tramps".

In Berlin yesterday we saw what looked like large farm trucks packed with men and women, all Nazis, who had been earmarked for forced labour. They were waiting to "take off" – goodness knows where. Other Nazi women are made to clear the streets of debris. The house in which the P.M. is living is owned, or was owned, by a banker and his daughter came to do the gardening and cleaning.

We wondered what had happened to the people who were living in the houses in which we are billeted. I can't help feeling that the people who lived in our house were rather nice and young and that they loved children, because the nursery, which Betty and Wendy are sharing is very attractive and the house has a good atmosphere. One felt that the people who lived in it were happy.

I asked Victor Nares if he knew what had happened to the people. He said they had been turned out by the Russians – those who had remained as the advancing armies approached. Others fled to the south – into Austria. Others, Nazi, who were caught were put into concentration camps.

Potsdam, for devastation, is worse, if that is possible, than Berlin and there is a frightful smell everywhere which they say is bodies decaying under the ruins. It was certainly an excellent idea to insist on us all being inoculated because we would certainly all be down with some sort of disease by now. Betty has gone into hospital today with tonsillitis. We were afraid she might have diptheria or typhus as she had a high temperature. Poor Betty.

There is no main drainage here and there is a dreadful smell of sewers just after lunch each day – such an excellent time – don't you think?

We are having excellent food but nothing like so luxurious as one reads in the paper. We haven't seen any strawberries and cream yet and we are getting good old English fare, extremely well-cooked and attractively served.

There is a lot more to tell you, but I think it should wait until we get home.

We have all got on very well; there have been no major squabbles and no disturbing influences always around us. In fact, I'm quite enjoying this Conference – perhaps more than any of the others as we have been able to get away from the usual Conference mob. I enjoyed Marrakech, of course, and one enjoyed Cairo and Quebec, but in a different sort of way. I'm enjoying meeting different people here.

Neil says he is not important enough for the powers-that-be to fly him here and he is hoping that I shall be able to fly to him. A remote hope I'm afraid!

Hope you are not being too busy and that you are having fun. When you write to Margaret please give her my love – I hope she is enjoying her leave.

Will be writing to dear old Foot, but not a long letter, because I expect you will show this to her. My love to Joan Mainprice, Bridghid, Margaret Fairlie and all the WAAFS. It will be good to see you all again.

Must go now as Wendy is champing for me. We want to go on a party together tonight. She says we have been chaste too long (actually, exactly two evenings!) Poor Wendy – she has been so busy.

Lots of love, Jacquey.
Olive

Olive was on a 'high', with all the excitement of the conference, the parties and the fun alongside the hard work.[78] She also lived with the expectation of shortly meeting up with Neil. They had finally made arrangements for her to have time off at the end to go on to see him for a few days in Vienna. But her hopes were shattered by the results back home of the General Election, which were declared on 26 July with a resounding defeat for the Conservatives and a landslide Labour victory. Although Stalin had solemnly assured Churchill that his sources predicted an eighty-seat majority for his Conservative Party, the outcome was an emphatic rejection of the man who had led the British people through nearly six years of war. His party defeated, Churchill was no longer Prime Minister, and Clement Attlee, who had been his wartime deputy, and was Leader of the Opposition, took on the direction of the conference, returning to Potsdam as Prime Minister to complete negotiations. The Allies set up a new system of rule for Germany and prevented it again becoming a military power; and the respective zones of occupation and reconstruction were made independent of each other. Everywhere people struggled for food and fuel, and, in time, the conference was followed by an 'iron curtain', brought down over parts of Europe by Stalin's brutal regime.

Amongst the delegates there was immediate shock at the Election result, gloom and despondency dwelt everywhere, and Olive was deeply affected by the outcome. Apart from her disappointment for Churchill, she had to leave Germany and return to London to join Hollis, which meant that her plans to visit Neil in Vienna were cancelled. Yet again the joy of meeting was put on hold, and it took several days before she could find herself ready to write about it all to Neil – though in doing so she did finally manage to cheer herself up:

London
2nd August 1945

My darling,

I'm feeling so miserable about so many things but I'm most miserable about not seeing you and I feel very guilty about not having written before to tell you I've been back in England since last Friday.

The results of the Election completely dashed what little hope I had of seeing you because the General came home to hear the worst and when the worst happened I was recalled immediately, after exactly two weeks in Germany.

I had a word in a very influential ear about the possibility of a "flight" being arranged for me and I think he would, at least, have done all he could although he held out no promise of being able to get permission for me to go to you. So there we are, or what is worse here I am! Not very well and with "Potsdam Blues". In fact, I think I returned to England in the nick of time, for I was the only one who remained completely well while we were away. Brenda, Betty and Maggie all went into hospital. Wendy only escaped it by sheer will power and because she was afraid of missing something! On the morning of our departure I woke up feeling like hell and with great difficulty survived the journey to the airfield – viewing the prospect of a four hour flight with the deepest gloom, for I was quite certain I was going to be ill. However, I sank back into the most comfortable seat I've ever had in a Dakota and slept more or less all the way home. We flew back in very bad weather and had a very bumpy trip, but I wasn't ill. The pilot murmured a few cheerful words about the possibility of trouble and what to do "In the event of", but as I was feeling the shadow of death anyway I was beyond caring. But I live, and life becomes more rosy every day.

I can't explain why I didn't write to you before but perhaps you will understand – missing you, not feeling well, the results of the Election, and so much work that I had to do night duty the day I got back as Jacquey had been on duty for three days and nights. I've had two nights at home since my return and tomorrow I'm going home until Wednesday – isn't it wonderful?

The fact that I have not seen you on this trip has only renewed the awful disappointment of the Malta affair. I suppose it's stupid of me but every time I think of you I want to burst into tears. To have you so near (comparatively) and not to be able to do anything about it was hell. I must confess that most of the joy of anticipation of the trip was caused by the possibility of seeing you. I let my imagination play tricks with me and now I'm back in England a disappointed woman – thinking of you and of what grand glorious fun it would have been together, even if only for a day. Your last letter "smacked" of the hotel brochure and was certainly an excellent advertisement for your present "quarters" ably aided and abetted by the photographs which you sent me and the wording on which everyone in the office seems to have read with the greatest delight. Jacquey said they kept her cheerful while we were away and she tried to pretend that they were for her! Actually she sent them on to me.

Now to tell you about the trip. I've already told you that the most excit-ing thing for me was the British Victory Parade in Berlin. Next to that I think I was most thrilled by all the parties and dances which were given for us. I've never before had such an absolutely wizard "Conference". There were parties and dances every night and the Army of occupation for the two weeks that I was there seemed to be occupied chiefly in entertaining all the girls on the Delegation. I went to three big dances – one at UfA Film Studios – of particular interest to me, of course, and in fact it was the only reason I went. Chief reaction to that was hearing "The King" played for the first time on enemy territory. The next big dance was given by 2nd Army Signals in their Officers' Mess which is a pub not far from Potsdam. I've never had so much champagne in all my life. The evening was literally flowing with it. The Mess seemed to be filled with officers when we arrived and we were all presented with flowers. I believe there were 35 men and certainly not more than 15 girls. Oh boy! I was extremely lucky because I got an excellent dancing partner. He was a most amusing person with a voice exactly like George Watson of Western Bros. His name was or is Dixon, Captain Dixon, and he had that evening been notified that he was the father of a daughter called "Angelina" and at the same time he was celebrating his promotion to Captain. Wot a party. He was great fun and I liked him because he came from Lancashire – lives at Southport now but knows Blackburn well.

The only snag about the dance was that apparently the lads had made a pact before we arrived that the girl they chose should be their partner for the rest of the evening and I must say I would have loved to dance with some of the others who were just propping the bar up. I danced from 9.30p.m. until 3a.m. I "fraternized" that evening too. The waiter in the Mess was German but was very interested in me and I discovered that he had been in England until the war broke out and up to 1939 for five years had been a waiter at the Metropole at Brighton. In the cloakroom there was a most charming girl to whom I talked. She was helpful and nice without being servile and was very interested in we English girls. All of us were wearing American frocks, silk stockings, etc. and she was obviously admiring our clothes. Her name is Hildegarde and she lives in Babelsburg. She is the sort of girl with whom I would be friends if she were English. I went up to the cloakroom later in the evening and she was reading. I asked her in somewhat halting German what she was reading and in equally halting English she managed to tell me that she was reading Spenser's "Faerie Queene" in German, and she was too!

I got into trouble with the General for "fratting" but he needn't have worried about me for most of the time I hadn't the inclination – the people weren't sufficiently interesting.

I found that the majority of the British soldiers and officers I met were not so keen on fraternization. Most of them would not speak to the Germans unless it was absolutely necessary.

I found too, that it was very difficult not to be sorry for our former enemies. Berlin has to be seen to be believed and I thought ahead to the winter. They will have nowhere to live, most of them, no food, no heating, none of the ordinary comforts of life. They will barter anything for food, soap, chocolate, etc., and the "Black Market" outside the Reichstag is an incredible sight. The barterers were mostly Americans and Russians – not many of our tommies were to be seen and I believe there is now a ban anyway on "bartering" in Berlin.

The next party, which everyone said was the best party ever given on any Conference, was one organised by Olive Christopher and paid for by her and 7 other girls. It was only incredible luck that the party was such a success.

We had chosen last Wednesday night – the day on which all the V.I.P.s returned to London for the election results and all the less important people were left behind with nothing to do. When we arrived in our house we decided it was just the place for a party – it had a large attractive drawing room, with a polished floor and the most wonderful piano. Divided from the drawing room by folding doors was another small room, also with a polished floor. And so the idea of a party was born. Did you meet Dickie Bird (otherwise Captain Bird) the Catering Officer at Malta? Anyway, he was Catering Officer on this show and he was a poppet. He organised all our drink and food for us and we decided we would borrow a radiogram from one of the other houses.

The day of the party arrived – and wot a day! We had sent out thirty special invitations and issued about eight more verbal ones. Brenda and I, however, discovered at tea in the afternoon that lots of people hadn't had their invitations and knew nothing about the party. We began to wonder whether anyone would come to it. In fact, we got "cold feet" proper. Wendy, as usual, kept our spirits up by having even colder feet and Brenda and I got ourselves entangled with a standard lamp which we were trying to carry from our bedroom to add a little glamour to the dance room. Anyway, I seem to remember that we sat on the stairs giggling hysterically quite a lot of the time. Wendy put a notice on the door "This house has a plague – go away". I should mention that we had given her pen and paper to write a notice with "GENTS" on it! We were giving a dinner party to four of the signals officers at 7.30 and at 6.45 Maggie and one of the WAAFS carried in the radiogram. Darling, it wouldn't work! Our party was due to start at 9.30 and we had no music. We sat in depressed silence for a while and then remembered 2nd Army Signals, to whose dance we had been. I rang Dickie and asked him if they could bring their dance band pianist along. He said "Pianist? Let's have the whole band – I'll ring you in half an hour to confirm". Half an hour later I was in the bath and he rang frantically to say that he had got the band but the Security Officer wouldn't let them into the Compound. That was simple! One of the WAAFS had a boyfriend in the Security Office and was bringing him to the dance, so we got her to ring him up and he "played". He said "Just tell the band to come to the barrier and I'll be there to bring them in". Even though we were quite sure our party was going to be a flop. We thought how silly we would look if we had a band and nobody turned up! However, Dickie and Ken and their two friends arrived frightfully late for dinner. We knocked back a quick drink, guzzled two bottles of wine and our dinner in about 20 minutes and tore over to the house at 9.25, only to find that band, food, drink, and four guests had arrived. As I walked in the door ten officers arrived from another Mess and, darling, at 9.40 <u>everyone</u> had arrived including two gatecrashers! One of them came up to me and apologised for gatecrashing. I just shook him by the hand and said I was delighted that we had "earned" a gatecrasher. There were 60 people at our party eventually and it was terrific. But the worst part was the kick-off because I counted 8 girls and 30 men and we were having bits of dances with people. However, I rang up the typing pool in desperation and managed to rustle together a few more girls.

We had tried to keep VIPs away as much as possible, inviting only men who had helped with the organisation of the Conference, such as Transport, Signals, Catering, etc., but VIPs trickled in and two rather obvious "non-party goers" said they were having a wonderful time and just couldn't tear themselves away.

We had 8 bottles of gin, 8 of whisky, champagne cup and punch and there was not a drop left over. Total cost £8.0.0. (Some of our guests had, I think lifted a bottle or two!) I announced the last dance at 1.45a.m. for I felt that if it went on any longer it would be too long. I gather that there were various parties in odd (very odd) places after that. I was invited to a boathouse party but didn't get that far. I seem to remember a somewhat romantic grotto by the lake (but with the wrong person). I pleaded tiredness and was taken home. I believe I was the first of our girls to reach home (said she piously) but I had a snoop round to see if anyone else was in and the house was dark and silent, except that just as I entered the door the 'phone rang – it was one of the lads at the local airfield who had heard that there was a wizard party at our house. He wondered if it was still going on and whether he could come over. This was at 3a.m.!

This conference gave me to think quite a bit. All the men I met, practically without exception, were terrific. The only one I didn't like was a middle-aged Lt.Col. who was very preoccupied with himself. He was quite sweet really but I'm afraid my thoughts were preoccupied with a ridiculously young and attractive Lt.-Col. whom I know and who is now cutting a dash in Klagenfurt.

Some of the lads who tagged along really were terribly nice and great fun but apart from liking them very much and having fun with them I found I was immune – so I think I really must be in love with you. Life was very difficult at times, I must say.

Have I ever really told you very much about myself since you went away. Perhaps I told you quite a lot after Quebec, but I made sure, this time, that there was no repetition of Quebec. Nothing very much happened in the interim except Dan Hunt's and Jack Donovan's homecomings. Dan Hunt I have seen and will continue to see because we like each other and are great friends. Jack Donovan I have not seen. Somehow we just haven't made it and I think it's mutual. He's just got engaged to Win, his nurse girl friend who has a T.B. throat and may not live. They celebrated their engagement three weeks ago. I shall of course see Jack in due course, probably this weekend. It will be good to see him again and he wants to hear all about you so I shall have lots of fun telling him about you.

What have I been thinking about while you have been away? You, chiefly, not much else. Vague ideas of writing, with no time and no mental energy in which and with which to do it. I wish I had a double track brain. I wish I could do my work and spend my spare time doing some real thinking and writing. But I can't. Quite often it's an effort to write to you. Not because I lack the inclination. I frequently start a letter to you and do not finish it. I just haven't the mental energy to complete it. In fact, I don't think I write as well now as I did when I first knew you – chiefly because what little brain I have is absorbed in my work.

Since we have been at Brighton I have found myself becoming less mentally hidebound. I have been able to think about things other than my work. I love being there. If only you could have been there to see all the lights go up for the first time. I was away in Germany but Mother and Enid wrote and told me about it. From my bedroom window, darling, the night is just the most perfect thing. Thousands of little lights winking in the distance. It was quite as thrilling looking out of my window that first night home as it was to see Malta, or Cairo, or Quebec, for the first time.

Come home soon, Neil. There is so much to see and do and there is so much to share with you. People love coming to our house now and it's such fun having Aunty so near us.

I wish I weren't so tired always when I'm off duty. I'm getting very lazy I'm afraid. I never go and see people but am quite content for them to come and see me. I think the truth is that I like my home very much these days, I see very little of it and hate being away from it.

Home. How much it means to people. It meant much more to me when I returned from Germany than ever before and I was only glad that the Luftwaffe hadn't been as thorough as the R.A.F. The sight of Potsdam, laid absolutely flat by the R.A.F. in 40 minutes. Berlin, with only a very small portion of it standing and the rest a complete and utter ruin. Homeless people, on the road, pushing all their belongings in a handcart, through the rain, or wind, or heat and dust, halting to look at us as we swept by in Staff cars at 50 or 60 miles an hour along the Autobahn. Yes. I felt sorry for them and then I remembered that it was only what they would have done to us.

I went to Berlin several times but the last time we did a sort of grand tour with the General. We drove down the Charlottenburger Chaussee to the Tiergarten and stopped at the Franco-Prussian War Victory Memorial. Our interpreter suggested that we climbed the stairs to the top to get a good view of Berlin. But as it was practically unlighted inside and we had to pass a number of very unpleasant people on the stairs, the smell being almost intolerable, I didn't make the top, and by that time I had got so high that I felt faint when I looked through a hole in the wall. We drove from there to the Reichstag which is just a ruin. From there we drove down the Unter den Linden, round into Wilhelmstrasse, which as you know, is Berlin's Whitehall, and to the Chancellery. I was not long enough in the Chancellery. I wanted to linger and think. In fact I wanted to sit there for at least two hours and think about it. It is a complete and utter ruin. It will have to be demolished, but enough of it existed in places to give one an idea of its former vastness and magnificence. A most terrific entrance hall, very long and very high, with a marble floor and lighted by candelabra on the walls and chandeliers from the ceiling. Just the kind of thing one sees on a Hollywood film set. It was very exciting to linger behind the General and watch him walking down the hall towards what were once large doors leading to Hitler's room at the end. Old documents and bits of paper were flapping about. There was a tattered gas mask on the floor and a German steel helmet amidst the rubble. Outside one could see a battered German tank.

Can you imagine a vast, vast reception room, with a ceiling and walls once white and gold, hung with two enormous chandeliers, in crystal and silver, shaped like two giant Christmas trees. A room magnificently furnished, with a soft pile carpet. Now there is an enormous hole in the roof, through which one can see the Red flag flying. What is left of the ceiling is just a mass of twisted iron girders. The chandeliers have fallen and people, myself included, have looted them for souvenirs. The plaster is off the walls, bits of furniture and torn furnishings are lying about. If one stands very quietly and listens one can hear the plop, plop of water dripping from the roof; there is a breeze and a bit of paper flaps against the wall. Hitler's room is just a heap of ruins and this was where the people who planned our destruction worked and lived.

It is something I shall never forget. I'm only sorry that I could not have spent more time there because I do not think I registered everything.

There is a great deal to tell you about this particular trip which cannot be put into a letter. I only wish that you could always have been here when I returned from my trips. There is always so much to tell you.

On the day we heard the results of the Election a trip had been arranged for us to go to Cecilienhof, the Palace of the German Crown Prince at Potsdam, and then on to Sans Souci, the old and new palaces of Frederick the Great. Cecilienhof is the most romantic place imaginable. It exudes atmosphere and tradition. Unfortunately we saw only the exterior as they were working there and we were not allowed to go over it. Sans Souci was very interesting, of course. But it is very ornate and rather tawdry. My great thrill was to visit Voltaire's room and sit in his chair (much to the amusement of the Russian guard with us!). It is an amazing room, with vast barbola work in pastel colours all over the ceiling and walls. Its chief beauty are the chairs which are of the most exquisite tapestry. A room typical of Voltaire, one felt. Extravagant, sensual and imaginative.

We got rather bored eventually as the curator, who was German, would insist on explaining every picture to us in very bad French. When we got back to the Office we learned that the General had telephoned recalling us to London and Maggie and I left at crack of dawn the following morning.

I seem to have written an awful lot without having told you very much! But I'm going to bed now, my poppet, as it's 12.30a.m. and I'm very tired.

Incidentally, I saw the Wing Commander at dinner the other night and he says "When are you coming home?" That's wot I says too. Can't you possibly get home by August 18th. Joan is coming down that day for a week.

We are going to have a wizard party (we hope at the Savoy) that night. Joan and I are spending the weekend in Town at Welbeck Palace. There will be 12 of us to dinner. Margaret Le Sueur is going to Washington and this is to be her farewell party. It is fortunate that it coincides with Joan's visit. Jacquey and I are organising the party. The General and Mrs. Hollis are going to be there, Dan Hunt, "Junior" (whom you know), Jacquey, Maggie and myself, Joan and Margaret and we need a few more men – two more, in fact. One I think will be Jack Donovan. Wot abaht you, chum? We are wearing evening dress and Joan is very thrilled.

Will write next time and tell you more about Joan's visit. I'm looking forward very much to having her stay with us and I will certainly give her a basinful of Sunny South! Please come and help me!

Before I go I must tell you I love you and I guess I always will – please come home soon because I'm missing you and I'm lonely without you.

God bless you always,
Olive.

Austria
6th August 1945

Dearest Olive,

I've just received your letter written from "London again" on the 2nd of August. I'm in the middle of an elaborate report on the nitration of glycerine – but I <u>must</u> write though honest injun I haven't the time.

I am a miserable little schoolboy right now, almost blubbering because you're gone away again. All this past ten days I've been telling myself you would come. On three successive nights I sat up till 3 in the morning because Sigs said it was the only hope of raising Potsblatz.[79] I finally got through by way of Munich & Berlin only to be told by a very patient Yank that he was sorry but the line was too faint. Now I've "had it" again, the sun has gone in again. Heigho & hells bells – damn, damn, damn, and damn again.

I haven't written to you because I too seem to have been in the same funny strange frame of mind as yourself. Can't explain it, quite – except that I thought I should be showing you my lovely Tyrol & that words were rather a waste in comparison. I wish with all my heart that I could get home – I <u>must</u> see you, I feel in such a clumsy, useless state of mind & nothing can revive me except your own lovable self and the joy of tangible, real things again. There are many occasions when I want to go right off the rails: when the only safety valve seems to be a raging, blinding drunk and to hell with the consequences.

I am coming slowly to the conclusion that I am a bad type & that all this is punishment. I remember reluctantly those last dark November nights in London when I received my posting instructions to go abroad & you were not there – you were on a conference. "My dear", twitter the jays, "what an interesting experience your fiancée is having – fancy being with MR CHURCHILL!" I remember a series of careful plannings in my tent in Caserta as to how to get to Malta & how to stop there long enough for the conference. I flew to Malta – not the aeroplane. Then the frantic scramble to the WVS HQ in Valetta – a sweet-eyed Betty, a kind-hearted Sylvia and news to make even an angel groan.[80]

You implore me to come home, I implore myself to do likewise but the chances are abysmally remote…

I've just read this letter. I'm sorry it's a dark one and you really mustn't take me too seriously. I shall come home soon, I shall move heaven & earth to try and get home on a temporary visit providing I can find a genuine reason. There are a number of things which justify a War Office chat, but the Brigadiers collect those & use 'em instead. I want you to know, before I return to my nitration, that I love you just as strongly as ever before, and that I will not let things get me down too much. I've been a silly ass on this occasion because I let go all sorts of age-old misgivings, and really believed you were coming.

My love comes to you down London streets and dodging round the crowded corners. It is here before you on these words that you are reading, and I am standing right beside you as you smile. Maybe I shall kiss the funny tilt of hair in the warm soft smoothness of your neck & then dissolve again into a stranger somewhere in Austria.

God bless you darling & be patient again.
Neil.

It was early August 1945. By devious routes and rumours, Olive knew a little about the Atom bomb, where at work it was known only through its code name. She knew all about the correspondence, but did not have access to it. When it was dropped on Hiroshima on 6 August she remembers it as a total surprise, and she did not have a sense of 'Well that's it – that's the end of the war with Japan' – not until much later. She was on a week's leave with her mother in Brighton and really only heard all about it once back in the office. Neil, in Klagenfurt, referred to it briefly in his next letter:

Austria
REAR 5 CORPS CMF
12ᵗʰ August 1945

Dearest Olive,

My last letter was a muddle of disappointments, to which I am now philosophically reconciled – although still sore. You will be pleased to note that I am eligible now for flying L.I.A.P.[81] and that there are reasonable prospects of my paying you a quick cuddle sometime before Christmas. In addition, I have some good news for you.

Apparently my work has created very favourable impressions here – (not difficult seeing that we have to contend with a lot of mug-wumps with white knees from Blighty). However, I was summoned to an elaborate conference in Klag.[enfurt], on Saturday, and informed that I was being appointed as Explosives Commissar for the whole of the British Zone. The appointment is a wizard chance of promotion, my terms of reference extend over a number of industries which use explosives for their work, and I shall also have the opportunity for lots of travelling. Cross your fingers for me, and wish me luck. If, as I think likely, I do get the extra pip, I shall think seriously of volunteering for a further period in Austria, drawing my £1500 a year, and getting my own house here. All this on condition that I can first have a month's leave in England, marry you, and bring you back to Austria with me. At the moment my pay is roughly £1000 a year – would you even consider doing the same thing on my existing prospects? Austria is a very lovely country and I am a very lonely bloke. Perhaps you think that by so-doing, I am only postponing the evil day of my final release from the Army, & my chances of starting up as a civilian again? There is a lot to be said either way, & I would like your views.

The news of an impending Jap finale is very cheering; I am sufficiently selfish to think mainly in terms of my younger brother, and the fact that he is now very likely to survive the Far East show, & concentrate on "home and beauty".

Joan writes to tell me of her coming session in the big, dark city & her trip to your home. It is a grand thing, & I do so hope that you both enjoy the occasion...

You avoid much comment on the election results. Knowing your rare loyalty for Churchill and your anxiety for his cause, I suppose that you prefer to swallow the pill without saying a lot. The few Austrians I have spoken to, submit their bewilderment at the British action, and suggest that we must all be slightly "crackers" to acknowledge a victorious leader in this manner. I have submitted vague mumblings about "democratic principles", and that "the man does not necessarily make the party". I find it difficult to reconcile Bevin and Eden;[82] by the same token I am rapidly coming to the conclusion that our finest over-seas ambassador is the British Tommy – notably because of his sincerity and gentlemanly instincts. The Austrians have quickly recognised his worth, and one feels that our intervention here, and our methods of restoring legitimate enterprise are welcomed by the majority and frequently admired. The same reception has not been extended in all other Allied Zones – but I leave you to draw your own conclusions.

The Atomic Bomb has cast a gloom in many officers' messes, and the main reaction is a dread of such discoveries, and their future deployment. In the sole charge of a good & wise nation it is a safeguard for the future and a tremendous argument for peace. I tremble to think of its use by the Hitlers of this small world…

I love Austria. It is my nearest memory of Scotland and the wild moors of Cumberland. It is helping me to "get-over" the morbid doldrums of Italy, and I am feeling heaps better for the change. If only you could be here to help me enjoy it, I think life would be almost ideal. As it is, remember that I carry your memory around with me, and project it from hilltops across all this loveliness, in frequent emotional daydreams and thoughts of days to be.

All my love darling, and my greetings to Joan on her arrival.
Keep smiling.
Neil.

With the surrender of the Japanese forces in the Far East, 15 August was the date that marked the end of war against Japan. That weekend Olive had arranged for Neil's cousin Joan to stay with her in Brighton: 'Lets have a weekend at the Savoy', she had said, and they gave a party on the Saturday night in London for as many friends as could come. VJ Day happened, the lights came on, and everyone celebrated as they had done on VE Day. General Hollis then invited Olive down to Haywards Heath, to stay the night at their private home, Birchlands. She had dinner with them at the nearby Birch Hotel, and Mrs Hollis lent her a beautiful pale green taffeta evening dress to wear – which unfortunately had a little wine spilt on it by the waiter, but Mrs Hollis did not mind.

From now on life was going to be very different. With the war over those in charge of planning for peace could move back to their central offices, and the Chiefs of Staff were not occupied as they had been before, so General Hollis as Secretary to their Committee felt a change. The Cabinet War Rooms, where everyone had worked so intensively since the start of the war, were no longer needed, and, when, on 16 August, the lights of the Map Room were finally switched off and the door locked, it was the first time since the rooms had become operational. The administrative rooms were stripped of their contents and returned to storage and service areas; but the Map Room, the Transatlantic Telephone Room, Churchill's Room and the Cabinet Room were left undisturbed, even with a memorandum typed by Olive herself left lying on a table.[83] She continued to work upstairs in Hollis's office, now looking forward even more to her future with Neil and the prospects that would open up for them. It would, however, still be some time before they could meet. Neil was doing important work in the reconstruction of Austria and there was still the question of whether he might after all be sent to the Far East:

Austria
REAR 5 COPS CMF
20th August 1945

Dearest You,
    …Today is the last in Klagenfurt for at least the next four weeks. I go to pastures new and an abomination of coalmines… as Explosives Commissar. This past week has been a "bit much", in view of Ve-J day, and the usual celebrations. The P.M.C. suddenly unearthed a stock of drink and good food which he has been hoarding for many weary months, and the entire mess, including self, proceeded to get 'orribly whistled…

    I must stop. Be good and God bless you. All my love.
    Neil.

Throughout August he sent a range of attractive postcards to Olive from different parts of Austria, each marked: 'on active service'. On one showing the main room of a hotel in Innsbruck he wrote:

Austria
27th August 1945

Dearest Twitter-patter,
    This is the local "boozer" this weekend. Light lager – take it or leave it. Met my new boss last night (COL CARVER), gather he used to work

with you & saw Quebec at the same time. We discussed you & passed a
vote of confidence. He asked to be remembered. Who is he anyway? Am
off to southern Tyrol crack a' dawn for about a week on wheels. Mail
has gone haywire it never seems to catch me up!! Hope you're behaving
yourself. Stick to my old address pro temp. Auf wiedersen. All my wot
not- Neil

PS. Have the Japs won or have we?

From here on the letters became even more focused on preparation for
marriage and Neil finding a job, which Olive thought she may have
organised for him through her contact with General Hollis:

London
27th August 1945

Hello Sweetie,

Yesterday I intended going to action on all outstanding correspondence
and the afternoon was to have been devoted entirely to writing to you. Just
after a very belated breakfast, however, the 'phone rang. It was Joni, one
of the WAAF officers here who lives in Brighton, and I got an invitation
to go over to tea – so I went – I hope you don't mind – because she and
her husband are charming people and great fun. Joni is 35, very vital and
attractive. A terrific sport and tomboy, and she has two sons, one aged 14
the other 12. I think you are going to like them all. They have a wonderful
house just off the edge of cliffs by Roedean College. The house is full
of mothers, aunties, uncles, nephews, nieces and sons. There are bathing
suits, air guns, scooters, bicycles, hoops, pebbles, seashells, buckets and
spades, and wonderful flowers scattered in great profusion everywhere.
As a family they are rather like the Hollis's. People come to stay for a
night and remain five years. I hope you and I produce a family and have
a house like that. It's great fun to be with such people.

Talking of the Hollis's – they are mainly the reason why I haven't written to you for such ages. There has been so much to tell you and with
Joan down for the week there has been very little time for writing a really
long letter. I will tell you about Joan later.

Now I must tell you about all the happenings of the last two weeks
which may affect our future. I will start at the very beginning which is
about 2 weeks ago today.

My chief was told he was in the running for a very big job outside his
present sphere. This job would involve travelling all over the world and he

would be able to take his wife with him – in fact, she would be a necessary adjunct, as it were. I can't go into great detail obviously, but they asked me if I would be prepared to go with them, as Private Secretary to him and also to help her out occasionally with organising dinner parties and helping them entertain their guests. Naturally, I could not give an answer right away, except to say that if I were not going to marry you immediately you come home, I would love it. It is a wonderful opportunity, of course, but you come first. Anyway, it appeared at that time that the new job would materialise in the next few weeks and "Mrs" asked me if I would see him launched into the new job at least until I got married and I said that of course I would do that – I was assuming that you would not be out of the Army until Christmas at the earliest and that we could not, in any case, be married until early next year.[84]

I was going to write and tell you about all this when I had a moment to spare and, in the meantime, I had an invitation to go down for the day and spend the night at Haywards Heath with the Hollis's. This incidentally coincided with V.J. day and I had a wonderful party with them, but I will also tell you about that later.

While we were at lunch that day they had a 'phone call from the Office to say that formal application for his services was being made and he had to go unofficially to see a bloke about it the following Sunday. There was great jubilation about this, because they are both Empire-minded and he wants to make a change. I was thrilled because it would be a wonderful job for me. We had lots of talks that day during the course of which they mentioned that you would not be wanting in opportunities and openings for a career.

I returned to London on the Thursday and Joan arrived on Friday, so I still hadn't had a chance of writing to you.

On Saturday we had our party at the Savoy when Margaret handed me your letter telling me about the possibility of another pip and your new job. I'm terribly proud of you, darling, and I was so excited (aided and abetted by a few Martinis!). Anyway, when everyone had simmered down the following morning, I told the Hollis's about it. We all stayed at the Savoy for the night and Joan and I went for a drink with them in the morning. I also told them about the conditions on which you would accept the job. Looking at it in the cold light of morning I had decided that perhaps it would not be a good thing - that it would only be postponing the evil day – that, if we were married, the first year of our married life would perhaps be marred by niggling thought that we had to get cracking on a career at the end of it. It's not that I mind – you know

I'm always ready to take a chance on things. You may have altered, but before you went away such things would worry you to death and only your complete happiness would make me happy. I could not bear to think of you worrying about what was going to happen to us.

I pointed this out to the Hollis's and they said I was crackers. Joan was present at the discussion and will, doubtless, tell you all about it. Anyway, they eventually convinced Joan and me that you should take the job, volunteer, if you had to, for another year, and if you stay on for another year, then it would be wonderful if we could marry and have complete happiness for the first year of our married life in the most ideal circumstances. They said we were not to worry about what was going to happen at the end of the year, because they would help you to "hit the trail"! They pointed out that one thing very often leads to another and in that year you might meet with a job that was right up your street and, in addition, it would be a wonderful experience for both of us. If God gave you that opportunity then it must be right and we should take a chance on it. Why they should be so interested in us both I just can't imagine, but they are, and Joan will tell you so too. Anyway, as I say, they had us convinced and I was going to write and tell you during the Monday what I thought about the whole thing. But, on Sunday night, they telephone me at home to say that he had been to see the "bloke" and the job was much bigger than they had thought. In fact, not only could they use me, but they could also use you, and he said he thought you were just the chap for the job. He also asked me to hold hard on writing to you for a day or so pending further developments – and so, again, the letter was not written. I hope I'm forgiven, but I just could not get around to writing to you with all this happening.

Joan and I went over to Haywards Heath to spend the day with them on the Wednesday and they suggested that we might be able then to formulate some plan. However, nothing new had transpired except that a report on this particular show had been received, prepared by a man whom I think you know. In passing, I would mention that this is a Government show.

I read the report, which is very meaty, and, again, I can give you no details in this letter – we would need a long talk to cover the ground. Out of the arrival of this report had arisen one development which affected you and you only. I am sending you, in a separate letter, a "tree" of the organisation which includes a Director of Production – a job which is right up your street, for the Director of Production is responsible for Films, Books, Music, Literature, Art, Lectures, and all types of propaganda. It is, therefore, just the thing for you, and I was told by "Mrs." that if it was at all possible, and you were interested, "Mr." would see that you got the job.

Since then there have been further developments in the shape of far greater potentialities in our present "sphere" and the new job will have to be made very attractive, particularly financially, to compete at all. The latest news is that things are in a state of flux and we are waiting for the final offer officially to be made. As soon as I know the decision I will write to you.

Now comes the snag. It would help enormously if you could get home, even if only for a couple of days, for a talk about all this. Until it is definite, however, I would not persuade you to make the effort to get home – much as I would like you here. Wot I mean is – I don't want you rushing home on a wild goose chase, only to be disappointed. Do you think it would be at all possible to arrange this as soon as I give you the word – I have been asked by my chief to sound you on this point as in any case he would like to see you? I'm not sure, but even if he did not take the job himself, I do not think there is any reason why you should not get into the organisation. It would mean, I think, our travelling all over the world – and it seems to me that it would be ideal for you. I think this might be another possible opening.

Then comes the question of your getting your release and I have been discussing it with Jacquey, who tells me that a friend of hers who was in the Army was very bored with his Army job and the organisation about which I have been telling you got to hear of it and opted for him. He was told by the Army that he would be allowed to take the job if he so wished, but actually he did not do so because he thought that, however bored he might be, there was a war on and he wanted to contribute something to the war effort. This, however, my sweet poppet, is a <u>peace</u> effort and, I can tell you, it's a big show, especially if you are keen on world organisation and are empire-minded.

So there it rests for the moment – if my chief takes the job – presumably there will be room for you and me in it. There is so much more to it, as you can well imagine, than I can tell you in a letter, but I have done my best to explain it without making it too complicated.

I think I have given you the "meat" of the thing. There will, of course, be disadvantages and various snags, but I think these might be ironed out, providing you are sufficiently keen. I think there is no doubt you and my chief would get on well and the same applies to his wife and myself. They seem very anxious to give us a helping hand and I feel so inadequate when I am with them. They are both so kind and affectionate – Joan felt the same too. Mrs. Hollis was so sweet to Joan – but then Joan herself is a

sweet person. I felt so miserable when she returned on Saturday morning to Lancashire. I enjoyed having her more than I can ever express. She
was so excited and got such a kick out of everything. She certainly was
a great success at our party, and Dan and Ian McEwan thought she was a
poppet. They were all amazed at Joan's ability to get around so well and
the General told me later that he asked her to dance, completely forgetting
that she had a game leg and he said he did not notice it until quite a way
through the dance when she stumbled slightly.

Darling, we had a wonderful weekend at the Savoy and I do wish
you could have been there. We went to the Ballet with Jacquey in the
afternoon – having had lunch with Sylvia and Jacquey. We got back to
the hotel and pottered around glamourising ourselves and we had to
go up to the Hollis's room at 7.15p.m. so that I could introduce Joan
to them before the party started in order that she might not feel so shy.
We had a drink with them and Mrs. Hollis made Joan feel completely
at home by pinning a flower on her frock. Joan said she felt shy, but she
certainly didn't look it. I had purposely arranged for her to meet Jacquey
too, before the party, so that she might not feel a complete stranger and
everything went so well. It really was a grand party, although I organised
it myself! (Said she!)

All of us, except the Hollis's and Eric went on to a nightclub afterwards
– the Astor – but it was very crowded and we had to wait ages. Having
waited half an hour Dan and I decided that we had had our party and he
organised a car and took Joan and me back to the Savoy. By this time it
was 2a.m. so we went straight to bed! Joan, by the way, was particularly
struck with Dan, as I was, because of his likeness to you. He doesn't look
like you, but he is kind and gentle and he loves books and poetry.

On Sunday morning we trickled down to breakfast in the "Pinafore
Room" about 10.15 and after a lazy morning went up to the Hollis's room
for a drink. We had lunch with them at the Savoy and we all travelled
down in the afternoon.

In the evening I took Joan around to introduce her to Auntie and we
had a drink with her.

On Monday, mother, Auntie, Joan and I all came to Town to lunch and
we saw the George Black show "Happy and Glorious". It was excellent.
An early night that night.

On Tuesday we went over to lunch with Dorothy, my school friend, who
lives at Brighton. That was very pleasant and I think Joan enjoyed it. In the
evening on our way back, we were walking along the front and we saw
some coaches lined up for an evening drive. So we had a two-hour drive

in a coach up to the dyke, down, through the most wonderful scenery, into the village of Poynings (where I want us to be married) and through some lovely old Sussex villages nestling in the downs, to Henfield. The coach stopped there for 40 minutes and Joan and I went into the local (very local) and had a gin to pass the time away. We got back home about 9.30, had supper and went to bed.

On Wednesday we went to Haywards Heath, as I have told you. We were met by car and they drove us through the wonderful old village of Lindfield to a pub called the Red Lion. We had a little drive round to show Joan the sights and then stopped for a drink for half an hour. It was Gran's birthday and she had prepared a wonderful lunch for us. She was a little tearful when we arrived as she had just had some birthday greetings (she is 84) but Joan was very sweet to her and greeted her with a kiss. Gran was so thrilled and said what a pretty little girl Joan was. The older members of the party went to sleep in the afternoon while Joan and I read. I had the report to read. We had tea and I went for a little walk with the dogs. We had another long discussion about the job, and another drink, and then he took us in the car to the station. We got home about 8.30, had a meal and a long gossip (I was showing Joan all the souvenirs and photographs from my trips) and we got to bed about midnight.

On Thursday we came up to Town again. Margaret, Jacquey and Maggie had invited us to lunch with them. We did a spot of shopping in the morning, met them for lunch at the Corvette, did some more shopping, had tea and got home by 6.30. We had to change very rapidly as we were due at Auntie's for dinner at 7.30. We had a very pleasant evening with her, aided and abetted by champagne and Benedictine, some music and Pandy's antics (he had followed us round to Auntie's house!).

On Friday we spent the day at Brighton but it wasn't very pleasant as the weather was so bad. We had lunch and tea out and looked at the shops, went home for an early evening meal and then went with Mother and Auntie to a Clarkson Rose show, very good indeed, called "Twinkle". It really was most amusing and we all enjoyed it.

On Saturday morning Joan returned home. She caught the 10.15 from Euston, got a seat easily, and 'phoned me in the evening to say she had arrived home all in one piece. Now I am missing her very much. She is a darling and I love her particularly because she is so like you. You will probably have guessed that Joan and Enid liked each other enormously.

By the way, talking of Enid, I probably haven't told you that she has been very ill ever since I returned from Germany. She had a temperature of 104 for four days during V.J. week and we were very anxious about her.

That was another reason why I haven't written to you. She has had tonsillitis very badly and will, I think, when she is fit enough, have to have her tonsils out. She is still very weak but went out with me for a little while on Saturday afternoon. She lost her job – which doesn't matter very much – as we don't want her to return to work for some time. She has lost over a stone in weight but I think she may be on the mend now.

Another bit of news – which I should have told you before – is that Betty Shepherd was married on August 11th to her Dutchman. She is very happy I think and Sylvia and I gave her a coffee set as a wedding present. She sends her love to you and says that when they are established in The Hague, you and I must go and visit them. Your gifts to me arrived – I'm so thrilled with them. 3 pairs of stockings, a blouse and a slip. Thank you my sweet – I wish I could give you a big hug and a kiss.

My wonderful V.J. night party was quite a surprise. When I arrived at the Hollis's, they had some friends with them who own the Birch Hotel at Haywards Heath. Betty and Dick said we must all have a dinner party and the women must wear long frocks. Of course I had precisely what I stood up in, which was a suit. However I tried on various frocks of Mrs. Hollis's and she finally lent me a lovely pale green taffeta Worth creation and a super fur cape. I wore deep red roses in my hair and I had a wonderful time. I believe I sang a great deal while Dicky played the piano. Anyway, despite the amount I must have had to drink I surfaced happily the next morning. Wot I did forget to tell you was that I poured champagne, Kummel and coffee down Mrs. Hollis's frock in rapid succession. Was I embarrassed! She was very sweet about it though, and had, in fact, already told me that as the frock suited me so well I could wear it at our Savoy party.

We had a lazy morning and I persuaded my chief to do some work. I sorted out all his photographs for him, and we had more drinks, lunch and I returned to Town.

I'm so glad you liked the photographs I sent you. Neil, there is <u>so</u> much we can do these days. I'm sure you and I, with a car, could fill three weeks' holiday easily just pottering around home. There is always something to see and do. A lovely walk, or a swim early in the morning, a lovely pub to drink at or a lovely church to creep into (very bad grammar – but you know what I mean). There are the wonderful romantic nights when we can gaze out of our windows at home over a valley of twinkling lights – or a moonlight walk over the Downs. It would be so good to have you home.

Your winter sports effort sounds exciting and I wish I could be with you. I thought of you very "hard" on V.J. night and guessed that you would be celebrating too. You and I have talked so often in the old days about the end of the war and now it is with us.

There was a scare last week that the 25's would be out in October and I got all steamed up about it but now, in the papers, one learns that they can only get the 23's out by Christmas, which means presumably that you will not be with us until January or February, but I certainly do hope that you can manage a "quick cuddle" before Christmas. I almost can't bear to wait and I'm scared to think about it too much.

I'm sure there is a lot more I should tell you – yes, the Marsdens are coming to London for a week on 10th September and they have invited me to stay with them for a night at the Savoy. We are going to the Ivor Novello show "Perchance to Dream" and are going to have dinner and a long gossip. Isn't it sweet of them? I'm so thrilled about it, darling. People are being so kind to us.

Alan I understood from Joan on Saturday, is not due home now until January, but more than that I do not know.

And now, my darling, I must go, because Jacquey has been doing all the work this evening so that I might write to you and she wants to go to bed.

Just remember that I'm very, very pleased about your new job – are you holding it only until you are demobilised? I'm so proud of you and I think you're wonderful. In addition to all that

I love you. I'm trying to be patient and have been keeping myself ticking over quite happily but I'm not complete without you.

Life is very exciting and I'm eager for the next move. I will let you have the "tree" in my next letter.

"Two Types" I think is excellent, but I wish you had sent it to me before.[85] I will certainly try and put it over but am wondering if it has not been overtaken by events, if you get my meaning.

Anyway, leave it to me and if you have any more bright ideas please let me have them. The W/Cdr. has just written a marvellous song which he will be publishing – so please do send me right away anything new that you have. There is still a vast amount of "chat" – but I must get this letter off to you.

God bless you – and take care of yourself – you are so very precious. Olive.

London
29th August 1945

These roses were from my garden – and I wore them tonight.[86]

I'm in a silly, sentimental mood and I want you to have them for I hope I've put in some very good spadework for us this evening.

God bless you – I love you.
Olive

London
31st August 1945

A much more sane me. I'm simmering down – in fact, everything is simmering down and I think I'm sorry, though its probably a good thing for you because I wouldn't be at all surprised if my letters to you become more frequent than in the past five weeks or so – or is that a good thing?

It's Friday and I've sent Jacquey home early as now that both wars seem to be over we do not have meetings on Saturday mornings any more, which means very little work on Friday nights. The General went down to drink at the "mystic hour" and signalled to me that I might like to pour myself a gin form his own private supply – so while writing this I am also drinking gin – wot a woman!

Everyone is leaving us and I'm very miserable. Margaret Le Sueur crosses the drink any moment now. "Junior" whom you have met, I think, and who is the "Ian McEwan" I mentioned in a previous letter, leaves us at the end of September to return to civil life. Our officers are disappearing rapidly and the office is fast disintegrating. Carver was the first one to hit the trail and I learn today that your paths have crossed, as they say. I thought it was very possible that you would meet him. Please give him my greetings and if his P.A. (Ivy Lewis) is with him please also give her the wotnots! I think, however, that right now she is in Rome. She is an amusing person.

Leslie Carver was one of the General's Staff officers, as a Lt. Colonel. I've known him practically all the war because he was a Staff Captain at the War Office when I was there. I'm glad that you have met someone who was recently at home and who also knows me.

The exodus of Junior makes me feel sad – not because I am particularly fond of him, but because we have covered a few thousand miles together with our respective Chiefs and he has been extremely kind to me on many occasions – one or two distressful ones! At home he is not so good – but tolerable. On a trip, with me, he has been a poppet and we have had lots of fun – in Cairo, Quebec, and Potsdam, in battleships and aeroplanes. We have had many rows and altercations but seem to have surfaced. I think I'm going to miss him.

I'm glad there is a Neil because if there were not you to look forward to I would be quite desolated. Nearly all the people with whom I have worked for years are leaving us and the team is breaking up. Tubby Earle is now an Air Commodore and is in Australia. His wife, incidentally, gave birth to a son yesterday morning. You might tell Carver. He will be interested. I really have become very fond of them all. This time last year was the "peak" and I grumbled, we all grumbled, at the long hours, the nights on duty, the flaps and the hard work – but it was well worth while and the country, perhaps, will never know what a wonderful team, with Winston Churchill at its head, helped to win the war. As I've told you before, I'm very proud to have been only a very small cog in the wheel.

I have purposely avoided commenting on the change of government. Quite honestly, it's something I don't really like to talk about very much. I can and will say this, that when we lost Churchill as leader it was, to everyone here, a personal loss, and we miss his inspiration and leadership more than we can ever express. But he kept many of us up to all hours of the night. He was at all times demanding but one never grudged a single minute of one's time to him and, what is more, he knew his job. I could lose interest now but my duty is to my General – I am responsible to him and if a mistake were made, the country might suffer.

I had not thought about it until a week or so back – on V.J. night – when the General was making a speech. He was complimenting everyone seated at dinner on the way they had done their bit in the Second World War. He spoke to each one in turn – and then he came to me and after talking about the "Buzz-bomb blitz" and the way his staff had carried on in the face of heavy enemy air attack through the most critical period of the war – he said "in spite of it all, in spite of air attacks, fatigue and possibly not feeling up to the mark, we struggled along and we did not make any major boobs – we were never shot down very seriously, were we?" It made me feel very proud, darling.

I'm a very lucky girl because I can look back on so many big moments, but its biggest moments have been since I met you – nearly three years ago now, and it is nearly two years since I last saw you. In some queer funny way, and certainly in a very nice way, you have influenced my life. Not in a material way, exactly, but I changed fundamentally after I met you and because of that change my life has, I think, been very different from what it might have been.

Remember Denis?[87] I believe he is in England on leave. He wrote to Enid and said he was going to look us up but he hasn't materialised yet. I won't be seeing him anyway. Roy Hall, by the way, was in Potsdam when I was there and I didn't know! I do wish I could have seen him. Did I tell you that I think there is a romance budding between him and Enid – only we have to keep very "mum" about it! I don't think Mrs. Hall knows – not that she would mind but we are not saying anything in case it embarrasses Roy who is expected home in September on a month's leave.

I had a letter from Joan yesterday saying that she is trying to settle down after her leave. Apart from some wonderful times with you I've never really enjoyed anything so much as my week with Joan. Giving happiness and pleasure to other people is such a joy to one's self especially when they appreciate it as much as Joan did. She got such a kick out if it and I do wish you could have seen her, Neil. She looked attractive when she arrived but at the party and when she went home she looked really lovely. She has one of the most beautiful faces I think I have ever seen, and she is so patient and kind. Everyone adored her and Mrs. Hollis and the General, and particularly Gran, thought she was the tops.

If everyone tried to give happiness and pleasure to other people the world would be a very much better place – I have not a very exalted opinion of myself on that score, and the week with Joan certainly made me think. I am looking forward now to building a future with you, but the world in its present state offers us very little and life is going to be what we make it. I would be so happy if we could achieve perfect companionship and happiness in our love for each other.

I wonder if we shall find each other changed? It would be frightful if we discovered that we didn't like each other after all, wouldn't it? I hope you haven't acquired too rosy a mental vision of me – late nights and hard work have traced a few lines around my eyes which were not visible before. I still love my books and my poetry when I get time to read them but I never do any writing now – I'm always too tired. One day, if I have nothing else to think about I shall start writing again – in fact, I'm always having ideas.

I smiled when I read your account of your encounter with the Junior Commander, A.T.S. You're so sweet and I love you.

I must tell you – I showed the General "Two Types" and he thought it was very clever. He did say, however, without any prompting from me, that he thought it might not have the pull now that it would have had six months ago but he proposed to show it to the WingCo. as an example of what you can do. Send me some more please.

I saw a Clarkson Rose show last night with mother and Enid at Brighton and I'm sending you one of the theme songs from it called "Once Upon a Time" – which I think is good.

I forgot to bring it up to town with me today, but I bought an extra copy to send to you and will post it on Monday. Did your Father ever send you any music – I asked him if he would.

I ought to send you some books – I have got one or two to post off to you. I'm afraid I have been very neglectful in recent weeks but everything has been in such a flap and I've been rushing around so much. I think I've lost pounds in weight. Jacquey is very much smaller than me – or was, and this week I have bought from her a very attractive lime green and white floral pattern silk dress for £6 and no coupons, which fits me perfectly. (I hope I don't put on weight again!) All my clothes are getting too big for me now. I always envied Mrs. Hollis her lovely slim figure but even her clothes fit me. She is trying to persuade me to go to Worth for my next suit. I want a really super black one for when you come home but as her suit from Worth cost forty guineas I'm thinking very hard about it! She said it's well worth saving for – to have one or two really good suits and dresses – and I couldn't agree more if I were the wife of a General, but as I'm only a temporary Civil Servant and am likely to be the wife of an impecunious potential "Mr." Margerison with no career I'm not very happy about it. What do you think, chum! Forty guineas seems such a lot of money for a suit. There is this to be said for it – it will have to last a long time – clothing coupons being what they are and the aftermath of war being what it is.

I'm having a new black coat made from some material of Grandpa's which Aunty gave me a long time ago.

I seem to have spent such a lot of money just recently and now I'm going to save some for a change.

Conversation (to change the subject) between old lady from Brighton and an American soldier in a Brighton-London train – "Well, and what do you think of we Brighton women?" – Gum-chewing American replies "Say lady – we bury our dead"!

Now that I'm seeing more of Brighton I've decided it's an interesting place. It has a great deal of historical interest, as you will know, but there are such amusing and attractive little houses and shops tucked away. Houses with frontages flush with the street, looking slightly rickety and with quaint little bow windows. Tiny cobbled streets and alleyways lined with tiny shops, hundreds of years old and smelling rather dirty and musty. One day soon you and I will prowl around. Outside one of the shops on certain days of the week sits a large monkey in a cage who shrieks at passers-by and attracts all the children.

I haven't told you about Poynings church yet. From the road it is most picturesque. It is very old I believe and on my next day off I propose either to cycle or walk down the dyke hills to it and explore. The village of Poynings is beautiful and in the most perfect setting. It is about 4 miles from us.

No more news yet about the job – Very 'USH!! You know what these things are and the people concerned have got the doldrums.

1st September 1945[88]

Your letter received this morning (the one written in convoy!) Liked your summing up of our mutual friend. My chief and I couldn't agree more and we were very amused. Could say a lot!

How right you are about the natural beauties of life. I'm never so completely at peace as when I'm away from towns and cities and the ordinary hustle and bustle of life. I envy you your mountains too. I haven't a head for climbing but I love to be within range of them and some of my most treasured memories are of the mountains of Persia and the Atlas Mountains. I have a superb photograph which was typical of the view from my bedroom at Marrakech – but I've told you all about that before. And anyway you know the Atlas Mountains yourself.

Neil – you're getting rash and I'm so pleased. There was a time when you were very security-minded – I expect you still are, but it would be wonderful if we could potter off for six months. I would like to go to the Balkans – Montenegro and Sarajevo. I would like to climb the mountains of Albania. I would like us to be able to pitch camp under the stars, to walk, to climb, to live, perhaps, for a while with the people in the villages. I have been reading a book about the Balkans – that is why I have this sudden passion to go there. I want to cover the whole of Europe, and with you, in a car, going as we please, not in luxury, because if one travels in luxury one misses a lot of fun. I can think of nothing better, at this moment, than a six-month's holiday with you. Will we ever do it, I wonder? We could put it to such good use. We could both write, and work, if we had to. Isn't life exciting? There is so much one can do if one puts one's mind to it. An attribute of ours is that neither of us are hidebound and that may lead to great things.

I'm talking a lot of nonsense, but I'm feeling bubbly too despite the fact that the sun hasn't shone for a week and it's just started to rain.

I've had a lousy lunch, a cigarette and I'm going to do some work and go home soon.

We hear rumours of the C.C. and Mil. Gov. debacle and yours is not the only criticism I have heard – but at least you are able to get around on the job – you are not confined to a stuffy office all the time. I envy you that and even I have been lucky.

You have probably heard by now that May has given up hope of seeing Alan before Christmas, so it seems that there won't be a wedding in the 'gerison family this year!

There is one thing I want to mention to you though I'm afraid there is nothing you can do about it. Jimmie, I understand from Joan, is being very naughty and Joan and May are both wishing that you and Alan were home to "give him a good talking to". He has been unkind and inconsiderate with your Mother and I gather that it's all off with Mary. I don't know whether you feel able to deliver a lecture without letting on that you have heard rumours about his bad behaviour. I do happen to know that he worships you and if you shot him down it might do some good. Joan and May say he is getting very conceited and rude. If only he would come to Town and I got an opportunity I would like to "have a go".

When are we going to meet again? Shall I write to Leslie Carver and get him to send you home on leave? Would he sponsor your application? The people one goes around with are great fun but it would be much more fun to be with you and, besides, I love you and I don't love them.

My hair is "up" and, when the sun comes out, it shines. See! I've got a photograph of you! Do you remember the small passport photograph you gave me in Gib.? Sylvia has a clever father who is enlarging and mounting that for me. Haven't received it yet but it is due any moment now. Sorry about the photograph of me but you know I make a lousy one, and you wouldn't want it around permanently. In fact, I'd be scared to send it to you – you might sue for a divorce. I sent you one photograph of me and you were very rude about it. I seem to remember that you said you didn't think I was altogether used to sitting on five-barred gates! I had some photographs taken in Germany and if they are good I will send you one.

In meantime I'm borrowing a camera, and getting some film, and will try and get a series of photographs of myself and our house and send them to you.

Think of me on Tuesday, September 11th, at the theatre and then the Savoy with the Marsdens. I wouldn't be at all surprised if the chief topic of conversation is Neil D. Margerison – so watch out, my poppet. The Marsdens have a soft spot for you, and once, when Mrs. Marsden was talking about our early marriage the usual subject of your career popped up. She gave me a significant pat on the shoulder and said "Something is going to turn up, isn't it, Olive"! And I wondered!

If only you could be with us.
Must go now, my love.

Course I still love you – despite several – not very serious – impacts. I want you with me as a permanency so hurry up and get your formal release from His Majesty. If you don't get it soon I shall pay him a call and plead with him on your behalf.

God bless you – and be good – funnyface. No "fratting" please! If you do, I shall retaliate and "frat" too.
Olive.

Austria
REAR 5 CORPS CMF
2nd September 1945

Dearest Olive,
I arrived back in Klagenfurt yesterday after seven hectic days of travelling. I found your letter dated the 27th awaiting me. I've read it carefully four times. Once when it was first delivered, once after dinner, once before going to sleep, and once on waking this morning. My immediate reaction was one of wild delight. The mood has been overtaken by a series of "ifs" and "buts", notably prompted by your remark:–
"Since then there have been further developments in the shape of far greater potentialities in our present sphere" and "the new job will have to be made very attractive, particularly financially, to compete at all"… What does it all mean?
However, here are my reactions. I am sticking them down in order of importance, as seen by me.
The Hollis's are tremendously impressed with your abilities. Successful men do not offer jobs on a "sentiment basis". Therefore realise your own worth fully. They do not know me from Adam. They know nothing of my abilities. The only reason they could offer me a job is in part acknowledgement of your abilities, not mine. The fact that they are prepared to do this makes me so much more proud of you, but at the same time makes me feel something of a "strap-hanger"?

Is it a good thing for you & I, as husband & wife, to be employed by the same man? Is it going to lead to jealousies, feelings of favouritism, possible discord? – I don't feel confident to take a firm line on this point, because I don't know the Hollis's.

It is just the sort of job I am looking for, and whilst doubting my initial abilities (six years of war makes one ignorant), I am sure I could do it well, & at the worst apply it as a stepping-stone for bigger things. The war, & the present international & economic chaos prevent any man from planning long years ahead. My attitude about marriage – and one's job – is solely that of the opportunist. I cannot see what will happen in, say, 5 years time. I am 'ruthlessly' intent on getting the best of happiness from time present. Hence my idea that you should come out to Austria & that we should at least have some measure of happiness in the midst of all the present muddle. This job of Hollis's will provide us at the worst with an interesting job, married life & a rare chance of seeing the world… At best it suggests all sorts of contacts, business offers, & vague ambitions which can easily occur as a result of our efforts & which will constitute the second stepping stone.

In conclusion, therefore, I am ready & willing to "start in", straight away.

I have avoided such pleasantries as "thank you very much" or "how terribly pleased" because you know me well enough to realise just how keen I am to find a "chance" in the world, & thus you can measure the extent of my reactions…

My chances of getting home to see Hollis (& yourself) are not very bright. The only lever I have is your letter. Viewed officially it is "third-person-reportage" & would not carry very much weight. A note from Hollis or a D.O. to Col Carver, or some-such, would quite definitely work the trick…

So much for business:–

I'm terribly glad that Joan & yourself hit it off so well together. I think your organisation was terrific & I wish you were here to be kissed. I always thought you were terrific; that you could assail mountains and reduce 'em to dust. This is but a further proof of my convictions. I always remember the solemn-faced cherub, way back in '43 who on being offered a new job looked carefully into my eyes & asked "Neil – could I do it – am I good enough?" & how I grinned & smiled inwardly at your sincerity & innocence, & all those other funny things implying love, – & I assured you that you were in fact the cat's purple pyjamas. AND YOU ARE!!

No more now, because luncheon calls. I have written a separate note to Enid. Look after her for me as well as yourself – & understand how anxious I am that she should get better quickly. I think it's a philosophical rather than a physical convalescence that she needs, & I believe I could make her really well again.

Write soon darling.
All my love,
Neil.

Austria
HQ BTA CMF
10ᵗʰ September 1945

Dearest You,

Many thanks for your latest letter & the rose (which had retained a most heavenly scent & reminded me of an English garden). The most lovely things are those which are spontaneous & thus retain an individuality…

My enthusiasm has been fired by your recent "job prospectus". Certainly I was a bit disappointed to find no reference to it in your latest letter…

You and I seem terribly remote at the moment, Olive. Maybe I pounce too viciously to your references to gin & lime, the Savoy & new evening dresses. Such things also are in strong contrast to my army life & the pettifogging nonsenses of a job & a Spartan existence. Your present life is wrong, 'orribly wrong – and so too is mine. I think we both recognise the falsehood. I can sense in your writing the constant yearning for a common denominator, & I wish to dear God that we could find the opportunity to go out together & look for it. Since the war ended I am finding myself thrown more & more into contact with civilians & civilian life. The English girl in "civvies" who was a rarity six months ago, now pleats her tweed skirts in the Officers Transit Hotel, talks the most awful twaddle & occasionally meets me in my work. I find I am utterly out of touch with such people. I think they are "crackers", they must think the same about me. The only feeling they encourage is a sexual one; to wit, a pretty girl, and English girl, nice clothes, & clean. The feeling is easily repressed but only heightens my realisation that I am (like so many blokes) out of harmony with our civilian selves, & in need of a refresher course. All this causes me furiously to think & I must needs start in & learn my manners again, train myself to talk intelligent cocktail nonsense, & to stop staring at every English girl I see as something out of a cracker. It's damn funny really as I (a) catch myself doing the wrong thing, (b) watch other officers puzzling over the same extraordinary problem. At the moment I can view the civilian objectively, an odd circumstance, & realise that I am not one of them, & that I don't altogether agree with all they do & say. I daresay you too must feel occasionally "air-borne", in another way at your society parties.

All this apropos of you & me & how I feel more & more the urgent need to see you, walk all round you, talk to you & say that I am still Neil. Fundamentally, we are still so very much the same & I cannot remember ever losing a fundamental knowledge that I was in love with you. Time then for Spring-Cleaning in both houses. I'm starting in straightaway rearranging the trimmings that house the basic "ME". Excuse all this, maybe it's mountain air. I love you & must get home damn quickly.

All me.
Neil.

London
18th September 1945

Lots of things to tell you, darling. I did not say anything about the job in my last letter because there was literally nothing to tell you. But here is a letter from the General in which I understand he says that, as far as he is concerned, the British Council job has fizzled out. I don't know what he has said to you but he did say to me that it might anyway provide an opening for you. So don't be disheartened, Neil.

The British Council I gather could not compete with the present job. Not financially, exactly, but in terms of guarantees, contracts, etc. I think they could not guarantee more than a certain period of employment and when you are aged nearly 50, in not very good health, and with a family and responsibilities I think you would have to think again. As the General said, if he were a wealthy man he would take it like a shot, but as he really does have to work for his living it ain't so funny, especially as they would be sacrificing £900 on his pension. Taking the job would have meant his leaving the service immediately and another few months will make him a full Major-General and entitled to a Major-General's pension. All very difficult.

It cannot be coincidence, can it, that I, for the past week or so have been thinking along the lines expressed by you in your last letter. It seems as if our thoughts and minds are completely attuned, despite the distance which separates us.

There are so many things which I find it difficult to express in a letter, but one thought of mine predominates and has done for a long time.

I do not want a "soft" existence. Short of your physical presence I have had practically everything I wanted for the past two years. I have travelled nearly all over the world – in luxury. (Quite a point that! When I travel again I'd like it to be by cargo boat, donkey, bicycle and my own two legs – it will be much more fun!) I've had comparative luxury, money to spend. Those very rare things, clothing coupons, have been handed out to me by a very kind-hearted Government and money with which to use them. I've had wild shopping orgies in countries where things like perfume, clothes and silk stockings are to be had if you've enough money with which to buy them. I've had love and kind people around me and I've not lacked for pleasant company if I've wanted it.

I'm not <u>dissatisfied</u> with it all exactly. It has been terrific fun. I quite realise that it has endowed me with something which will be useful to me in our future, but apart from that, and the travelling and the affection of kind friends, I don't give a damn really for all the other things. I haven't had to fight for any of it – unless you can call it the fruits of all the early lean years! My one big fight has been to prevent myself from being "bogged" down mentally, and ultimately physically, by the feather bed existence.

I've discovered that life means nothing to me unless I've got to fight for every inch of it. I always thought that, and now I've had a chance of proving it. In that somewhat turbulent year we had together before Cairo separated us, I told you often that I didn't want security and I don't, not yet – not until I'm well past the age of 50. Then security will mean something – if I have worked for it.

You and I will start off from scratch – perhaps some kind person will give us a good push and then we're going to fight all the way and, as I've said so often before, our greatest pleasure and happiness will be in achievement. If it's any comfort to you I'm sure that adversity brings out the best in me!

Money is very important, of course, but the money we shall appreciate most will be that for which we have worked and if we can use it to give a little happiness to other people as well as ourselves then it will pay great dividends. Our mutual happiness, and a delightful and intelligent family, if we are to be blessed with one, is my chief goal. Everything depends on it and we must have confidence in each other and an inner contentment.

Frankly, I haven't got "inner contentment" right now only because, as I say, I don't seem to have had to put up a fight for anything for such a long time.

I've thought about it so much and I ought to be doing something about it – but I haven't found an answer to that one yet. I've had these phases before and have postponed them, as it were, saying to myself "It will be alright when Neil comes home"!

I've expressed myself very badly, I'm afraid, and I hope you will understand.

How right you are about the "common denominator"!

Perhaps you have not experienced it but I, personally, have not met anyone in all the time we have been separated to whom I can really talk, as you and I talk to each other. Perhaps the Almighty intended that it should be so! I'm sure the way you and I think and talk must be quite peculiar to us.

Other people pretend to enjoy the things that I love, but one always knows when they are not sincere. They might endure but they don't really like the wild winds and the lashing rain of the hills, or being enveloped in a sea or valley mist in a silence broken only by the bleating of sheep or the call of a ship at sea. They don't like tramping through the mud and getting wet and having untidy hair or wearing old clothes, or striding home, soaked, with shoes caked in mud, for a hot bath and tea beside a blazing fire.

I shall do all that again when you come home. Wootton Hatch symbolised everything for us didn't it?

I haven't got anyone to think with or talk to as I talk to you, but I manage to crystallise my thoughts from time to time and my one wish at the moment is to get to grips with life again and get down to something that really matters.

You must realise this, if you don't already, that I'm not a very wonderful person really but I do love you and I will never wittingly let you down.

Life, it seems, would be very simple if we could be together. But it is not long to wait – at least it is in the foreseeable future. I feel that you, darling, have all the nonsenses, with few alleviations and I think it will be a little difficult getting yourself adjusted. If you had had a definite career and a sort of "cut and dried" existence before the war it would be rather different – you would probably slip back very easily. I'm sure you will adapt yourself rapidly to a completely new existence but there are bound to be difficulties.

You won't have seen any of the "demob" suits!

Austria
HQ BTA CMF
11th October 1945

Dearest You,

For once in a very long while I feel in a bolshie mood. This is notably prompted by the latest news confirming that I shall be required to stay on in the army for a period of four months after the date of my release. This means that unless I get a LIAP vacancy, it will be mid-Summer before I can expect to see England and beauty again. It appears perfectly obvious that the various Theatre commanders have put up such a strong bleat to the War Office saying that they will be unable to undertake a satisfactory charge of their duties if men continue to be released at such an alarming rate, that the War Office has bleated to Government, and Government has had to climb down several feet... there is a great shortage of technical men for work in occupied Europe... and it is therefore terribly unfortunate for chaps like myself...

One serious effect of all this, is that I feel rather browned-off with life in general, and that even when the odd opportunity offers, I feel in no mood to write letters either to yourself or the family. I feel very worried that you should have to wait so very long before we can think of establishing a home, and almost feel prompted to renounce all claims to you, in your own interest; knowing that these procrastinations are so constant, and that there are so many difficult corners to tie up, before we can really get down to the business of marriage. That is only one side of me talking however, and you mustn't take the mood seriously...

Now I must stop, and get back to the job. Sorry I'm in such a lousy mood – I must try and snap out of it. I haven't really replied to Hollis yet, but will do so this weekend...

I have stuck in a further application for FLIAP, but am not really eligible, having been less than 2½ years abroad. Anyhow, here's hoping, before I go really mad and take solely to the bottle.

All my love,
Neil.

London
[no date]
1st Pages missing

You sure are going to be a heartthrob my poppet. Colonel Weber-Brown came in the other day in his "civvy" suit and we shrieked with laughter. To go with it he had a bright blue striped shirt, and a brilliant blue and red tie. He said he couldn't cope with a collar to match the shirt so wore one of his own white ones.

The hats are a dream and you even get a raincoat too!

I've never seen you in civilian clothes – do you realise that, but Boy, OH Boy! Won't it be wonderful when you <u>do</u> come up for inspection!

I gather that you're worried about me and my "society parties". I was very amused at that! Didn't you know – I don't go much on society. One could hardly describe the General and Mrs. Hollis as "society". They are far too unassuming for that. They both love parties but in their own home and Mrs. Hollis dislikes intensely having to come up to Town "all tarted up" as she terms it for some public function. She is at her happiest and looks her best in the country and so does he. He is very good looking and looks splendid in his uniforms but much nicer in an old pair of grey flannel slacks and a tweed jacket. They, and indeed, you and I, can go "society" if they have to but they loathe it and it doesn't mean a thing to them.

Parties of the Savoy type are a great treat for everyone and happen probably once in six months. It was a great occasion when the General and Mrs. Hollis spent the weekend at the Savoy – it was something they hadn't done for years because they couldn't afford it and <u>they</u> had to count their pennies.

They are celebrating their wedding anniversary tonight. They have been married 24 years. She was married before and had two daughters, one four the other 18 months, and they married when he was 23 and she 26. They had a Royal Marine's subaltern's pay on which to live and they lived and educated two children on practically nothing at all. <u>They</u> have had to fight for everything they have now, darling, and will go on fighting. That is why they are so interested in us.

I don't "gin and lime" with my friends, except now and then on special occasions, and I have only one evening frock, wot you've 'eard all about.

If I do "gin and lime" and go glamorous at the Savoy occasionally I enjoy every minute of it but one doesn't do these things too often or they would lose their savour.

I've talked lots of nonsense in this letter but before I go I must tell you that I had a wonderful evening last Tuesday with the Marsdens. We saw the Ivor Novello show "Perchance to Dream" which was delightful, and then we had drinks – "gin and <u>orange</u>" – in their room at the <u>Savoy</u> (tee hee!) and went down to supper. After supper which was very amusing, we returned to their room again for <u>more</u> drinks and about 12.30a.m. Mr. Marsden walked down to the Office with me. They presented me with a beautiful bunch of pink roses and I enjoyed the evening enormously. I wore a new black and rather elegant dress, with one of my diamond clips and the family pearls! The dress, you will be amused, and doubtless relieved to learn, came from Simpsons in Piccadilly, was Utility and cost 48/-! So there!

I had, in fact, been looking for a black frock for which I anticipated having to pay £14, but as I saw exactly what I wanted for 48/- so why bother to pay £14!

Anyway, I'm embarking on an economy campaign.

Enid seems to be getting better but her throat is not well yet and she goes to a specialist to-morrow morning.

I've had the enlargement of the photograph of you which Sylvia's father did for me, put in a white and gilt leather frame and I'm delighted with it.

Again, I envy you your mountains. You must read a book of mine by Anne Bridge called "Singing Waters". The General is reading it at the moment but I will send it to you if you will keep it and bring it back with you.

I wish I could be with you – to share the mountains, the snow, the pines, and your little room with the yellow pine bed.

There is much more to say and I long for the time when we can be together and talk and talk.

For now – I love you, and will always love you, very dearly.

God bless you, my darling,

Olive.

I think Mary is Jimmie's "trouble". I'm not sure that I agree with you entirely – but you know best.

I'm glad you got the rose – was it censored? I wondered if I should have declared it!!

Austria

HQ BTA CMF

23rd October 1945

Dearest Olive,

Things have been getting out of hand lately, due principally to the fact that Headquarters have been closing down in various places, and setting up again elsewhere…

To comment on your own latest letter. Firstly, you must never, never start a letter to me with "would you like to come home on leave"! The shock to the nervous system is tremendous, even now, my hands are shaking so fiercely, that I must have recourse to a battered typewriter. It's rather like asking a small boy whether he would like a barrel of pink ice cream, with vanilla flavouring. Secondly, to put you in the picture on the prospects of leave… I am hard-pushed… without an office staff, and without transport… being called upon to do far too much, and that I am not being given adequate assistance, and that it might do a lot of good to realise that the departure of one Margerison will be accompanied by lots of unpleasant consequences for the mining world.

I therefore suggest that a request be made for my accelerated return to England on LIAP. Reason for the acceleration being Genl. Hollis's desire to grant me an interview… I want to come home and thus receive the opportunity of landing a job.

Stealing around the house here the other evening, when all respectable people were abed, I fell to thinking how heavenly it would be to own this little place, and to be able to find your presence haunting this home of mine. It is perhaps my most popular daydream – to take my environment, and "add Olive". It's not a very good thing, because it always makes me so horribly homesick, but maybe now, I can look forward with more surety, to such a prospect – and in the not too distant future. Up till very recently, I had become horribly morbid and pessimistic of really ever achieving this. I seemed to vacillate between moods of super-sentiment and a "black gloom" which got me right down in the dumps, and usually resulted in going out and going "wild". One good reason is that, like yourself, I am feeling extremely tired-out. I would give all my money for the chance of a month with you, doing absolutely nothing, and having nothing to worry me. I am coming to the conclusion that there are only two people in this world who can stop me worrying. One is your dear self, and the other is a bloke called Grieg,[89] who died too soon, and too long ago. It is only to you I can talk out my hundreds of problems, and find their solution. At the moment they stand up like so many tank-traps before the view. They seem to prevent most things, but most especially, my ability to relax. I hope, so very hard, that the day will come, when we can find that mutual sanctuary of quietness that we know to exist, and that the day is close at hand. Having been together already, I think we shall find the way back – but I do know that I seem incapable these days of finding it alone.

Chin, chin, my poppet, & let me know the outcome of the latest developments.

Neil.

Austria
No 18 TOWN MAJOR CMF
3rd November 1945

Dearest Poppet,

I have just returned to find your latest letter. I went to the APO and sent off telegrams to mother and yourself, which I hope have cheered you up. I was very sorry to read of you in such a depressed state of mind, and felt a great urge to be with you at that time, to cheer you up, and to reassure you... it is rather a wonder to me that you have maintained such a constant standard of happiness for so very long. Be miserable for a while, poppet, it will do you good. Relax, let down those maidenly tresses, allow someone else to worry, and by and large, prepare yourself for the homecoming of one cock-eyed officer.

I heard the glad tidings on Wednesday afternoon. A "voice" rang from Vienna and told me that I was due my LIAP. There followed a wicked two days during which the Powers that be decided whether they could let me go... then they said I might go, but must delay it as long as possible...

Do you realise my darling what all this means. Do you know that I shall be looking at a real live "you", in a few more weeks; that we can actually go some place where we are alone and together, and can remain like that for days, and days, and days. I can nip you, tweak your hair, tickle you till you're purple, make you laugh or cry, or hysterical, or good, or naughty. You have HAD IT in a very large way. I think you had better go and lie down right now, and rest and rest until I send for you... I am tremendously happy, my height is ten foot six, I have just been told that they won't hang me after all. I am coming home, and my name is NEIL DIARMID MARGERISON.

What shall we do; I've got a whole month – the first leave for five million years. You will apply for special leave and we shall go away somewhere together for at least a week. I have many things to do. My family to see for a part of the time, your home to visit in Brighton, business claims, "bad types" to meet – it's going to be difficult to fit it all in; but what I do insist upon is a complete period of you and me (nobody else). It must also occur in a countryside of hills and valleys and woods and things. Places to walk, good country folk, and beds that melt in a dream of eiderdowns and feather pillows...

Tonight I am all alone... it's all wrong... If only the door would open and you were to pop your dark head round the door. We would dine together... I would play to you, some Grieg and some Schumann.

Then we would sit by the bubbly stove and talk about everything. Not so much what we have missed apart, but rather what we planned to do in the hazy future.

If you were here – but oceans still separate that yearning, and I must indeed wait years, or so it seems, until we are together.

Here I stop, and must go to sleep alone, bearing with me your dearest wishes, and a funny feeling of happiness which I always get whenever I think seriously about you. Together we are not afraid of the years ahead, together I think that we are complete. That's why after two years abroad you are still here, deep in my thoughts, and closest to my sense. God bless you, funny one, and see you at Victoria sometime.

Till then, be patient.

Neil.

The telegram, dated 5th November 1945, read:

GRANTED FLYING LIAP FOR 28 DAYS HOME THIS MONTH NEIL – MARGERISON.[90]

Postscript

Olive was beside herself with joy. Neil was coming home at last, she would see him soon, and they were to be married – though quite when was yet to be settled, as he would not be demobbed until the spring. She would not work once she had become Neil's wife, so she could give up as soon as possible with three months' notice.

And then, to make her cup of happiness even more overflowing, she received the following letter from No. 10 Downing Street, Whitehall:

3rd December, 1945.
Personal and Confidential
Please quote this reference in your reply
14/732/B.E.5.

Madam,

I am desired by the Prime Minister to inform you that it is his intention, on the occasion of the forthcoming list of New Year Honours, to submit your name to the King with a recommendation that he may be graciously pleased to approve that you be appointed a Member of the Order of the British Empire.

Before doing so, the Prime Minister would be glad to be assured that this mark of His Majesty's favour would be agreeable to you, and I am to ask that you will be so good as to communicate with me accordingly at your earliest convenience.

Yours faithfully,
T. L. Rowan.[1]
Miss O. M. Christopher.

Olive replied on 6 December that she was 'deeply honoured' and 'can assure you that this mark of His Majesty's favour will be entirely agreeable to me'; and it was on her wedding day that confirmation arrived.

On 6 February she received, from the Central Chancery of the Orders of Knighthood, St. James's Palace, SW1, the 'Warrant under The King's Sign Manual' granting her 'the dignity of a Member of the Civil Division of the Most Excellent Order of the British Empire'[2] and informing her that the insignia had been sent to her under separate registered cover. It arrived in a package with a letter from Buckingham Palace, signed by the King:[3]

> I greatly regret that I am unable to give you personally the award which you have so well earned. I now send it to you with my congratulations and my best wishes for your future happiness. George R.I.
> Olive Margaret, Mrs Margerson, M.B.E.

With great excitement, Olive finally met Neil at Brighton station on Saturday 1 December, and overnight they decided to get married as soon as possible without even waiting till he was demobbed. He had only a month's leave, so they had two weeks to prepare for the wedding, which they fixed for 15 December, then a week's honeymoon and a week in Blackburn with his parents. On the Sunday evening he made an appointment to see the priest for a special licence. Olive arranged the clothes she would need, and had a coat made for "going away" out of a length of material given to her by Aunt Daisy. It was a beautiful length of pre-war tweed, which had been kept by her grandfather. Her friend Evelyn Low's father's best friend was a tailor who made it up, in Streatham. General Hollis and his wife were invited to the wedding and he agreed to give Olive away. The hectic fortnight passed quickly and amongst all the cards and good wishes Olive was sent the following very special one:

> OFFICES OF THE WAR CABINET,
> GREAT GEORGE STREET,
> S.W.1
>
> Olive,
>
> With our very best wishes for your future happiness from
> Laura, Joan Bright, Joan M, Joan Cluney, Olwen, Winnie

15 December turned out to be a bright, chilly day, and the wedding passed off as everyone hoped and planned.[4] A report in the local paper[5] read:

Charming Scene at Patcham

There was a charming bridal scene at the picturesque old church of All Saints, Patcham, on Saturday, when Lieut.-Colonel Neil D. Margerison, son of Mr. and Mrs. James B. Margerison, of 28 Adelaide-terrace, Blackburn, Lancashire, married Miss Olive M. Christopher, daughter of Mrs. H. Christopher, of "The Wolds", Redhill-drive, Brighton.

Given away by Major-General L. C. Hollis, C.B., C.B.E., Royal Marines, the bride wore a becoming dress of soft pink silk with a silver fox fur, and matching hat of feathers and veiling. She carried a sheaf of pink and white carnations.

Attending her were her sister, Miss Enid Christopher, attired in a pale blue silk dress, with a nigger brown hat and veiling decorated with a bird in blue feathers, and the bride-groom's cousin, Miss Joan Swarbrick, in a silk dress of deeper blue and a similar head-dress decorated with a bird in pink feathers.

The duties of best man were undertaken by the brother of the bride-groom, Lieut. J. Margerison, R.N.V.R., and the fully choral service was conducted by the Rev. S.H.P.Ensor.

The reception was held at "Dormans", Dyke-close, Hove, the home of the bride's aunt, and the honeymoon is being spent at West Chiltington.

We learn from Deeson that: 'Letheby and Christopher catered for a modest buffet for forty guests which included 3 bottles of whisky, 3 of gin at 26/- a bottle, sherry £1 a bottle and 100 cigarettes for 11/8d. The buffet was charged at 7/6d a head and the total cost was £48.1.8d for the event. Aunt Daisy paid the bill, being a Director of the family firm'.[6] The week's honeymoon was spent at the Roundabout Hotel, West Chiltington, near Pulborough, in West Sussex, where the bill for six nights came to £19.0s.7d.[7] The seventh night, however, was passed in the greater luxury of the Savoy Hotel, London, where the bill for the one night alone came to £19. They then made their way by train up to Blackburn to spend the final week with his parents, before Neil went back to Austria and Olive returned to work in London.

At the time of their wedding Olive was asked by the War Office what her plans were; Neil was to be demobbed at the end of March, so she gave in her three months' notice at the end of December. A farewell party was fixed for 31 March and Neil was home just in time for her to bring him along to it. They were to spend the day and stay over with General Hollis and his wife, and his two stepdaughters, going in the evening to the Mill Roy, run by Harry Roy.[8] Neil was jealous of Harry Roy making a pass at Olive, and flirting with the young daughter, so he remonstrated with him and punched him on the nose!

They settled for their first years of marriage in a flat in London, where Neil had been finally helped into a job through a contact of General Hollis. He was working for one of his friends, a former spy, Wing Commander Peter Kochde Gooreynd, who had business interests in 3D photography in Paris, which he wanted to expand in the UK. Other opportunities subsequently opened up and they moved north. Olive's mother-in-law kept a newspaper cutting of a short interview Olive gave a while later, in which she talked about keeping in contact with her wartime friends:

> Back to the Washing-up
>
> What makes a woman give up a career that offers travel, responsibility and the confidence of the famous? A wise answer comes from Mrs. Neil Margerison, who spent the war years as one of Churchill's private secretaries, and is now a Worsley housewife.
>
> Then, she went to conferences at Cairo and Marrakech, and was one of the few British women who had met Stalin at Teheran. Now, as wife of the North-West Regional manager of Philips Electrical Ltd. she enjoys nothing more than "a day trip to London".
>
> When I met her she had just returned from one. "They are my way of keeping in touch with old friends", she told me. One of her "old friends" is secretary to General "Pug" Ismay of N.A.T.O.
>
> Does she regret losing the excitement of her career? "Of course I do. But then I remember to ask myself what has an unmarried career woman of 40 got to look forward to? Just losing her job. Marriage is still the best career of all".[9]

In fact, Olive had missed working when she was first married and became social secretary to Nancy Lancaster,[10] a charismatic American in London, who was an interior decorator working for Colefax and Fowler. Later years were spent travelling extensively with Neil as he moved through a variety of interesting and demanding executive positions, particularly with Philips. His wartime experience had not lessened his talent in the arts and he continued to play the piano, composing, writing poetry and painting in oils and watercolours. They led a busy social life, much of it in the world of entertainment and an extended period in Hong Kong before their return to London, where Olive worked in the BBC. She never lost touch with the Cabinet War Rooms colleagues, who now met as close friends every so often, and she remained devoted to Winston Churchill, whose memorial service she attended in St. John's Cathedral, Hong Kong, on 1 February, 1965. Her wartime experiences were forever to provide vivid memories.

It was therefore a great pleasure, and a welcome surprise, to hear that the Imperial War Museum was acting as an adviser to the Department of the Environment on a project to restore the Cabinet War Rooms to their original war-time condition, preparatory to opening the rooms for public viewing. Jon Wenzel,[11] who was instrumental in getting it going, wrote to Olive saying that, in addition to the restoration work, the Museum was also anxious to build up a comprehensive record of the life and routine of the staff, and indicated he would be delighted to hear any recollections that she might have. She did of course have much to offer, and a copy of the girls' spoof 'Operation Desperate' became one of the exhibits. At the official opening the Prime Minister, Mrs Margaret Thatcher,[12] spent some time with the former secretaries, asking many questions and gently probing about what they had done there. Olive particularly remembers her saying quietly to them: 'You make me feel very humble – but what I'm interested to know is how did you manage with the loo?!' They all laughed, recalling that conditions had indeed been pretty hard going in certain areas.

Neil died of a heart attack in 1988 so never knew about the Churchill Museum, nor that Olive was invited, as one of the few veterans, to the royal opening by Her Majesty Queen Elizabeth II on 10 February 2005. It was the year marking the fortieth anniversary of Sir Winston Churchill's death, so a fitting time for the world's first major museum dedicated to his life and achievements. In the Cabinet War Rooms alongside, the Queen met many of those who had served under him, including Joan Bright Astley, Elizabeth (Layton) Nel, and Olive herself.[13] The Director Phil Reed, a dynamic force behind the new museum, had organised a nostalgic meeting for the remaining 'girls' who had worked so hard there during the war as clerks, stenographers, telephonists and secretaries. They chatted and gazed about feeling nothing had changed, and they were unanimous in their respect and affection for Churchill, who they felt was always very kind and considerate to them being civilian staff. They agreed that he and the Allied leaders, like Eisenhower and Roosevelt and their own generals, were men of exceptional ability and dedication. Above all, they considered themselves fortunate to have been in the right place at the right time, and privileged to have been part of that victorious team fighting in its own way to win the war from Churchill's War Rooms.

Through Olive's story this book pays tribute to them all.

Notes

PART ONE

[1] The Churchill Museum and Cabinet War Rooms, Imperial War Museum, Clive Steps, King Charles Street, London, SW1 2AQ; www.iwm.org.uk

[2] Churchill, Sir Winston Leonard Spencer (1874–1965) had become Prime Minister in May 1940, formed a Coalition government, and led Britain against Germany and Italy, and Japan, in the Second World War. Much of the operational planning had taken place here in the Cabinet War Rooms. See Plate 2, and below. He had a profound influence on Olive's life both then and after, and her admiration and respect for him has been life-long.

[3] Olive Christopher. See Plate 1.

[4] Osterley Park, in Isleworth, South London.

[5] Bridge, Frank (1879–1941), English composer and conductor, born in Brighton.

[6] See Plate 4, Herbert, Margaret and Olive Christopher, 1920.

[7] The company exists even now as part of the Compass Group, a leading group of caterers. See Deeson, A.F.L. *A Refined and High Class Business. The Story of Letheby and Christopher Ltd.* Unpublished thesis, University of Sussex, 1990.

[8] See David Gould, *East Grinstead and its Environs*, Stroud: Tempus, 2001, pp.28–9.

[9] These letters, dated in the 1930s, are in Olive's private possession.

[10] Olive wished to introduce Denis Ford. See below.

[11] Chamberlain, Neville (1869–1940) had become Prime Minister in 1937. For the sake of peace, and with the country unprepared for war, he essayed 'appeasement' of Italy and Germany, and made the now famous radio speech (1 October 1938) after the Munich Agreement. In the end, having pressed on with rearmament, he was constrained to go to war in 1939.

[12] Dormans Park Hotel never reverted to a hotel; after the war it was demolished and the area built over.

[13] See Gould, *East Grinstead*, 2001, pp.33.

[14] Grandfather William was buried in Brighton and in his Will he stipulated that a reception should be held at his, by then, famous Whitehall restaurant, East Grinstead, for all friends and associates. Aunt Daisy could not bring herself to act as hostess and asked Olive if she would represent her.

[15] Astley, Joan Bright, received the OBE and married after the war. See Joan Bright Astley, *The Inner Circle: a view of war at the top*, London: Hutchinson, 1971. Olive later wrote to Joan: 'You being my mentor at the time... it seems appropriate to remind you, if you need reminding, that if it had not been for you my career would have followed a totally different course.' (22 October 2002).

[16] MO9: the Military Operations arm of MI5.

[17] David Niven (1910–83), army officer during the war, but well-known English actor.

[18] Taped interview with *Fareport Talking News* reporter Dilys Griffiths. 2001. Tape in Olive's private possession.

[19] Bright Astley, *The Inner Circle,* 1971, pp.40-41.

[20] Information about the Cabinet War Rooms from: *Imperial War Museum. The Cabinet War Rooms.* Foreword by Robert Crawford. London: Imperial War Museum, 2001; and *Imperial War Museum. Churchill Museum and Cabinet War Rooms.* The Trustees of the Imperial War Museum, 2005; www.iwm.org.uk.

[21] Hollis, General Sir Leslie Chasemore (1897–1963), known as 'Jo'. In 1936, then a major in the Royal Marines, appointed Assistant Secretary to the Committee of Imperial Defence; later, as Brigadier, became Senior Military Assistant Secretary in the Office of the War Cabinet (1939–46). Chief Staff Officer to the Minister of Defence (1947–49). Olive became his personal assistant in 1943. See General Sir Leslie Hollis, *One Marine's Tale.* London:Andre Deutsch, 1956, and James Leasor, *War at the Top,* London: Michael Joseph, 1959.

[22] Hollis, *One Marine's Tale,* 1956, pp.57-8.

[23] Ismay, General Hastings Lionel, 1st Baron (1887–1965), known as 'Pug'. He was Chief of Staff to Winston Churchill as both Prime Minister and Minister of Defence. He became Secretary-General of NATO (1952–1957). Joan Bright worked for him, and Betty Green stayed with him as personal assistant after the war.

[24] The Courtyard Rooms have now become the Churchill Suite, opened to the public in 2003, and the large complex of rooms forms the Churchill Museum, opened 2005.

[25] Cited by Phil Reed, Director of the Churchill Museum and Cabinet War Rooms, Imperial War Museum, London, in Fyson, Nicola, 'Winston's Secret World', *The Lady,* 13-19 May 2003, pp.41. He has worked for the IWM since February 1975. He rose to become Deputy Keeper of the Department of Documents, before taking on the job of Director of the Cabinet War Rooms. He was the driving force behind the campaign to create the Churchill Museum at the CWR since 1995.

[26] Bridges, Sir Edward Ettingdon (1892–1969), later first Baron Bridges. Civil servant. Secretary to the Cabinet since 1938, also Permanent Secretary of the Combined Offices of the Cabinet, Committee of Imperial Defence, Economic Advisory Council, and Minister for the Coordination of Defence. Became Permanent Secretary to the Treasury and head of the Civil Service (1945). It is his signature on Olive's CWR Pass. See Plate 5.

[27] Bright Astley, *The Inner Circle,* 1971, pp.59-60.

[28] Brooke, General Sir Alan, later Field Marshal Lord Alanbrooke (1883–1963), as Chief of the Imperial Staff he was Churchill's principal military adviser; Cunningham, Admiral Andrew Browne, Viscount Cunningham of Hyndehope (1883–1963), known as 'ABC'; Laycock, General Sir Robert (1907–1968); Mountbatten, Admiral Louis, Earl Mountbatten of Burma (1900–79); Portal, Charles, Viscount Portal of Hungerford, (1893–1971), became Air Chief Marshal in 1943; Pound, Admiral Sir Alfred Dudley (1877–1943), became First Sea Lord in 1939.

29 D'Orville, Jacqueline/Jacquey Reepmaker, now Lady Iliff, became a close friend of Olive.

30 See Plate 6, Cabinet War Rooms Typing Pool in Room 60A, where the girls worked.

31 Olive remembers that Churchill insisted on noiseless typewriters, which she believed were specially produced by Remington.

32 Eisenhower, General Dwight (1890–1969), assumed command in 1942 of the Allied forces mustered for the amphibious descent on French North Africa.

33 Bright Astley, *The Inner Circle*, 1971, pp.62-63.

34 Nel, Elizabeth: As Elizabeth Layton, she was Churchill's Personal Secretary during the Second World War. She began work at the CWR on 5 May 1941 and continued working there till November 1945. She married after the war. Olive knew her well. See Nel, Elizabeth, *Mr. Churchill's Secretary*, London: Hodder and Stoughton, 1958, pp.9.

35 Joan Bright Astley, cited by Harris, 2003, pp.39.

36 Olive still has a packet wrapper for a pair of *Roman Stripe Stockings, knit of DuPont Nylon*. They were more hardwearing than silk.

37 The Antelope: this was one of Neil and Olive's favourite eating-places. They would sometimes see the artist Augustus John who frequented the restaurant. Nearby was the 'safe house' for agents coming secretly to London. See Bright Astley, *The Inner Circle*, 1971, pp.85-6.

38 Churchill had arranged to leave on 17 June 1942 to meet President F. D. Roosevelt in Washington.

39 Evelyn Low met Olive in 1935–6 when they worked together. They became very close friends.

40 Moonshine: illicit homemade alcoholic spirits.

41 See Plate 3, Neil Margerison, 1943. This was Olive's favourite photograph and she carried it in her purse throughout the war.

42 His army number was 134025. A letter, found in a family folder, dated 19/10/40 reads: [To] Lt. N.D. Margerison, R.A.O.C. The War Office have telephoned to instruct you to report first thing on Monday morning to D.D.O.S. (A) War Office to fill a vacancy for a Staff Captain. Posting Orders have been sent today to cover your move. Will you therefore report at this H.Q. tomorrow morning for a warrant to make final arrangements with me. [From] W.H.P. Bungeat, Capt. Adjutant, Military College of Science. [sent from] H.Q. 'Franklands', Queens Road, Pentshull[?], S-O-T. Later Neil would be with the R.A.O.C. in the Central Mediterranean Forces in Gibraltar, North Africa and Italy. He became Major in 1941, and eventually was promoted to Lieutenant Colonel in 1945 when he moved from Italy to work in Austria.

43 Buckmaster, Maurice James (1902–1992), joined Special Operations Executive (1941) and became head of the independent French section, dispatching agents into France. Promoted Colonel by 1944.

44 Bright Astley, *The Inner Circle*, 1971, pp.75-60.

45 It was a building on the corner off George Street, and they entered the Cabinet War Rooms from Storey's Gate. Clive Steps, where the museum's modern entrance is now found, is a little way along.

46 Hollis, *One Marine's Tale*, 1956, pp.72.

47 Bright Astley, *The Inner Circle*, 1971, pp.88.

[48] First Quebec Conference: 17-24 August, 1943, codenamed 'Quadrant', with Roosevelt, Churchill, MacKenzie King.

[49] See Plate 1, Olive Christopher passport photo, 1943.

[50] Eden, Robert Anthony, Lord Avon (1897–1977), Secretary for War (May 1940), then appointed Foreign Secretary (December 1940) by Churchill.

[51] Harriman, William Averell (1891–1986), Roosevelt's Special Envoy to administer Land Lease, soon to be US Ambassador to Moscow, 1943-46.

[52] Stalin, Joseph (1879–1953), Soviet leader, pressing for a 'Second Front' in Europe to relieve the strain on his outnumbered forces. He aimed to exploit the unwarranted Anglo-American fear that Russia might withdraw from the war.

[53] Roosevelt, Franklin Delano (1882–1945), President of the USA, keen to meet Stalin.

[54] Bright Astley, *The Inner Circle*, 1971, pp.86-7.

[55] Bright Astley, *The Inner Circle*, 1971, pp.89.

[56] The same maroon trousers were also worn on *HMS Jervis*.

PART TWO

[1] Chiang Kai-Shek (1887–1975), Chinese general and statesman, commander-in-chief of China united against Japanese aggression. His unexpected early arrival with his wife and a party of twenty delegates upset the original plans.

[2] Greer Garson (1904–1996) starred as a village housewife surviving the blitz in *Mrs Miniver*, (1942, dir. William Wyler), Hollywood's tribute to the home front in wartime Britain. Churchill apparently considered her performance to be worth more than six divisions.

[3] William Wordsworth, 'Tintern Abbey' (1798), ll. pp.88-102.

[4] Letter to Mrs Margerison, 12 February 1944.

[5] Carton de Wiart, General Sir Adrian (1880–1963), Churchill's special representative to Chiang Kai-Shek.

[6] Ranfurly, Hermione, *To War with Whitaker: Wartime Diaries of the Countess Ranfurly, 1939–45*, Mandarin, 1995, pp.200. Olive knew Lady Ranfurly when she worked in the War Office.

[7] For example, the *Guide* stated: 'All delegates are the guests of his Britannic Majesty's Government and they are requested to make no payment for any meals, drinks or services supplied, or to tip the hotel or villa staffs'; 'All laundry will be undertaken and no payment will be made'; and 'All delegates have been made honorary members of the Gezira Sporting Club, situated on Gezira Island, and the Turf Club, situated at Sharia Adley Pasha.' It all sounded very attractive to the secretaries.

[8] Ranfurly, *To War with Whitaker*, 1995, pp.200.

[9] Leasor, *War at the Top*, 1959, pp.258.

[10] Bright Astley, *The Inner Circle*, 1971, pp.120.

[11] Taped interview with *Fareport Talking News* reporter Dilys Griffiths. 2001.

[12] Letter to Mrs Margerison, 12 February 1944.

[13] Bright Astley, *The Inner Circle*, 1971, pp.120.

[14] Letter to Mrs Margerison, 12 February 1944.

[15] See Plate 7, Churchill, Roosevelt, Stalin, Teheran, 1943.

16 The Sword of Stalingrad was made by Leslie Durbin (1913–2005). It was over four foot long. In October 1943, long queues had waited to see it exhibited, first at Goldsmith's Hall, and then at the Victoria and Albert Museum. At the end of the month it was displayed at Westminster Abbey. Olive heard that Stalin, unpractised in swordsmanship, held the hilt downwards, so the sword slipped out of its scabbard. It was caught just before it hit the ground.

17 Taped interview with *Fareport Talking News* reporter Dilys Griffiths. 2001.

18 Nel [Layton], *Churchill's Secretary*, 1958, pp.126.

19 The US 5th Army landed at Anzio on 22 January 1944.

20 Letter to Mrs Margerison, 12 February 1944.

21 Beaverbrook, Max (William Maxwell Aitken), 1st Baron (1879–1964), founder of the 'Beaverbrook Press'; Minister of Supply (1941–42), Lord Privy Seal, and Lend-Lease Administrator in the USA

22 Olive later wrote to Neil's mother: 'I eventually curled up on Mae Wests [inflatable flying kit and safety harness] and parachutes in the bomb-bay and had a most amusing trip'. Letter to Mrs Margerison, 12 February 1944.

23 See Hollis, *One Marine's Tale*, 1956, pp.120-1.

24 Nel [Layton], *Churchill's Secretary*, 1958, pp.130.

25 Cooper, Sir Alfred Duff, 1st Viscount Norwich (1890–1954), Ambassador to France 1944–47. Villa Taylor in fact belonged to an American who had placed it at Roosevelt's disposal.

26 Montgomery, General Bernard Law, 1st Viscount Montgomery of Alamein (1887–1976). He was appointed commander of the ground forces for the Normandy invasion in 1944.

27 Letter to Mrs Margerison, 12 February 1944.

28 Letter from Joan Umney-Gray, 4 January 1944.

29 I.e. the New Year party at Villa Taylor.

30 Taped interview with *Fareport Talking News* reporter Dilys Griffiths. 2001.

31 Jenkins, Roy. *Churchill* , London: Pan Macmillan, 2002, pp.728.

32 Open letter to the Margerison family, January 1944.

33 Joan was a cherished cousin. She later visited Olive in London. Dr Porteous was the family doctor.

34 Hollis, *One Marine's Tale*, 1956, pp.130.

35 See below, letters from Neil: 6 July and 13 October 1944.

36 Olive did not see Evelyn Low again for a long time. She continued working overseas with the US, went through France and Germany, and ended up working for the US Attorney General at the Nuremberg Trials, where she met and married the lawyer, David Pitcher.

37 Olive had been promoting Neil's song writing talents, with a view to future employment.

38 Bowery: a New York accent.

39 Merries: the London club where they met.

40 He would never really be able to put this behind him, suffering after the war from similar conditions when placed in stressful situations at work, particularly in Hong Kong. It was there that a doctor informed him that his nervous disorder led back to the wartime injuries, and he was advised to reduce the stress and, finally, to return to England.

41 The first V1 flying bombs had landed on Britain on 13 June.

42 Wing Commander Peter Koch de Gooreynd, the friend of General Hollis
referred to earlier, would eventually give Neil a job.

43 The First Quebec Conference (August 1943) had set the date for D-Day and
reorganised the South East Asia Command.

44 King, William Lyon Mackenzie (1874–1950), Prime Minister of Canada (1935–
48) had successfully hosted the first conference in Quebec.

45 Bill Sutherland had been considered dead on the battlefield at Monte Cassino;
taken to the mortuary, he was resuscitated after being seen moving, and hos-
pitalised. Some months later Olive remembers Bill phoned her, saying: 'I shall
never forgive you! You never told me you were going to Canada! But can I
meet you now? Lunch again at the Berkeley Buttery?'

46 The brochure is in Olive's possession: 'Water Wings (By Waff out of Element)',
owned by M.A.E.West, ridden by 'Brown… I. Carus'. One 'horse' in the steeplechase was 'Scanties (By Silk out of Sight)' owned by 'A. Kestos' ridden by
'Green… E. Lastic'; another in the hurdles was: 'Gin (By Juniper out of Bottle)',
owned by 'Gordon Seager', ridden by 'Green… A.L.Cohol' .

47 *The Gazette*, Montreal, Monday, 11 September, 1944. Early edition.

48 See Plate 8, Canadian National luncheon menu.

49 See Plate 9, Quebec Conference Pass. Bright Astley, *The Inner Circle,* 1971, 151.

50 See Plate 10, a Chateau Frontenac dinner menu. It was the best Quebec hotel,
and rose to the occasion so not only its most important visitors enjoyed its fine
menus. See Nel [Layton], *Churchill's Secretary,* 1958, pp.143.

51 See Plate 11, letter from Olive (16 September 1944).

52 The Morgue: their name for the Royal Empire Society (Commonwealth
Society), Northumberland Avenue, London.

53 Henry Morgenthau, Jr., served in President's Roosevelt's cabinet from 1934–
1945, and became Secretary of the US Treasury. He was a close and trusted
friend of the President.

54 Arnold-Forster, Mark. *The World at War*, London: Pimlico, 2001, pp.212.

55 See Plate 12, Olive with General Hollis and Maggie Sutherland at Lake
Beauport, Quebec, September 1944.

56 'Penny' was a gambling game with bets laid on pennies rolling along the floor
following the movement of the ship.

57 Neil had been working on one of the wartime ammunition films directed by
Bladon Peake.

58 Olive did not of course go to Moscow because at the last moment Hollis stayed
in the UK with Churchill who was unwell.

59 See Plate 13, letter from Neil (4 October 1944).

60 Eisenstein, Sergi (1898–1948), Russian film director. Neil's interests in film-
making had not diminished.

61 Yalta Conference: 4-11 February 1945. Most of the important decisions
made remained secret until the end of the war, but they included demanding
Germany's surrender and the division of the country.

62 This had been the site of fierce battle between the German and Russian armies.
Roads, buildings and gardens had been specially restored. See Bright Astley, *The
Inner Circle,* 1971, pp.183-4.

63 Wendy worked for General Sir Ian Jacob (1899–1993).

64 Olive had this material made up into a coat at the time of her wedding.

65 Truman, Harry S. (1884–1972), elected Vice-President in 1944, became President for the next seven crucial years, when he would make many historically important decisions.

66 Belsen and Buchenwald: concentration camps.

67 Mussolini, Benito (1883–1945), Italian dictator. On 28 April 1945, he and other Fascists were caught by the partisans at Dongo on Lake Como, and, after some form of trial, were shot.

68 All available evidence suggests that Adolph Hitler (1889–1945) and his former mistress/wife, Eva Braun, committed suicide, and that their bodies were cremated on 30 April. Soviet troops had reached the Berlin suburbs on 21 April, with the link-up of the Eastern and Western armies on 25 April. 'The crumbling of Germany is fast…The end must come soon'. 1 May 1945, in Alanbrooke, Field Marshall Lord. *War Diaries 1939-1945*, edited by Alex Danchev and Daniel Todman. Berkeley and Los Angeles, University of California Press, 2001, pp.685.

69 *The Manchester Guardian,* Tuesday, 8 May, 1945, 1.

70 Jenkins, *Churchill*, 2002, pp.795.

71 See Plate 14, Berlin/Potsdam Conference photograph of Olive with General Hollis and colleagues.

72 See Plate 15, Berlin/Potsdam Conference Pass.

73 See Plate 16, Olive's own photograph of the ruined Reichstag, Berlin 22 July 1945.

74 Churchill had viewed the ruins on 16 July, and later recalled his impression of the German crowd watching him: '[Except for one old man] who shook his head disapprovingly, they all began to cheer. My hate had died with their surrender and I was much moved by their demonstrations, and also by their haggard looks and threadbare clothes'. Cited in Gilbert, Martin. *Churchill: A Life*, London: Minerva, 1991, pp.850.

75 The invitation read: 'The Commanding Officer and Officers of Second Army Signals request the company of Miss Christopher at a dance to be held at their mess at 2030 hrs. on Friday, 20 July. R.S.V.P.'

76 Victor Nares, an interpreter, was part of the delegation.

77 Olive's piece of this red marble sat heavily in her hand till she gave it away to friends.

78 Olive has a note, dated 30 August 1945, from the Delegate Accountant: 'TERMINAL (Potsdam) Conference. Herewith final statement of a/c. for Wines etc supplied during the above Conference, together with your signed chits substantiating the charge. Early settlement of amount due, forwarded to me for transmission to His Majesty's Treasury, would be appreciated.' It totalled '£1.4s.4d'. Olive still has the fourteen chits listing: '1 gin and orange, 1 gin and vermouth, 1 sherry'; '1 gin and Italian 1 lemon squash'; '1 gin and lime 1 bottle soda'; '2 gins 1 bottle soda'; '1 gin and orange 1 soda'; '100 cigarettes'; '3 lime juice'; '1 brandy 2 lemon squash 2 bottle soda'; '2 cointreau'; 'martini'; 'benedictine'; 'whisky'; 'gin and lime'; 'gin and orange'.

79 Sigs: Signals. Neil was trying to telephone Olive in Potsdam.

80 I.e. that Olive was not there after all.

81 L.I.A.P.: Leave In Addition to Python. The end of the war left numbers of troops with an urgent desire to go home but there was an acute shortage of transport to take them. In a cunning move to diminish the complaints, some-

body invented LIAP to cater primarily for those who had served for several years and thus been away a long time. It meant special leave, but with return to barracks still awaiting demobilisation.

82 Bevin, Ernest (1881–1951), Foreign Secretary in the Labour government (1945051); Eden, Sir (Robert) Anthony, 1st Earl of Avon (1897–1977), Deputy Leader of the Opposition during this time.

83 See *Churchill Museum and Cabinet War Rooms* (2005), pp.21. In 1948 an Act of Parliament declared the CWR a site of national significance, and the Government formally undertook to preserve the rooms. The Imperial War Museum finished the project to restore the site. The parts in use in 1940 were opened to the public in 1984. In 2000 the IWM was granted permission to occupy the remaining areas and a major restoration programme followed. Phase One of the expansion was completed in 2003. Phase Two, the Churchill Museum, opened in 2005.

84 This new job was for Hollis to become Chairman of the British Council. The proposal for Neil was that he be interviewed for the post of one of the four Heads of Division, ie. Production Director, with responsibility for books, films, press, drama, music, lectures, visual publicity and periodicals. Olive sent him a sheet noting titles of the British Council Executive Committee and heads of divisions.

85 "Two Types" was a humorous poem written by Neil.

86 See Plate 17, letter from Olive (29 August 1945).

87 Denis Ford, her former fiancé.

88 This is a continuation of the same letter.

89 Grieg, Edvard (1843–1907) Norwegian composer.

90 See Plate 18, Telegram from Neil (5 November 1945).

POSTSCRIPT

1 Leslie Rowan was one of Churchill's principal secretaries.

2 See Plate 19, warrant for MBE. CENTRAL CHANCERY OF THE ORDERS OF KNIGHTHOOD. *St. James's Palace, S.W.1. 1ˢᵗ January*, 1946. The KING has been graciously pleased to give orders for the following promotions in, and appointments to, the Most Excellent Order of the British Empire:– *To be Additional Officers of the Civil Division of the said Most Excellent Order:–* Miss Olive Margaret CHRISTOPHER (Mrs. MARGERISON), clerical assistant, Offices of the Cabinet and Minister of Defence.

3 See Plate 20, Letter from Buckingham Palace signed by King George VI.

4 See Plate 21, Olive and Neil. Wedding, Patcham, Sussex, (15 December 1945).

5 Cutting in family folder. Paper and reporter unknown.

6 Deeson, A.F.L. (1990), pp.69–70.

7 Residential terms of £2.10s 0d for 6 nights; with teas, coffees, and liqueurs charged separately.

8 Roy, Harry (1900–1971), a popular musician and bandleader.

9 Cutting in family folder; newspaper and interviewer are unrecorded.

10 Lancaster, Nancy Keen (1897–1994), a niece of Lady Astor, and at this time Mrs Ronald Tree.

11 Jon Wenzel, first Curator of the Cabinet War Rooms, 1984–1993.

12 Mrs Margaret Thatcher, Leader of the Conservatives, Prime Minister until 1990; then became Baroness.

13 Other veterans there, who had served Churchill, included: Patrick Kinna, Jo Countess of Onslow, Lady Williams of Elvel, Sir Anthony Montague Brown, Doreen Pugh, Jacqueline Lady Iliff, Wendy Maxwell, Ruth Ive, and Lieutenant Colonel Anthony Mather. A dinner was held for them the night before at the Hyatt Regency Churchill Hotel, Portman Square.

Select Bibliography

Works consulted specifically in the preparation of this edition of the Olive Christopher letters.

Chambers Biographical Dictionary, edited by Magnus Magnusson. Edinburgh: Chambers, 1990.
Oxford Dictionary of National Biography, edited by H.C.G. Matthew and Brian Harrison, Oxford: Oxford University Press, 2004.

Alanbrooke, Field Marshall Lord. *War Diaries 1939–1945*, edited by Alex Danchev and Daniel Todman. Berkeley and Los Angeles: University of California Press, 2001.
Arnold-Forster, Mark. *The World at War*. London: Pimlico, 2001.
Astley, Joan Bright. *The Inner Circle. A view of war at the top*. London: Hutchinson, 1971.
Boston, Anne & Jenny Hartley. *Wave no Goodbye*. London: Virago, 1999.
Colville, John. *Footprints in Time*. London: Collins, 1976.
— *The Fringes of Power: Downing Street Diaries 1939–1955*. London: Weidenfeld and Nicholson, 2005.
Deeson, A. F. L. *A Refined and High Class Business. The Story of Letheby and Christopher Ltd*. Unpublished thesis, University of Sussex, 1990.
Focus, the journal of the military defence, no.60, June, 1994, pp.14
Fyson, Nicola. 'Winston's Secret World', *The Lady*, 13-19 May 2003, pp.41.
Gilbert, Martin. *In Search of Churchill*. London: Harper Collins, 1995.
— *Churchill at War. His" Finest Hour" in photographs 1940–1945*. London: Carlton Books, 2003.
— *Churchill: A Life*. London: Minerva, 1991.
Gould, David. *East Grinstead and its Environs*. Stroud: Tempus, 2001.
Harris, Carol. *Women at War, 1939–1945*. Stroud: Sutton, 2001, & 2003.
Hollis, General Sir Leslie. *One Marine's Tale*. London: Andre Deutsch, 1956.
Imperial War Museum. *The Cabinet War Rooms*. Forward by Robert Crawford. London: Imperial War Museum, 2001.
Imperial War Museum. *Churchill Museum and Cabinet War Rooms*. The Trustees of the Imperial War Museum, 2005.
Jenkins, Roy. *Churchill*. London: Macmillan, Pan Books, 2002.
Jones, Helen. *British Civilians in the Front Line. Air raids, productivity and wartime culture, 1939–45*. Manchester: Manchester University Press, 2006.
Leasor, James. *War at the Top, based on the experiences of General Sir Leslie Hollis KCB, KBE*. London: Michael Joseph, 1959.

Nel, Elizabeth. *Mr. Churchill's Secretary*. London: Hodder and Stoughton, 1958.

Mathers, Jean. *Twisting the Tail of the Dragon*. Lewes: The Book Guild, 1994.

Mayle, Paul D. *Eureka Summit: Agreement in Principle and the Big Three at Tehran, 1943*, University of Delaware Press, 1987.

Ranfurly, Hermione. *To War with Whitaker: Wartime Diaries of the Countess Ranfurly, 1939–45*. London: Mandarin, 1995.

Reynolds, David. *In command of history: Churchill fighting and writing the Second World War*. London: Penguin, 2005.

Roberts, Andrew. *Eminent Churchillians*. London: Phoenix, 1995.

Sinclair, Andrew. *War Like a Wasp. The Lost Decade of the Forties*. London: Hamish Hamilton, 1989.

Soames, Mary, ed. *Speaking for Themselves: the Personal Letters of Winston and Clementine Churchill*. London: Doubleday, 1998.

Summerfield, Penny. *Reconstructing Women's Wartime Lives*. Manchester: Manchester University Press, 1998.

Taylor, A.J.P. *The Origins of the Second World War*. London: Harmondsworth, 1964.

— *English History 1914–1945*. London: Penguin, rpt. 1982.

Wheeler-Bennett, John Wheeler. *Action This Day. Working with Churchill*. London: Macmillan, 1968.

List of Illustrations

Index

References with the suffix 'n' refer to Notes (e.g. 245n).

Subheadings are arranged in chronological order where appropriate.

The following abbreviations are used:

OC – Oliver Christopher.

NM – Neil Margerison